Foreign Direct Investment and Corporate Networking

NEW HORIZONS IN INTERNATIONAL BUSINESS

General Editor: Peter J. Buckley
Centre for International Business,
University of Leeds (CIBUL), UK

This series is aimed at the frontiers of international business research. The study of international business is important not least because it gives researchers the opportunity to innovate in theory, technique, empirical investigation and interpretation. The area is fruitful for interdisciplinary and comparative research. This series is established as a central forum for the presentation of new ideas in international business.

Titles in the series include:

Foreign Direct Investment and Corporate Networking

A Framework for Spatial Analysis of Investment
Conditions

Robert L.A. Morsink

NEW HORIZONS IN INTERNATIONAL BUSINESS

Edward Elgar
Cheltenham, UK • Northampton, MA, USA

Published by
Edward Elgar Publishing Limited
Glensanda House
Montpellier Parade
Cheltenham
Glos GL50 1UA
UK

Edward Elgar Publishing, Inc.
6 Market Street
Northampton
Massachusetts 01060
USA

A catalogue record for this book
is available from the British Library

Library of Congress Cataloguing in Publication Data

Morsink, Robert L.A., 1961–
      Foreign direct investment and corporate networking:
   a framework for spatial analysis of investment
   conditions / Robert L.A. Morsink.
         (New horizons in international
   business)
      Includes bibliographical references and index.
         1. Investments, Foreign—European Union countries.
      2. Business networks—European Union countries.
      3. Investments, Foreign. 4. Business networks.
      I. Title. II. Series.
      HG5422.M67   1998
      332.67'3'094—dc21   98–27886
                                                              CIP

ISBN 1 85898 983 3

Printed and bound in Great Britain by
Biddles Ltd, Guildford and King's Lynn

Contents

Figures

Tables

Acknowledgements

The foundation for this book was laid in 1989 when my professor, Willem Molle, asked me to present a paper with him at a conference in Geneva. Our joint research resulted in a first outline of analysing intra-EU foreign direct investments with a gravity-type model. Then in 1990, the European Commission assigned us a project to investigate whether monetary integration could foster foreign direct investments. To this end, we improved the analysis and presented the results at a workshop on monetary integration. After this interesting exercise, Willem Molle encouraged me to undertake a dissertation study, in which I should develop the analysis further and give it some more theoretical substantiation. Later, when we both had the privilege of working with Professor Leo Sleuwaegen on industrial strategies, the fruitful idea was born to include corporate strategy elements in the analysis.

Working with Willem Molle and Leo Sleuwaegen proved to be highly stimulating. Without their guidance and support it would have been very difficult to find my way in the voluminous literature on this subject. Their comments have inspired me to explore new thoughts on my investigations and have disciplined the consistency of these revelations. Therefore, I am most indebted to both.

My gratitude extends to my current employer, the Social–Economic Council, and my previous employer, the Netherlands Economic Institute. Both institutions gave me appropriate facilities to work on my dissertation. In particular, the opportunity of spending one day per week on my study proved invaluable. I also thank my colleagues at both the Council and the Institute, who kindly tolerated my absence. Special acknowledgement goes to the Council's library staff. Without their help in finding the appropriate literature, finishing this book would have been far more difficult.

My indebtedness extends also to my family and friends. My parents encouraged me to continue and never complained that my visits to them were infrequent. However, at family get-togethers I cherished their love and understanding, which gave me new energy to proceed. In addition, the numerous pleasant gatherings with many friends ensured that I did not lose sight of the rest of the world. I shall always remember their friendly enquiries about the progress of the dissertation and their understanding at each new postponement.

Last, but certainly not least, is my gratitude to Elena Konovalova who helped me with so many things and encouraged me to maintain sufficient momentum until the end. When my motivation was at its lowest, her vitality and humour gave me fresh impetus; her neverending efforts on my behalf, regardless of her own work, persuaded me to carry on. Finally, I would like to thank her for her patience in putting up with me while I spent long hours studying and working at my computer.

Krimpen aan den IJssel, 17 July 1998

1. Introduction

This introductory chapter will describe the background of foreign direct investment flows and indicate the perspective from which it is analysed. To this end, the next section will discuss the internationalisation phenomenon in a historical perspective. After this, the growing attention of economists for analysing foreign direct investments will be discussed. Then, the aim of this study will be specified together with the main features of the methodology. Next, the scope of the study will be indicated. The chapter will finish with an outline of the subsequent chapters.

1.1 DEVELOPMENTS IN INTERNATIONALISATION

The theory of international trade states that each country or region specialises in the type of activity that fits best with locationally available endowments. Companies located there, trade the result of that activity with another country or region. This may create new endowments, as companies may be able to benefit from cheaper imported inputs. As a result, more regional specialisation becomes possible. An important assumption in the theory of international trade is that factor endowments are immobile and cannot be transferred to foreign locations.

The immobility of factor endowments is an acceptable simplification in the theory of international trade, but common practice is otherwise. Labour and capital move across regional and national borders. As a result, regional specialisation not only follows from trade linkages, but also from other types of linkages in geographical space. It may be the case that trade between two regions is not possible, but a company may consider the sales of a product in another region attractive. The company seeks other types of arrangements, for example it transfers labour and capital to initiate local manufacturing. It may also be the case that a company considers the provision of cheap inputs in another region an important strategic asset. Labour and capital can be transferred to take control of input production in the foreign region and its shipment to the home base. These are only a few examples of the many types of relations that can be established.

It seems appropriate to group the many types of relations under the common denominator 'internationalisation'. Internationalisation relates to the organisation of economic activities in an international perspective and can be defined as the phenomenon of creating and sustaining linkages by economic actors in one country with economic actors in other countries throughout the world. The way in which linkages are organised, depends on the corporate strategy companies want to pursue for achieving their (long-term) goals.

The phenomenon of internationalisation is not new. Wilkins (1970, p. 3) argues that around 2500 BC the Sumerians had already found it appropriate to have men stationed in foreign regions to help them with the trading of their products. The Greeks and the Romans developed trade with other regions along the Mediterranean and established (trade) colonies. Later, the same happened with sea going nations in Europe, such as Britain, Spain, Portugal and the Netherlands. They transferred production factors (labour and capital) to colonies, at first in order to create trade posts, later to establish companies producing goods destined for the home market.[1]

Times have changed, but the internationalisation phenomenon has remained. Production processes have developed into complex systems of geographically dispersed, but interlinked economic activities. Each activity requires inputs from other economic activities and sells its products (goods and/or services) to others. The production and distribution of a product can thus be seen as a network of geographically dispersed, but interlinked, economic activities. Examples of these economic activities range from input production, the manufacture of semi-finished products and finished goods, to the actual transportation, distribution and marketing of the product to the consumer. New trade and investment relations between economic activities have emerged together with new forms of industrial organisation.

The move to internationalisation gained serious momentum in the latter half of the last decade. World foreign direct investment flows amounted to about US$168 billion annually during 1986–90 compared to an annual average of US$48 billion in 1981–85, an annual growth rate of 24 per cent on average.[2] Mergers and acquisitions constituted a large part of these investments.[3] During 1991 and 1992 a temporary reduction occurred, which was due to a stagnating world economy. By 1993, however, the strong upward trend resumed. Also, the number of strategic alliances, joint ventures and other cooperative agreements among companies increased considerably over the years. Another kind of internationalisation, world trade, showed a similar, but less strong growth pattern. It grew by 12 per cent on average during 1986–90, stagnated at the beginning of the 1990s and has continued growing at a moderate pace since then.[4]

1.2 DEVELOPMENTS IN ANALYSING FOREIGN DIRECT INVESTMENT

Over the years, economic theorists recognised the existence and the growing importance of factor mobility. Already during the 1960s and 1970s, more and more economists had started to investigate the occurrence of factor movements, in particular foreign direct investments. In the late 1960s, analyses were made by Scaperlanda and Mauer (1969) and d'Arge (1969). Scaperlanda and Mauer tried to find determinants of US investments in the then European Economic Community. D'Arge considered the relation between customs unions and foreign direct investment. At the beginning of the 1970s, Schmitz (1970), Schmitz and Helmberger (1970) and Schmitz and Bieri (1972) studied the relation between trade and investment.

With the strong increases in foreign direct investment flows, especially during the 1980s, the number of economists dealing with foreign direct investment proliferated. Theoretical insights were developed further and many empirical analyses were made. For example, Dunning developed an 'eclectic paradigm' and Kojima presented a 'Japanese model'.[5] Empirical analyses were made by, among others, Pelkmans (1983), who studied intra-EU investments, and Sleuwaegen (1984), who wrote a dissertation on location decisions of multinationals. More recent analyses were done by Culem (1988), who attempted to find determinants for foreign direct investments among industrialised countries, and Jansson (1994), who considered the occurrence of multinationals in Asia. Also, special units at the United Nations and the OECD started to deal with this subject.

Many studies investigate the time dimension: how and why internationalisation develops. The geographical dimension, the question why internationalisation occurs on certain geographical relations and not on others, seems to get less attention. According to Krugman (1991a), this dimension was even neglected. For trade, this observation may not be entirely true, as quite a number of studies try to explain geographical patterns in international trade flows. For foreign direct investment, Krugman's statement seems more appropriate. Many studies consider possible determinants in home and host country for specific investment relations in a time perspective. Some studies try to deal with the geographical dimension in an indirect way by comparing the results of time-series analyses for specific investment relations with each other. Studies on foreign direct investment that deal with the geographical dimension more directly, seem to be scarce.

To a certain extent the modest attention given to the geographical dimension is strange. Internationalisation has a spatial impact. In pursuing their corporate strategies, companies are able to cope with the spatial dimension adequately as they assess endowments at different geographical locations and decide to engage in internationalisation on a regular basis. With continuing economic integration processes – also a phenomenon with a particularly spatial dimension – the need for spatial interaction, especially among the countries concerned, seems to grow. Molle (1994, pp. 136 and 226) advocates that economic integration in Europe has given an impetus to intra-EU trade and foreign direct investment. Therefore, it seems justified to analyse foreign direct investment patterns more consistently in view of their spatial dimension.

1.3 AIM OF THE STUDY AND METHODOLOGY

The aim of this study is to identify determinants that could explain the mosaic of macro-economic foreign direct investment patterns in geographical space with a model specifically developed for this purpose. The model is of the gravity type, which is known in economic geography as a simple, but appropriate tool to analyse various types of spatial interaction. It combines elements from the theories of international production and economic geography into a set of potential determinants for foreign direct investment flows.

With the model an attempt is made to identify differences in the set of determinants for different spatial clusters of foreign direct investment flows. The results from the analyses made with the model should be consistent with those of other studies that try to identify determinants for foreign direct investment flows. This allows an assessment of the model's ability to explain spatial investment patterns appropriately. In particular, it is necessary to consider whether the results of the macro-economic approach chosen in this study are consistent with the results of studies assessing investment flows at a meso-economic (industry) or micro-economic (enterprise) level.

Another aim of the study is to derive the prevailing corporate strategy of multinational enterprises behind macro-economic foreign direct investment patterns. This is done by comparing the set of investment determinants that emanates from the analyses with the determinant profiles of three main types of corporate strategy. These strategy types differ in terms of the extent of possible internationalisation of economic activities and the potentials of networking. As different spatial clusters of foreign direct investment are analysed, the study can try to identify differences in corporate strategies by multinational enterprises for the various spatial investment clusters. This may give a view on the level of integration of economic activities in a geographical region in international production networks.

Finally, the study aims to identify possible implications of the results for national and international policy-making. This is done by assessing the consequences of the results of the analyses for policies of home and host countries and of international institutions. The assessment is made by considering the results on foreign direct investment determinants and prevailing strategies for the various spatial investment clusters. As the implications are likely to vary with the set of identified determinants, the study may specify different policy implications for different prevailing corporate strategy types.

1.4 SCOPE OF THE STUDY

With the above aim this study tries to contribute to the existing insights in international business-making and the role of foreign direct investment in it. This is done by developing an analytical tool for analysing the mosaic of geographical patterns in foreign direct investment flows using elements from the theory of international production and the theory of economic geography. In particular, the latter theory allows the geographical dimension to be considered in a more direct way.

Although, the study will focus more on the geographical dimension than on the time dimension, the latter cannot be neglected altogether. Spatial differences are subject to dynamic changes over time and thus influence changes in the mosaic of spatial investment patterns. Therefore, the emphasis lies with geographical differences in available endowments without forgetting their dynamics in the time dimension.

The study will not try to analyse the choice for the foreign direct investment mode of internationalisation *vis-à-vis* other modes. This would also require an analysis of geographical patterns in other types of internationalisation and a comparison of the results explaining those patterns. Including such analyses would increase the complexity of this study considerably. However, the possibility of changing internationalisation modes has to be taken into account.

Another limitation is that the study will analyse foreign direct investment flows on a macro-economic level. It would be more appropriate to analyse flows at a lower level of aggregation, for example the meso-economic (industry) level or the micro-economic (enterprise) level. However, this would require data on investment flows by type of industry or by enterprise specified according to their geographical relations. Such data are not (yet) sufficiently available. Another reason for limiting the scope of the study in this respect is that this would add a third dimension to our study: the type-of-industry dimension. In view of the relatively unexplored field of analysing the geographical dimension of foreign direct investment patterns directly, this was considered less advisable.

1.5 OUTLINE OF THE STUDY

In Chapter 2 an attempt will be made to develop a theoretical framework. It will describe how the spatial dimension in the theory of international production can be made more explicit by borrowing spatial differentiation elements from the theory of economic geography. Further, it will go into some spatial dynamics that could arise from developments in knowledge, regional synergies, economic integration and networking. Also, the role of corporate strategies is discussed. Three strategy types are introduced, in which opportunities that arise from spatial differences and spatial dynamics in available endowments are used differently.

The third chapter will develop MOSAIC, the MOdel for Spatial Analysis of Investment Conditions. This model is of the gravity type and allows the testing of potential determinants that could represent (changes in) spatial differences. First, the chapter will develop the specification of the model by translating potential determinants into testable hypotheses. Then, this chapter will identify the relation between the potential determinants in the model and the three corporate strategy types. Finally, it will explain how the model is estimated and how the results are presented.

Chapters 4 to 8 will present the results on the relevant determinants for the geographical patterns in foreign direct investment flows and their underlying corporate strategies which follow from MOSAIC estimations. Chapter 4 will describe the results for foreign direct investments within the European Union. Conclusions are presented distinguishing between core and periphery regions within the Union. Then, Chapter 5 will delineate the results for investment flows originating from the United States heading for three world regions: Western Europe, South and Southeast Asia and North and South America. Chapters 6 and 7 will deal with foreign direct investments from Japan and Germany to the same three regions. For the Netherlands, data availability allows the model to be tested only for investments in some European countries plus the United States and Japan. Results of the model estimations for this home country are the subject of Chapter 8.

The assessment of policy implications that emanate from the study results will be made in Chapter 9. Policy implications for national governments will be discussed by the type of overall corporate strategy multinational enterprises appear to pursue. Further, some implications for international policy-making will be presented.

In Chapter 10 an evaluation will be made of the validity of the results in this study. The extent to which the theoretical framework holds, will be assessed. Also, the use of MOSAIC will be evaluated by considering its consistency and its ability to identify determinants. The chapter will end with some ideas for future research.

Finally, Chapter 11 summarizes the main conclusions of the book.

NOTES

1. For an interesting review on the colonisation of America and the earliest investments from Europe to America, see Wilkins (1989).
2. Based on total world outflows of foreign direct investment. See United Nations (1994, Table I.4, p. 12).
3. The United Nations estimates the ratio of majority-held cross-border mergers and acquisitions in the world to world foreign direct investments in the range of 30 to 70 per cent. See United Nations (1996, p. 40).
4. Based on total world imports (fob). See: United Nations (1993d, Special Table A).
5. Dunning started to present his ideas in Dunning (1973). In the following years he developed his paradigm further. See Chapter 2 for a more extensive review. Kojima developed his model in Kojima (1978).

2. A Theoretical Framework for Foreign Direct Investment

2.1 INTRODUCTION

After having specified this study's subject in the previous chapter, this chapter will consider it in more detail and will put it in the perspective of the theories of international production and economic geography. An attempt will be made to come to a theoretical framework which could explain the mosaic of geographical patterns in foreign direct investment.

As was discussed in the previous chapter, the internationalisation phenomenon has two dimensions: a temporal dimension and a geographical space dimension. The temporal dimension is obvious as it considers the development of (international) production over time. The spatial dimension considers the allocation of production in space due to spatial differentiation in available endowments.

Two interesting scenarios describing the growth process of corporate structures show the complexity of combining time and space dimensions and the many determinants relevant for this growth process. The first one, drafted by Vernon, presents a geographical process of locating a product's manufacturing units in various stages of its maturity. This became known as Vernon's product cycle (Vernon 1966). In particular, it indicates the influence of knowledge creation and application and decisions on the way of market servicing. The second scenario, developed by Håkanson (1979), describes the geographical pattern of a corporate structure, which grows from a local company into a multinational corporation using different modes of internationalisation. Among other things, it demonstrates the relevance of distinguishing between various types of (subsequent) activities in the production process and decisions to be made on the way to organise the interlinkages between these activities.

Sleuwaegen has developed a formal comprehensive micro-economic decision model of a multinational enterprise, in which both the temporal and the spatial dimension have been included (Sleuwaegen 1984, p. 1). The model describes the behavioural dynamics of a multinational enterprise that wants to optimise its allocation of production in space and its spatial marketing strategy. It includes ideas from the theory of international production and from theories on localisation strategies.

It is not the intention in this study to develop another formal theoretical model describing a company's decision-making process on investing abroad. Testing such a model would need an analysis of micro-economic data on foreign direct investments and on other modes of internationalisation. This is beyond the scope of this study, which tries only to identify the determinants that could explain the geographical pattern in macro-economic data on foreign direct investment flows. In view of this scope, it suffices to develop a general theoretical framework from existing theories.

Both the theory of international production and the theory of economic geography deal with the space dimension. The theory of international production includes spatial differences in available endowments in the so-called locational advantages. The theory of economic geography deals particularly with the organisation of economic activities in geographical space in view of spatial differences in available endowments (Krugman 1991a, pp. x, xi and 1). These differences influence three important economic variables for location decisions: the possibilities of getting sales revenues from a market (market revenues), the efforts to be made to produce a good or a service for a market (production costs) and the efforts to be made to bring a product to a market (transaction costs).[1] The latter may relate to costs of transportation, communication, coordination and so on.[2] If it is a foreign market, this may also relate to various kinds of costs from exchanging currencies, border formalities, administrative procedures or, when such applies, trade barriers (for example, import tariffs).

In the subsequent sections of this chapter, the theoretical framework for analysing foreign direct investment flows will be developed. First, the theory of international production will be described with an emphasis on geographical allocation. The reasons for choosing the foreign direct investment mode of internationalisation are explained in the section on internalisation advantages. Further, some dynamic changes that can alter the geographical allocation of international production are dealt with. Then, international production is put in the perspective of corporate strategies. Finally, this chapter will summarize the theoretical insights obtained and put forward a hypothesis on the influence of spatial differences in available endowments on the geographical allocation of foreign direct investment flows.

2.2 THEORY OF INTERNATIONAL PRODUCTION

The theory of international production as developed by Dunning provides the major elements for a theoretical framework for foreign direct investment. Dunning (1981) has combined existing theories on internationalisation into an eclectic theory of international production. This theory became known as the Ownership-Location-Internalisation (OLI) paradigm. It is a descriptive analysis of the possible advantages of foreign production. Dunning's paradigm states that a country's direct investment position (and changes in it) is determined by three groups of advantages:

1. *ownership specific advantages*: the extent to which an enterprise in a country possesses, or can gain access to, assets or rights which local firms in foreign countries do not possess or to which they cannot gain access (so easily);
2. *locational advantages*: the extent to which enterprises find it profitable to locate any part of their production facilities outside the country due to locational attractions or location specific endowments;
3. *internalisation advantages*: the enterprises possessing assets that determine their ownership specific advantages and having access to endowments in foreign locations that give them locational advantages, want to internalise the use of these assets in these locations.

Dunning derived the idea of having ownership advantages from Hymer and Kindleberger.[3] The idea was first developed by Hymer, and was later elaborated by Kindleberger. According to this view, advantages relate to a broad concept of knowledge:[4]

- in product markets (product development, marketing skills);
- in factor markets (management techniques, patented technology, technology and knowledge embodied in employment);
- in economies of scale (integration of production, distribution and sales);
- in economies of scope (product differentiation).

Locational advantages indicate the attractiveness of a (foreign) location for specific economic activities. They determine whether it is profitable for a company to use its ownership advantages in the foreign location. The locational advantages originate from a large variety of spatial differences in available endowments. For example, they relate to market strength if a company is looking for new markets or to available resources or production factors if a company is interested in available inputs.

Internalisation advantages relate to the question of keeping certain activities under a company's control. If a combination of ownership and locational advantages in a foreign location is attractive to a company, it has to decide on internalising this combination within its corporate structure. Dunning puts an emphasis on the reasons determining this decision, particularly regarding knowledge-orientated factors available to the company. In his view, companies should keep knowledge and its application internal to the firm.)

Over the years Dunning has developed his OLI paradigm in various ways. Two developments are important here. First, he distinguishes between two types of ownership advantages: asset advantages and transaction advantages (Dunning 1988b). Asset advantages determine mainly the level of production costs; transaction advantages particularly relate to transaction costs. Hence, as the theory of economic geography distinguishes between these cost types, Dunning creates a linkage with this theory. Second, he extends his paradigm by introducing strategy variables. He considers them as 'dynamic add-on' variables. In his opinion, they are unrelated to the existing OLI variables (Dunning 1993, p. 97). However, some relation must exist, as strategies are likely to be at the basis of decisions on developing ownership advantages, on using locational advantages and on internalising interesting combinations of ownership and locational advantages.

2.3 THE INTERNALISATION QUESTION

In Dunning's OLI paradigm the internalisation question is particularly important for foreign direct investment. If a company does not want to internalise a combination of ownership and locational advantages, other modes of spatial economic interaction can materialise. Therefore, it is relevant to go deeper into the internalisation question.

2.3.1 Modes of Internationalisation

The relation between an economic activity in a country and economic activities beyond the country's borders can be manifold.[5] A continuum of modes exists varying from the simple utilization of spot markets to the extensive governance of wholly owned subsidiaries. Following Dunning, they can be grouped into three types of internationalisation.[6] These are:

- international trade;
- non-equity agreement; and
- foreign direct investment.

In the international trade mode the relation between a company and another economic entity is limited to the selling or buying of products. The company can export its output to entities in foreign markets. These can be trading companies (wholesale and retail trade) or final consumers in the foreign market. The company can also import its inputs from a foreign entity. These inputs can be raw materials, semi-finished products, machinery and even labour services. If the company is a wholesaling or retailing company the 'input' can be a final product.

The attractiveness of the trade mode is the limited responsibility between a company and a foreign entity. The foreign entity has to pay only the invoice for the delivery of products. Or, in the case of input provision, the company may want to order from another firm next time if the foreign entity's deliveries are not satisfactory. However, for strategic reasons the company may want to influence the operations of the foreign entity, which brings the other modes into perspective.

A non-equity agreement is a mode of going international in which a company has no or limited equity involvement in the foreign entity. The most commonly known types are licensing and franchising in which a company sells technical and/or managerial knowledge about particular economic activities to foreign firms.

Various strategy considerations can be at the basis of a non-equity agreement. A company may want to sell its product in a foreign market, but does not have sufficient production capacity at home and may not have the financial resources to invest in new capacity. It may also judge investing in the foreign market too risky. Another possibility is that trade and investment barriers block other modes of internationalisation.[7] By licensing knowledge on the production of certain products to a foreign entity, the company is able to evade the need for capacity increases or the perceived investment risks. In general, the foreign firm producing the product with the company's knowledge pays a fee for using this knowledge (for example, a license fee).

Foreign direct investment is generally appraised as a far-reaching mode of internationalisation. In essence, it is similar to the non-equity agreement mode. The main distinctive feature of foreign direct investment is *control* on the management of another enterprise abroad. In most cases the equity involvement is a majority share.[8]

A foreign direct investment can be motivated by strategy considerations which are similar to those for non-equity agreements. Selling in the foreign market may be attractive, but natural or political barriers may block access to this market via trade. In addition, reasons for preferring the control feature determine the choice of the foreign direct investment mode. A company may want to exert full or extensive control on the foreign operations, for example, the proper distribution and sales of its products in the foreign market. Similarly, a company may want to secure the input provision for its production process.

A company can choose from two ways of foreign direct investment. Either it can create a local production facility by setting up a new facility (greenfield investment), or it can take over an existing facility (merger or take-over investment). This choice is again based on various strategy considerations. In the case of a merger, the company may be able to strengthen its existing ownership advantages by combining them with interesting assets of the foreign entity. Also, a merger may incorporate a previous competitor. An advantage of a greenfield investment may be that new production capacity can be created, which complies fully with the corporate structure's needs.

2.3.2 Choosing a Mode

The previous section indicates that two important strategy decisions have to be made by a company that wants to internationalise. The first one is the decision on where to produce (production in the home country versus production in the host country). The second decision relates to the extent of control needed on the economic activity in the host country (see Table 2.1).

Table 2.1 Deciding on the mode of internationalisation

Internationalisation mode	Production location	Extent of control in host country
International trade	Home country for output Host country for input	None
Non-equity agreement	Host country	None/limited
Foreign direct investment	Host country	Full/substantial

Many strategy considerations and evaluations of (potential) market revenues and (future) production and transaction costs are at the basis of these decisions. Buckley and Casson (1981) have developed a model in which choosing the mode of internationalisation is described. They specify particular production and transaction costs, namely non-recoverable set-up cost, recurrent fixed cost and recurrent variable cost as determinants of the internationalisation mode. Other influences are also relevant. Among these are considerations on how to cope with risk and uncertainty.

Changes in a company's environment may incur a need to switch from one mode to the other. This was already obvious from the two scenarios of Vernon and Håkanson. In the model of Buckley and Casson, developments in market revenues are introduced as a dynamic element, which makes mode switching necessary. However, it is shown that mode switching causes adjustment costs, which may postpone the switch. By including uncertainty on market growth and on the real exchange rate in the model of Buckley and Casson, Capel (1993, p. 86) shows that uncertainty also causes postponement of mode switching.

The decision on the extent of control is based particularly on reasons which can be derived from Rugman's theory of internalisation. This theory claims that goods and factor markets are imperfect (Rugman 1980). Trade barriers distort product markets; certain factor endowments and knowledge such as human capital, information, marketing and management techniques, cannot be traded freely on factor markets. As a result, companies are forced to create an internal market which replaces or supersedes the regular imperfect external market.[9] When the company continues to rely on the external market, it encounters high costs caused by the purchase of the necessary endowments and by market barriers. In line with the model of Buckley and Casson, a company chooses the foreign direct investment mode because it allows the creation of a more efficient and less costly internal market.[10]

The mode of internationalisation may also depend on the type of economic activity. For some activities, scale economies are very important and imply a heavy geographical concentration of production in specific locations. Servicing foreign markets may then favour the trade mode. For other activities, proximity to (foreign) markets may be more important. This may incur a dispersion of production in geographical space. In that case the foreign direct investment mode (or the non-equity agreement mode) may be favoured.

2.3.3   Complementarity of Modes

In the scenarios of Vernon and Håkanson, foreign production ultimately replaces production in and export from the home country. This is in line with the theoretical analysis of Mundell (1957, pp. 321–2). He demonstrates that in a two-country two-commodity two-factor model substitution of commodity trade for factor movement is complete, when production functions are homogeneous of the first degree and identical in both countries, factor proportions in the production of the commodities are different and factor endowments in both countries are equal. Kojima (1975, pp. 2–4) applies Mundell's analysis to internationalisation, in particular foreign direct investment. He calls this type of investment 'trade-destroying' or 'anti-trade-oriented'.

Purvis shows that foreign direct investments may not be of the trade-destroying type, but can also be trade creating. In his view, factor movement can complement commodity trade, when the assumption on identical production functions in the two countries in the model of Mundell is relaxed (Purvis 1972, p. 991). Kojima (1975, pp. 4–6) argues that this is the case when an industry in one country has entered into a situation of comparative disadvantage for the manufacture of a product in the home country: there must be comparative advantages in improving productivity of the host economy. The transfer of production to the host economy allows both countries to specialise in products in which they have comparative advantages. As a result, in line with international trade theory wealth will increase. Such investments are 'trade-oriented', as they incur trade between the two countries.

According to Markusen (1983) a complementary relation between trade and factor movement is the norm. More recent research supports this. For example, Pearce (1993, p. 106) concludes that production in a company's foreign facility is likely to have a net positive relationship with exports. In his view, this is probably due to increasing intra-group exports of intermediate products, which outweigh a weaker substitution effect for final product exports of the parent company.

The modern world is far more complex than in the above models. Extending the ideas put forward and applying them to the modes of internationalisation distinguished here, the following relations between host-country production (either by way of foreign direct investment or by way of a non-equity agreement) and international trade can be derived (see Table 2.2).

Table 2.2   Host-country production and the relation with trade

Company strategy	Relation with trade	Character	Strategy orientation
Provision of host-country market	No trade	Substitute	Markets
Use of home-country intermediates	From home to host	Complement	Processes
Input for home-country production	From host to home	Complement	Resources / production factors

Both the non-equity agreement mode and the foreign direct investment mode have either a positive or a negative influence on international trade. A company may decide to sell its product on the foreign market by using a local production facility, which replaces the export of the product from the home base to the foreign market. The company's strategy orientation on the foreign production facility is market orientated. If the company decides to engage a foreign firm for manufacturing its product locally, the company's exports to the foreign market may continue, when the foreign firm uses intermediate products made at the company's home base.[11] The strategy orientation regarding the foreign firm is then more process orientated. If the foreign firm manufactures an input for the company's production process at the home base, the company continues to import these inputs, irrespective of the company's involvement in the firm. Strategy orientation in this case relates to the provision of resources or production factors.[12]

2.4 DEVELOPMENTS IN KNOWLEDGE

Developments in knowledge can result from various sources. A distinction needs to be made between internal knowledge creation and external knowledge creation (SER 1995, p. 9). Internal knowledge creation is achieved by engaging in, for example, own research and development, own market research and own training of employees. Also, the accumulation of working experience can be considered as such. External knowledge creation is achieved by purchasing or hiring knowledge from outside the company. An important source is knowledge incorporated into new production means (for example, machinery, equipment and inputs) and new employees (human capital).[13] Further, engaging in internationalisation is an external source of knowledge. Sources are licensing, mergers and acquisitions and cooperation, such as joint ventures and strategic alliances.

Knowledge creation allows companies to generate new or improved ownership advantages, which enables them to strengthen their competitive position. It results in new or improved production and transportation possibilities, management techniques, organisation principles and so on. It is obvious that decisions on knowledge creation are an important element in corporate strategies.

The creation of knowledge may also have an impact on locational advantages and internalisation advantages. If in a specific location the knowledge intensity is high and increasing, this may be an interesting locational endowment for certain types of economic activity. By locating there, the high knowledge intensity may become an important source for (external) knowledge creation. New knowledge may also influence the internalisation question, if it creates new circumstances for the strategy decisions on host-country production and on the extent of control on foreign activities.

New knowledge has a geographical impact if new opportunities to combine ownership advantages and locational advantages in foreign locations arise. Pearce has identified a positive relationship between R&D intensity and internationalisation.[14] Audretsch, Sleuwaegen and Yamawaki (1989a, p. 234) found some evidence that a country's R&D expenditures are associated with its exports. If the new combinations have internalisation advantages, they result in new foreign direct investments. This is also the case when the internalisation advantages of existing combinations change (mode switching).

The geographical impact is particularly obvious if new knowledge creates possibilities for lifting or circumventing existing barriers in economic interaction across national borders. New or improved production and marketing techniques may diminish the relevance of differences in demands in separate markets (cultural barriers). New or improved transportation techniques can erase transport barriers, for example, a river. New or improved manufacturing techniques may reduce the impact of a political barrier. In some cases, techniques are developed specifically with the purpose of circumventing such barriers.

2.5 ECONOMIC INTEGRATION

According to Yannopoulos (1990, p. 248), the consequences of integration on the ownership and organisation of economic activity is a central issue in the theory of international production. He argues that this is also the base for a comprehensive framework for linking the theory of economic integration with the theory of foreign direct investment.

The theory of economic integration basically deals with the lifting of political barriers, or, in the words of Molle (1994, p. 8), 'the gradual elimination of economic frontiers between independent states'. If two countries achieve a situation of full integration, their economies end up functioning as one integrated economic space, where only natural barriers prevail.[15]

The extent of integration between any two nations depends on the extent of barrier elimination. Molle identifies six stages of increasing economic integration (see Table 2.3). The stages depend in particular on the lifting of political barriers in three types of interaction: the movement of products (goods and services), the movement of production factors and the level of policy coordination.[16]

Table 2.3 Impact of the integration process on product and production factor movement and the extent of policy coordination within the integrating area.

Integration → ↓ Interaction	Separated markets	Free trade area	Customs union	Common market	Economic and monetary union	Full economic union
Product movement						
Trade	None	Free	Free	Free	Free	Free
External tariffs	Different	Different	Common	Common	Common	Common
Production factor movement	None	None	None	Free	Free	Free
Policy coordination	None	None	Limited	Growing	Extensive	Full

Source
Molle (1990, pp. 12–13).

Economic integration clearly has a direct impact on internationalisation. The lifting of political barriers lowers transaction costs. This creates new opportunities for companies to benefit from locational advantages in the foreign market and combine them with their ownership advantages. They can also adapt their strategies, which is relevant for the internalisation question. If internalisation advantages exist, they foster foreign direct investment.[17] Additional impacts on internationalisation can be identified when considering the level of economic integration in the three types of interaction.

When economic integration in the field of product movement is achieved, this may result in trade with new foreign markets. This opens a way to benefit from scale economies at home. Similarly, it creates opportunities to purchase cheaper or better inputs from foreign sources. This allows a company to strengthen its ownership advantages at the home base.[18] As a result, additional possibilities for combining them with locational advantages elsewhere are created.

Integration on factor movement creates – in addition to the possibilities from integration in product movement – opportunities to concentrate activities in a particular (foreign) location within the integrated geographical space. Again, scale economies may strengthen ownership advantages. However, concentration of production may imply increased transaction costs, as the production unit has to service (more distant) customers in a larger integrated market. Again, new possibilities for combinations of advantages can arise.

Policy coordination adds to the opportunities from integration in both product and factor movement. This may stimulate companies to develop their corporate strategies. The need for strategy formulation for specific countries declines, whereas the need for strategies applicable to the integrated area becomes more important. This opens new perspectives regarding the internalisation question. New internalisation advantages may occur for both existing and new combinations of ownership and locational advantages.

The past decades have shown that lifting political barriers gives an impetus to internationalisation. Considerable trade liberalisations were achieved in various rounds under the General Agreement on Tariffs and Trade (GATT). This contributed to the strong growth in world trade during the past decades. In view of complementarity between trade and other modes of internationalisation, there is an inclination to believe that the liberalisation of trade has also created opportunities for foreign direct investment. Companies, continuously assessing their combinations of ownership and locational advantages, may decide to engage in foreign direct investment if internalisation advantages *vis-à-vis* the trade mode occur. However, despite the liberalisation process trade barriers continue to exist.

Another example of economic integration fostering internationalisation can be found in Europe. Within the European Union, trade and investment within the Union have grown strongly. For trade, Molle (1994, pp. 136 and 226) concludes that the integration of economies of EU countries has led to a stronger increase in mutual trade and investment than in trade and investment with third countries. Sleuwaegen (1996) reaches a similar conclusion on foreign direct investment.

It should be noted that the theory of economic integration does not deal with the integration of market demands. Differences in market demands throughout the integrating area, for example from cultural differences, may continue to exist despite the level of economic integration. However, one may expect that in the long run the free movement of people within the integrating area may lessen these differences.

2.6 REGIONAL SYNERGIES

The theory of economic geography indicates that economic activities in geographical space form in such a way that hierarchies develop.[19] Krugman (1991a) uses this idea and describes how production concentrates in geographical core regions due to the existence of transportation costs. This is shown by introducing a typical natural barrier, the distance between two locations, in a hypothetical environment without any further barriers. A situation of regional divergence emerges in which a dichotomy evolves, distinguishing between core and periphery regions.

Krugman (1991a, pp. 14–23) also shows that by minimising transportation costs, companies tend to locate where potential customers are and labour availability is sufficient. This is due to what Krugman calls the 'concept of localisation'. This concept means that synergies are created in core regions in the field of labour skills, input provision and information (including technological spill-overs).[20] Krugman emphasizes that these synergies create additional locational advantages for the core region, enlarging the difference between core and periphery region.[21]

Sleuwaegen puts forward a similar concept when he argues that locational endowments, in particular those relating to general conditions in the country, may stimulate the competitiveness of companies located within its boundaries (including foreign owned). Such general conditions may relate to the availability of good education facilities, skilled labour, reliable capital markets, effective industrial policies and so on. In his view, these locational endowments create specific intangible assets, which are incorporated in indigenous companies as an external source of knowledge (Sleuwaegen 1987, pp. 256–7). Hence, they become additional ownership advantages *vis-à-vis* (foreign) competitors.

It is obvious that the occurrence of regional synergies influences internationalisation processes. Transportation costs, a major determinant of transaction costs, can be lowered when companies locate in regions where the bulk of their customers and their production factors are situated. This already creates locational advantages. In addition, the concentration of customers and production factors enables the occurrence of synergies, which may strengthen both ownership and locational advantages. Further, synergies may cause adaptations in corporate strategies and, as a result, in internalisation advantages. New opportunities for internationalisation in general, and foreign direct investment in particular, can arise.

By introducing political barriers in his hypothetical environment, Krugman (1991a, p. 86) indicates that two nations can develop independently a core-periphery structure in the spatial allocation of economic activity. Already a border between two nations implies different circumstances and different legal systems, which can make transaction costs for economic interaction prohibitively high. Political barriers can relate to other aspects of economic interaction as well, for example measures intended to favour a certain type of activity within a nation.

Krugman's observation stresses the importance of economic integration. Policies aimed at eliminating political barriers result in a new integrated dichotomy from existing national core-periphery structures. Its geographical scope is not the individual country any more, but encompasses the area of the countries participating in the integration process. One may consider (parts of) the European Union as a good example (see Chapter 4).

2.7 NETWORKING

In previous sections some indications have already been given that linkages between (subsequent) stages in the production process may be relevant. This phenomenon needs to be developed here because it also has consequences for foreign direct investment initiatives.

2.7.1 Definition of a Network

A network can be defined as a number of distinguishable economic activities engaged in a significant amount of interaction with each other (Oerlemans, Dagevos and Boekema 1993, p. 167). For the purpose of this study, this general definition needs some further specification. The theory on value chains and value systems as developed by Porter (1990) can be helpful for this.

In Porter's theory, economic activity is considered as the combination of a variety of constituting factors, such as inputs, raw materials, labour, capital and other production factors, into an output or a product. Porter calls this the value chain. Inputs can be the products of other (upstream) economic activities or value chains; outputs can be the input of other (downstream) economic activities.[22] Each economic activity has a complex set of interlinkages with other economic activities. This is the network, or, as Porter describes it, the value system. If the network goes beyond national borders, one may speak of an international production system.

The interlinkages of economic activities in a network can relate to many types of interaction, varying from product delivery to cooperation in research and development or decision-making. Figure 2.1 gives a simplified view on interlinkages. They may have both vertical and horizontal orientations. A vertical orientation is when the activity delivers its product as an input to a downstream activity. A horizontal orientation arises when an activity starts to cooperate with similar activities elsewhere.

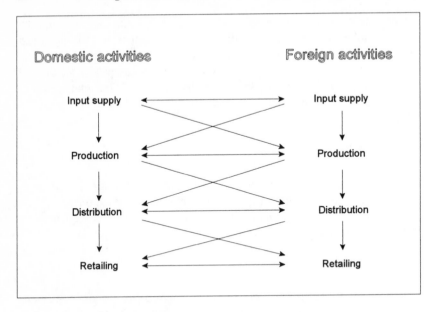

Figure 2.1   Interlinking economic activities

The geographical dimension of a network is obvious. In general, a set of interlinked economic activities is not located at one specific point in geographical space. Locations for each activity are chosen by searching for the optimal combination of ownership and locational advantages. The existence for each activity of internalisation advantages determines whether its combination becomes a foreign direct investment.

Networking implies coordination among economic activities on the exchanges to be made, which may increase with the complexity of the network (Hertz 1992, pp. 106 and 118). This may imply a stronger influence from transaction costs in the geographical allocation of economic activities. Transaction costs are the subject of transaction cost theory, which stresses the interorganizational relations among economic activities (Oerlemans, Dagevos and Boekema 1993, p. 169). The most important representative appears to be Williamson (1985), who shows that there is a direct relationship between coordination mechanisms and networking.

It may be the case that economic activities integrate into larger units (see Figure 2.2). Hertz (1992, p. 108) gives an extensive description of the reasons for integration of economic activities into a whole. The key function is to increase effectiveness not only for the integrated activity at any position in the network, but also for the whole network. The improved effectiveness is the result of various scale economies in the use of resources. This strengthens the ownership advantages of all activities in the network.

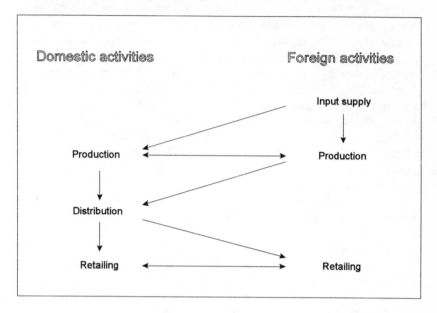

Figure 2.2   Integrating economic activities

Integration of economic activities may have a geographical impact. Perhaps, the integrated activity will relocate within geographical space if a new optimal combination with locational advantages elsewhere can be achieved. Again, internalisation advantages determine whether this new combination results in a foreign direct investment.

2.7.2   Modern Networking

So far, nothing has been said about how the linkages between economic activities are organised. In principle, for each linkage any of the modes of internationalisation distinguished in the theory of international production, and combinations of these modes, can apply.[23] However, traditionally, strategies are aimed at organising networks of interlinked economic activities in large multinational corporate structures. Apparently, the advantages of internalisation and thus the (perceived) gains from substantial control on all production, distribution and sales activities, were considered great.[24] This is generally known as the 'Fordist' approach and can be identified as 'traditional networking'.

Currently, new forms of industrial organisation occur (OECD 1990). The traditional types of industrial organisation have proved not to be beneficial in all cases. New organisation principles show a trend away from strategies that focus on internalisation. These principles are much more orientated towards ideas emanating from the Japanese '*keiretsu*' system, in which very strict relations between interdependent activities seem to prevail. Activities are undertaken by separate independent companies, subcontractors or just suppliers. Their relations are based on strong mutual responsibilities towards each other rather than on control (Oerlemans, Dagevos and Boekema 1993, p. 168). These integrated relations combine the strengths of all entities involved, creating synergies and thus strengthening the ownership advantages of all constituting activities. Therefore, the new types of corporate organisation can be considered as a new variety of networking: 'modern networking' (Etemad 1995).

The United Nations (1993b, pp. 125–7) mentions some important developments that fostered the growth of modern networking:

- advances in information and communication technology have enabled a decrease in transaction costs by creating cheap coordination possibilities among activities throughout the network. In addition, new management practices have contributed to this;
- convergence in consumer tastes has enabled the creation of world products, which can be sold, with minor modifications, in various markets throughout the world. This has created opportunities for scale economies lowering production costs. The convergence is caused by the spread of communication technologies, increased tourism and educational and cultural exchanges;
- intensified international competition, not only by a sustained decline in tariff barriers, but also by accession of new transnational corporations from more and more countries.

Jacobs extends the developments put forward by the United Nations. He argues that several trends (in ownership advantages), particularly in modern management and organisation techniques and progress in information and communication technology, form the basis of the new ways of networking (Jacobs 1994, p. 38). Companies seek economies of scale not only in production, but also in other activities necessary for bringing products to markets. These can relate to activities such as common promotion, marketing and sales. Technological developments, necessary to gain ownership advantages, become increasingly more complex and require larger and larger investments. Sharing the risks of these investments is much more acceptable and thus common R&D projects emerge, which may even lead to strategic partnerships. Consumer demands may also force companies into networks. Quality guarantees towards the consumer have become an important strategic asset, but require good connections with downstream activities in distribution, wholesaling and retailing. Another important drive may come from increasing ecological pressures safeguarding environmentally friendly production, which requires control on all necessary activities. Finally, according to Jacobs, one could mention tendencies like public private partnerships, deregulation, self-regulation within industries and needs for common information retrieval, education and management development.

Modern networking does not basically change the internationalisation scenarios of Vernon and Håkanson. Vernon has reconsidered his product-cycle scenario in view of the occurrence of multinational companies operating in large global networks. He concluded that the basic elements of his scenario still hold, as it continues 'to provide a guide to the motivations and response of some enterprises in all countries of the world' (Vernon 1979, pp. 255–67). The scenario of Håkanson already contained networking elements, since he distinguished various types of (subsequent) activities in production processes. Also, the geographical dimension of modern networking is not fundamentally different. Economic activities continue to search for optimal combinations of ownership and locational advantages and relocate if necessary. If internalisation advantages exist this results in new foreign direct investments.

In this study an emphasis is put on networks which are controlled by large, multinational corporate structures: the traditional type of networking. This is due to the fact that foreign direct investments are taken as the main subject of analysis. However, corporate structures are dynamic in nature, which implies continuous evaluation of the mode of internationalisation for each linkage of economic activities in the network. A foreign direct investment can be transferred easily into an independent company and vice versa without exiting from the network.[25] Therefore, analysing foreign direct investment flows may also give some insights into modern networking.

2.8 CORPORATE STRATEGIES

The theory of international production shows that internationalisation is based on decisions on how to combine ownership, locational and internalisation advantages. These decisions are generally made in the light of company strategies. In a strategy a company formulates the guidelines for using their advantages in the most optimal way. In decision-making a company weighs a wide variety of aspects.

Prahalad and Doz (1987) have formulated a grid in which two fundamental dimensions of corporate strategies are incorporated (see Figure 2.3). One dimension, which is on the vertical axis of the grid, is the need for integration of economic activities. This need follows from possible economies of scale that could lower production costs by integrating activities. The other dimension, which is on the grid's horizontal axis, is the need to meet local demands as much as possible, which could increase market revenues: a company's market responsiveness. These demands are determined by specific local requirements of customers, prescribed by public authorities or set by specific local circumstances.

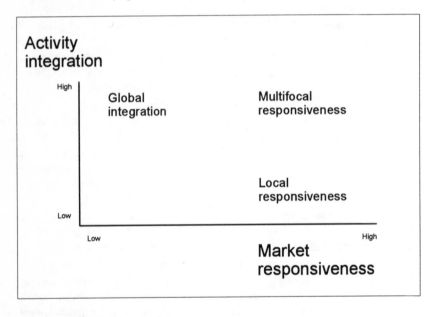

Source
Prahalad and Doz (1987, pp. 18–24).

Figure 2.3   Integration-responsiveness grid

In practice, a company tries to seek a balance between activity integration and local market responsiveness somewhere in the grid (economies of scale and scope). When markets require high responsiveness, a company tries to locate in such a way that it is close to the market, but is still able to attain some benefits from scale economies (local responsiveness). When certain activities require a large scale in their operations, a company may want to locate in such a way that it can benefit as much as possible from activity integration economies, but can still meet some market requirements (global integration). The company's strategy may become multifocal, when it can meet with specific market requirements and achieve a high level of scale and scope economies.

The United Nations (1993b, p. 117), by assessing a large volume of literature on corporate strategies, has distinguished three types of strategies, which corporate structures can pursue. They can be discussed using the above integration-responsiveness grid.

Table 2.4 Evolution of strategies and structures of transnational corporations

Strategy	Types of intra-firm linkages	Degree of affiliate integration[a]	Degree of economic and political integration[b]
Stand alone, e.g., multi-domestic	Ownership, technology	Weak	Host country accessible to FDI; significant trade barriers; costly communications and transportation
Simple affiliate integration,[a] e.g., outsourcing	Ownership, technology, markets, finance, other inputs	Strong at some points of the network, weak in others	Open trade and FDI regime; non-equity arrangements
Complex international production, e.g., regional core networks	All functions	Potentially strong throughout the network	Open trade and FDI regime; information technology; convergence in tastes; heightened competition

Notes
a. Affiliate integration refers to the integration of the affiliate's (economic) activities into the transnational corporate structure.
b. Economic and political integration refers to the (economic) integration processes between countries.

Source
United Nations (1993b, Table V.1, p. 117).

Stand-alone strategies prevail in situations in which a high local market responsiveness is required. This can be due to considerable natural (for example, specific customer demands or high transport costs) or political barriers (for example, trade barriers or local content requirements). The foreign unit is likely to be a stand-alone production unit servicing the domestic (host) market. It may use the parent's technology. There is little integration with other activities of the transnational company and the need for coordination is fairly limited. The company only seeks to reap the benefits from a (protected) host market by manufacturing and selling in a local unit. This can be considered the optimal combination of ownership and locational advantages. If internalisation advantages exist, the local unit is established by way of foreign direct investment.

Simple affiliate integration strategies can be pursued if some economic integration has enabled activity integration. This may be due to an open trade and foreign direct investment regime between home and host country or to allowing various kinds of non-equity arrangements. The transnational corporation may outsource some economic activities to a production unit in a foreign country. This type of strategy requires a more intensive coordination than in stand-alone strategies. It is not possible to achieve full integration, as for some activities barriers remain. The company seeks to create additional ownership advantages by trying to benefit from scale economies resulting from the integration of particular activities. Foreign direct investment occurs when new optimal combinations of ownership and locational advantages arise that need to be internalised.

If there is full or well-advanced economic and political integration between home and host country, *complex international production strategies* become possible. Depending on the extent of integration in market demands, the responsiveness of economic activities may be either 'global' or 'multifocal'. Activities dispersed over locations in home and host countries are able to integrate into one new integrated network of economic activities: a complex international production system. The transnational corporation is able to allocate its activities to wherever optimal combinations of ownership and locational advantages arise. These result in foreign direct investment relations if internalisation advantages exist. Coordination is crucial in such a production system.

In a multi-product and multi-country world, the extent of integration is not everywhere the same. Not all products can be made in complex corporate structures; not all countries have reached a high state of development and have not gone through a process of regional economic and political integration. Hence, the situation differs from one product to the other and from one country to the other.

A transnational corporation's overall strategy has a *multi-country orientation* when it has to pursue stand-alone strategies or simple affiliate integration strategies in different host markets or regions. This can be due to particular national or regional tastes or habits (market responsiveness), trade barriers or any other barriers which inhibit activity integration. The corporate strategy's character is mainly local responsiveness with an inclination to move towards multifocal responsiveness.

A *regional orientation* in a corporate strategy prevails when the transnational corporation is able to integrate economic activities for a grouping of countries within a geographical area. This can be done when within this grouping barriers regarding the free movement of goods and services, people, capital and technology, have disappeared or at least substantially diminished, either by way of knowledge creation within the transnational corporation or by way of removing political barriers in economic integration.[26] Also, integration may have diminished differences in market demands throughout the geographical area. As a result, the need for market responsiveness may have declined to some extent. The corporate strategy is of the complex international production type, in which affiliates and subcontractors are active in various countries within the region. The transnational corporation has organised a complete integrated system within the region: a regionalised international production system or a regional core network.[27] Such a network can be defined as a complex set of interlinked complementary economic activities within a world region in which a reasonably high level of integration among the countries in this region is achieved or in which the corporate structure has sufficient advantages to circumvent any existing barriers.

A *global orientation* can be reached for a transnational company if it is able to organise and integrate its activities in different geographical world regions. Activities do not encounter substantial barriers of any kind across national or regional boundaries. Differences in market demands between world regions do not seem to require high market responsiveness. The resulting production systems or networks go beyond these regional boundaries and can be qualified as global networks or regional core networks encompassing more than one world region.

2.9 A THEORETICAL FRAMEWORK FOR FOREIGN DIRECT INVESTMENT

This chapter has made an effort to make the geographical dimension of foreign production in Dunning's theory of international production more explicit. This has been done by specifying spatial differences in available endowments as a major source of locational advantages. Also, the geographical impacts on ownership, locational and internalisation advantages from some dynamic forces have been assessed. These forces relate to knowledge development, economic integration, regional synergies and networking. Further, the chapter has explained the role of decisions on combining advantages in the perspective of corporate strategies. From these

elements the following theoretical framework for foreign direct investment
emerges (Figure 2.4).

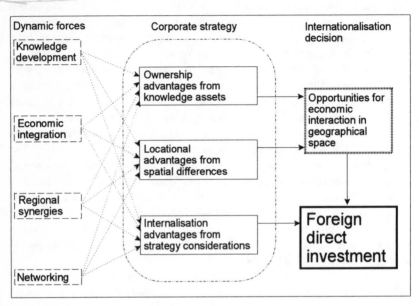

Figure 2.4   Assessment of a foreign direct investment

A foreign direct investment implies that an optimal combination of
ownership, locational and internalisation advantages exists. Ownership
advantages originate from a company's stock of knowledge. Locational
advantages are determined by spatial differences in available endowments.
Both ownership and locational advantages create opportunities for economic
interaction in geographical space. Opportunities materialise in a foreign
direct investment if strategy considerations make corporate structures to
decide in favour of this mode of internationalisation.

The three types of advantages are subject to four major dynamic forces,
which mutually influence each other: knowledge development, economic
integration, regional synergies and networking. These forces influence the
three types of advantages. As a result, they create new opportunities for
economic interaction in geographical space, which may become foreign
direct investments. Strategy considerations are also subject to the four
dynamic forces. This implies that the internalisation of existing combinations of ownership and locational advantages can change as well.

Many factors determine the three types of advantages and influence the four dynamic forces. These determinants can be grouped into four main categories:

- *push factors*: variables that give a push to the occurrence of a foreign direct investment flow from a home country;
- *pull factors*: variables that attract a foreign direct investment flow towards a host country;
- *stimulus factors*: variables which are typical for a bilateral relation between a home and a host country, and which give a *positive* impulse to the occurrence of foreign direct investment on this bilateral relation;
- *friction factors*: variables which are also typical for a bilateral relation between a home and a host country, but which give a *negative* impulse to the occurrence of foreign direct investment on this bilateral relation.

In order to verify the validity of the above theoretical framework, a hypothesis needs to be formulated. The hypothesis is that *different countries offer different opportunities to corporate structures to internalise optimal combinations of ownership and locational advantages via foreign direct investment*.

Testing the hypothesis requires a tool which allows an explicit introduction of the spatial dimension. In economic geography, gravity models were recognised for their success in analysing many different types of geographic interaction (Olsson 1965, p. 43). As foreign direct investment flows can be considered as a specific type of geographic interaction, it seems appropriate to use a model of the gravity type here as well. Therefore, in the next chapter MOSAIC, the MOdel for Spatial Analysis of Investment Conditions, will be developed to analyse the geographical mosaic of foreign direct investment flows and to test the hypothesis put forward here.

NOTES

1. See the derivation of a simplified model for the spatial organisation of economic activities in Lloyd and Dicken (1977, Chapter 2).
2. The simplified model of Lloyd and Dicken considers only transport costs incurred by distance. Jansson (1994, Chapter 2) argues that not only transport costs are relevant, but also costs of communication, organisation (both internally and externally), control on information, behaviour, output and input and so on.
3. Hymer presented his ideas in 1960 in a dissertation and they were publicised in Kindleberger (1969). Later, he revised his dissertation and published it as Hymer (1976). See Agarwal (1980, p. 749).
4. For an extensive description of a broad concept of knowledge, see SER (1995, pp. 6–12).
5. For a discussion on the alternative modes of internationalisation, see United Nations (1989, Chapter IV).

6. Dunning (1981, p. 32) uses a different terminology, as he distinguishes three alternative modes of servicing markets: foreign direct investment, exports and contractual resource transfers. These are only horizontal and vertical forward linkages. Because backward linkages are also considered in our study, a more general terminology has been chosen.
7. Mundell (1957, p. 329) has shown that trade barriers will stimulate factor movements.
8. However, the OECD Benchmark Definition also considers minority shares as foreign direct investment, when it is clear that some influence is exerted on the other company. See Appendix I.
9. Rugman refers to Hymer (1976).
10. According to Agarwal (1980) the 'internalisation of markets across national boundaries leads to FDI, and this process is continued till the benefits and costs of further internalisation are equalised at the margin'.
11. Note that this also applies in the case that the foreign firm engages only in local distribution and marketing of a company's final product made at its home base.
12. For an illustration of the complexity of such relations in practice, see Chesnais (1995, p. 9).
13. See also Bondt and Sleuwaegen (1988, p. 25).
14. This is the case in the trade mode of internationalisation, and what Pearce (1993, p. 152) calls the 'overseas production mode'.
15. 'Integration' originates from Latin, in which '*integratio*' initially meant 'renovation'. Later on its meaning changed to 'combining parts into a whole'. See Machlup (1976, pp. 61–3).
16. Molle derived the six stages from Balassa (1961). In the second edition of his book Molle revised the six stages to some extent. See Molle (1994, pp. 10–12).
17. It is obvious that for existing combinations of ownership and locational advantages for which internalisation advantages were present, economic integration may create internalisation disadvantages. This can imply a disinvestment.
18. Note that production at the home base can also be considered as an optimal combination of ownership, locational and internalisation advantages.
19. This notion has already been put forward in location theories by Von Thünen, Christaller and Lösch. See Lloyd and Dicken (1977, Chapter 2).
20. Krugman (1991a, pp. 36–8) refers to Alfred Marshall, who identified these three reasons for localisation.
21. Others call this 'agglomeration forces'. See Olsson (1965, p. 7).
22. For example, steel is an input to automobile production, but it is the final product of a steel mill.
23. Multinational companies seem to engage regularly in licensing agreements with their foreign affiliates. See Morsink (1992, pp. 169–71).
24. In this respect, Dunning's emphasis on internalisation was not surprising.
25. See the discussion on 'de-internalisation' of a multinational enterprise in Rugman, Verbeke and D'Cruz (1995, pp. 107–28).
26. The corporate structure can attain a certain level of integration despite existing barriers, by using its ownership advantages from technical, organisational or other innovations to circumvent them. It may also be the case that existing barriers are irrelevant to the company's activities.
27. Note that the parent company is not necessarily located within the region: for example, an American transnational company can have a complete production system in the European Union. See United Nations (1993b, p. 129).

3. A Model for Analysing Geographical Investment Patterns: MOSAIC

3.1 INTRODUCTION

Having developed a theoretical framework for foreign direct investments in the previous chapter and having formulated a hypothesis on the geographical diversity in investment opportunities, it is now time to develop an analytical tool for testing the hypothesis. To this end, this chapter will develop the gravity-type model MOSAIC, the MOdel for Spatial Analysis of Investment Conditions.

The history of gravity modelling shows that gravity models have been used to analyse a wide variety of social and economic interaction in geographical space (see Appendix II). Gravity models have been particularly developed for investigating some types of internationalisation. Tinbergen, Pöyhönen and Linnemann have been among the first to use gravity modelling for analysing international trade flows. Other applications on trade flows can be found in Pulliainen, van Bergeijk and Ménil and Maurel. Vanderkamp has used a gravity model to explain migration flows. Heijke together with Klaassen, and Molle together with van Mourik have developed gravity models for explaining labour movements (for references see Appendix II). To date it appears that foreign direct investment flows have not been analysed with gravity models very often.

It seems appropriate to use a gravity-type model also for analysing geographical patterns in foreign direct investment flows. If the model is successfully applied to many spatial phenomena, in particular in the field of internationalisation issues such as trade and migration, it may provide a satisfying tool for investigating international investments as well. Further, it seems to be a flexible tool in which the many push, pull, stimulus and friction factors identified in the theoretical framework can be included easily.

In most applications of the gravity model a formal derivation is lacking. Bergstrand appears to be the only one to have made an effort. He derives a gravity equation from a general equilibrium model for world trade (Bergstrand 1985). In this model, the 'generalized' gravity equation results, when all markets are in equilibrium. The equation is a function in which re determined by income in home and host countries, transport riff rates and the exchange rate. Later, when he extends some of his ptions, Bergstrand (1989) derives a gravity equation, in which exports a function of national output, capital and labour stock in the home country, income and per capita income in the host country and transport costs, trade tariffs and the exchange rate between both countries.

It is not the intention here to develop a formal derivation of a gravity model for foreign direct investment. It is tempting to reformulate Bergstrand's model into one for foreign direct investment, as it is an alternative mode of internationalisation *vis-à-vis* trade. However, Bergstrand uses a general equilibrium framework, which implies that he assumes perfectly competitive markets. Caves (1982, p. 128) shows that multinational enterprises do not operate in such markets. Hence, deriving a formal model for foreign direct investments requires a framework in which market imperfections exist. Developing such a framework is very complex and would require a separate in-depth study, which would go beyond the scope of this book.

The structure of this chapter will be as follows. First, the many push, pull, stimulus and friction factors that could approximate the influences put forward in the theoretical framework will be presented. These factors will be transformed into specific hypotheses on foreign direct investment determinants, which can be tested using MOSAIC. Next, the relation between investment determinants and corporate strategies will be discussed. Finally, an outline will be given on the way in which estimations will be made using MOSAIC and how the estimation results will be presented in subsequent chapters.

3.2 HYPOTHESES ON DETERMINANTS OF FOREIGN DIRECT INVESTMENTS

3.2.1 Knowledge Transfer Hypothesis

In the previous chapter it was shown that knowledge plays an important role in establishing ownership advantages. In addition, it contributes to creating new networking opportunities from which additional ownership advantages can arise. Further, new knowledge can be used to overcome existing (political) barriers.

As was already indicated in the previous chapter, the creation of new ownership advantages in the home country is an important push factor. It provides new opportunities for combining them with locational advantages of host markets. This implies a knowledge transfer from the home country (*i*) to the host country (*j*). When internalisation advantages exist, the new opportunities will become foreign direct investments.

The following knowledge creation indicators will be used in the analyses:

- gross domestic expenditure on R&D in the home country as a percentage of GDP;
- business expenditures on R&D in the home country as a percentage of the domestic product of industry.

A positive relation of these indicators with foreign direct investment is to be expected. The higher the level of knowledge creation in a home country is, the more companies within this country are inclined to exploit the obtained ownership advantages abroad via foreign direct investment:

$$\frac{\partial FDI_{ij}}{\partial R\&D_i} > 0. \tag{3.1}$$

3.2.2   Market Potential Hypotheses

A particular locational advantage is the attractiveness of the market in the host country or the demand potential. This is determined by the number of (potential) customers and their level of income or purchasing power. This constitutes a potential for (future) market revenues. Hence, foreign market potential is an important pull factor.

Market potential hypotheses have various links with similar hypotheses described by Agarwal (1980, p. 746). First, he identifies the 'market size hypothesis', which states a positive relationship between the size of the foreign market and foreign direct investment. Second, Agarwal mentions the 'output hypothesis', which argues that with growing sales volumes determined by the number of potential customers and their income, companies are likely to engage in foreign direct investment.

In the analyses, two hypotheses will be tested: a market size hypothesis and a per capita income hypothesis. As an indicator of market size or demand potential in the foreign market, the population size in the host country (*POP*) seems most appropriate. For per capita income the level of gross domestic product per capita in the host country (*GCA*) seems the obvious variable. Another variable is the growth in GDP per capita in the host country. Investors could consider the growth in per capita income a stronger pull factor than its level. There is likely to be a positive relation of these indicators with foreign direct investment. The larger the size of the host market and the higher its per capita income (growth) the more foreign companies are inclined to engage in foreign direct investment:

$$\frac{\partial FDI_{ij}}{\partial POP_j} > 0. \tag{3.2}$$

$$\frac{\partial FDI_{ij}}{\partial GCA_j} > 0. \tag{3.3}$$

3.2.3 Labour Cost Hypothesis

Another locational advantage may be that the host market provides attractive inputs for a company's production process. A company can consider moving production to the host country and internalising the input provision in its corporate structure. In his product cycle, Vernon (1966) indicates the availability of cheap inputs, in particular cheap labour, as an essential determinant for moving production capacity abroad. Hence, cheap inputs attract foreign direct investments and can thus be interpreted as a pull factor.

As an indicator for input availability, the average real labour costs per employee in the host country will be used. Effectively, this limits the input orientation hypothesis to one of labour availability only, but data limitations prohibit the inclusion of other input indicators. Various specifications are used:

- the level of labour costs per employee in the host country in real value terms or as an index;
- the level of labour costs per employee in the host country as an index of the level of labour costs per employee in the home country;
- the percentage change of labour costs per employee in the host country.

Low labour costs per employee in the host country (*WAGE*) will attract more foreign direct investment to this country, which implies a negative relationship:

$$\frac{\partial FDI_{ij}}{\partial WAGE_j} < 0. \tag{3.4}$$

However, in Krugman's theory on regional synergies, it is argued that in core regions synergies are created in the field of labour skills. This is a quality aspect of labour, which generally translates into a higher wage level. A company may choose a location with skilled labour, accepting the higher labour costs. This may imply also that a positive relation between labour costs per employee and foreign direct investment could exist.

3.2.4 Return on Investment Differences Hypothesis

Some theories on foreign direct investment have concentrated on portfolio-orientated determinants. In particular, the differential rate of return hypothesis and the portfolio hypothesis should be mentioned here (Agarwal 1980, pp. 741–46). These hypotheses are based on theories in which the cost of capital determines the allocation of investments.

The differential rate of return hypothesis is based on the traditional theory of investment, in which the firm seeks profit maximisation by equalling the marginal return on capital and the marginal cost of capital. It can be expected that investment funds will flow from countries with low rates of return on capital to those with high rates.

The portfolio hypothesis is based on the same line of thought, but now considers foreign direct investment to be a special form of international portfolio selection because the investor will try to diversify the risks on all assets in his or her portfolio.[1] Hence, investment funds will flow not only to countries with a higher yield on capital, but also to those with limited risk on investments.

A linkage with this study's theoretical background arises when differences in the rate of return on capital give an indication of the existence of internalisation advantages. Return on capital can be considered as an indication of the balance of revenue flows from a market and production and transaction costs to service that market. An investor will engage in foreign direct investment if he or she expects the return on this investment to be higher than the return from other modes of internationalisation.

The indicator that will be used to approximate return on investment is the difference in the real average yield on long-term government bonds (*RLDIFF*) between home and host countries. Real average yield is determined by correcting the nominal yield (*RL*) with the GDP deflator (*P*):

$$RLDIFF_{ij} = (RL_j - P_j) - (RL_i - P_i). \tag{3.5}$$

If the real rate in the host country $(RL_j - P_j)$ is higher than the rate in the home country $(RL_i - P_i)$, then *RLDIFF* is positive. This will incur foreign direct investment flows from the home to the host country and makes *RLDIFF* a stimulus factor. When *RLDIFF* is negative, investments from the home to the host country will be restricted and the real rate difference becomes a barrier or friction factor. Hence, companies will invest in host countries, where the difference *vis-à-vis* return on investment at home is largest:

$$\frac{\partial FDI_{ij}}{\partial RLDIFF_{ij}} > 0.$$ (3.6)

However, although relevant for investment decisions, it can be considered questionable whether a company builds its foreign direct investment decisions on the net return as a major determinant. In view of corporate strategies, long-term sustainability of market revenues and efficient production and distribution are likely to be more important. Therefore, if return on investment is identified as a determinant of major importance, the question can be raised whether the investment really has a corporate strategy orientation. An investor may have a portfolio orientation instead.

3.2.5   Taxation Differences Hypothesis

A hypothesis that could be related to the previous one is the taxation differences hypothesis. If the level of taxation in a host country is substantially lower than in the home country, a company may want to invest more in the host country in order to benefit from a higher after-tax return on investment due to lower tax levels. When taxation in the home country is lower than elsewhere, investors may want investment capital to stay in the home country to get a high after-tax return. Relatively high taxation in the home country may force investors to seek investment opportunities in countries where the taxation pressure is lower than at home.

Various authors have studied the relation between taxation and foreign direct investment. Devereux and Freeman (1995, p. 97) identified the after-tax cost of capital as a relevant investment determinant. They derive this from estimating the impact of taxation on foreign direct investment for seven countries during the period 1984–89 by using the real rate of interest in the home country and the tax wedge between home and host countries. Slemrod (1990, p. 112), in studying inward investment flows into the United States from seven major investing countries, identified the effective rates of taxation in the United States as a relevant investment determinant.

The indicator which will be used is based on analyses made by Devereux and Pearson (1989). They have measured differences in taxation between any two nations by comparing their rates of return before taxation required to get a net after-tax return of 5 per cent. Dividing this required rate in the host country with that in the home country gives a measure of taxation difference between both countries. When the ratio is about one, taxation differences can be considered minor. When it is larger than unity, taxation in the host country is more severe than at home, which implies taxation to be a barrier or friction factor for investment flows from the home country to the host. When the index is less than unity, taxation becomes a stimulus factor. Taxation abroad is less than at home, which causes investors to transfer capital abroad. Hence, the relation between taxation differences and foreign direct investment is likely to be negative. Foreign investors are inclined to locate in markets where taxation is lowest:

$$\frac{\partial FDI_{ij}}{\partial TAXDIFF_{ij}} < 0. \tag{3.7}$$

The taxation differences hypothesis is similar to the return on investment differences hypothesis. Both hypotheses approximate the actual result following from revenue flows and production and transaction costs. Instead of a gross result in the return on investment differences hypothesis, the taxation differences hypothesis stresses the net result. Again, the question on portfolio orientation could be raised whether a strong influence is found.

The taxation differences hypothesis may also indicate a relevancy of favourable taxation policies. If the difference in taxation between two countries influences foreign direct investment considerably, it may be the case that favourable taxation policies exist in host countries.

It should be noted that Devereux and Pearson estimated their indicators only for a specific period and made several assumptions in deriving these estimates. This calls for a careful interpretation, if this variable is identified as a relevant investment determinant.

3.2.6   Transport Cost Hypothesis

Transportation costs are an important component of transaction costs in economic geography. Other transaction costs could relate to costs of coordination and communication and costs to transfer funds.[2] As a foreign direct investment flow can be seen as a transaction, transport costs are a relevant determinant.[3] Therefore, a transport cost hypothesis, in which transport costs are a friction factor, puts forward a negative relation between foreign direct investment and transport cost.

As a proxy for transportation costs the straight-line distance in kilometres between the most important economic centres of countries (*DISTANCE*) will be used in the analyses.[4] It is clear that a negative relationship with foreign direct investment is envisaged:

$$\frac{\partial FDI_{ij}}{\partial DISTANCE_{ij}} < 0. \tag{3.8}$$

A qualification needs to be made regarding the relation between trade and foreign direct investment. In the case of trade from the home country to the host market, goods have to be transported physically. Distance thus incurs transportation costs, which are highly relevant for the price of the product on the host market. In the case of foreign direct investment replacing this trade relation, physical transportation is obviously of less importance. The physical distance may even have stimulated the choice for the foreign direct investment mode.[5] However, in the previous chapter it was argued that in practice the pure trade substitution case is less common. In most cases, the trade relation continues to exist and so does the relevance of physical transportation costs.

3.2.7   Cultural Differences Hypothesis

Another hypothesis which could influence foreign direct investment decisions, deals with the existence of cultural differences. In the case of a large cultural difference between the home and the (potential) host countries, an economic interchange may be blocked. Cultural difference is a friction factor to host-market provision.

For the foreign direct investment mode, cultural differences could be a stronger barrier than for other modes. This is due to the fact that a foreign direct investment is a far-reaching mode of internationalisation, as in this mode the foreign owner takes full or substantial control of the foreign entity. If local habits and customs of employees in the host country are very different from those of the managers from the home country, serious conflicts could arise.[6] This could lead to high production and transaction costs.

Measuring cultural differences is not an easy task. At the beginning of the 1980s, Hofstede (1984) made an elaborate comparative study of cultural differences between countries, distinguishing four dimensions for which he constructed indices:

- power distance index: extent of hierarchical inequality between a boss and his or her subordinates in a country;
- uncertainty avoidance index: extent of tolerance towards future uncertainties in a country;
- individualism index: extent of dominance of individuals versus that of the collectivity within a society;
- masculinity index: extent of a nation's population to endorse goals usually more popular among men than among women.

Cultural differences (*CULTDIFF*) can be measured by dividing the indices for host and home countries:[7]

$$CULTDIFF_{ij} = \frac{CULT_j}{CULT_i} \qquad if\ CULT_j > CULT_i$$

or   (3.9)

$$CULTDIFF_{ij} = \frac{CULT_i}{CULT_j} \qquad if\ CULT_j < CULT_i.$$

When the resulting index is about equal to one, there is little cultural difference. An index substantially larger than one represents a large difference. Hence, a negative relationship with foreign direct investment is likely. Foreign investors are inclined to invest in host markets, where the difference with their own culture is lowest:

$$\frac{\partial FDI_{ij}}{\partial CULTDIFF_{ij}} < 0. \qquad (3.10)$$

Unfortunately, Hofstede made his analysis for only one period. No updates have been made available so far. Therefore, caution is required when interpreting results from analysing the relationship between cultural difference and foreign direct investment.

3.2.8   Trade Intensity Hypothesis

Although this study does not analyse the determinants of the trade mode, it is relevant to consider the relation between foreign direct investment and trade. In Chapter 2 it was shown that the relation between host-country production and trade is complex. Trade is only replaced in the case of a horizontal investment, servicing the market of a host country from a local production unit. In other cases, which generally relate to vertical investment relations, there is likely to be a complementary relationship. Creating a local production facility will incur new trade flows: imports of inputs and semi-finished products for local assembly and exports of manufactures from the local production unit.

In the scenarios of Vernon and Håkanson and in the model of Buckley and Casson, the foreign direct investment mode of internationalisation is chosen when a certain level of trade is achieved. The company has obtained sufficient knowledge about the foreign market and has reached a market volume of sufficient substance to consider changing the internationalisation mode.

$$TRI_{ij} = \frac{TRD_{ij}}{TRD_i} + \frac{TRD_{ij}}{TRD_j}. \tag{3.11}$$

Various indicators can be used for the intensity of trade relations. A first indicator is the sum of relative trade shares (*TRI*). This is measured as the share of the bilateral trade flow in total home-country exports plus the share of the bilateral trade flow in the host-country imports. If there is no trade between two countries the indicator is zero; if bilateral trade is the only foreign trade both countries engage in, then the indicator amounts to two. Another indicator is the share of the trade flow between the home and host countries in the total of the home-country's exports. This also gives an indication of the importance of the host country for companies in the home country. A third indicator is the growth rate of the trade flow between the home and host countries. If this variable is found of relevance, investments may be stimulated by the strong growth in mutual economic relations.

In general, a positive relation between foreign direct investment and trade is expected, because complementarity with trade is considered the norm. It is likely that this relation is lagged: the decision to switch to the investment mode is based on the intensity of trade having reached a sufficient level in the past. Further, in the previous chapter it was argued that adjustment costs and uncertainty may postpone the switch. Hence, it is probable that it takes some time before this decision leads to an actual investment:

$$\frac{\partial FDI_{ij}}{\partial TRADE_{ij}^{t-1}} > 0. \tag{3.12}$$

Sometimes a negative relation may occur if trade substitution prevails. Trade intensity is not high and may even decrease, when the foreign direct investment materialises. Following Bergstrand, this may even point to the existence of trade barriers.

Trade intensity may also be considered as an indication of the level of trade liberalisation or economic integration between any two countries. One may expect a positive impulse to mutual trade when trade barriers are removed.[8] Further, one may expect a high trade intensity when integration processes have reached higher stages of economic integration (see Table 2.3).

3.2.9 Exchange Rate Hypotheses

Lizondo (1991, p. 74) and Agarwal (1980, pp. 756–8) mention some economists who have theorised on the relation between foreign direct investment and currency fluctuations. One of these economists, Aliber (1970 and 1971), postulated a relation between foreign direct investment patterns and the relative strength of currencies. Firms from strong-currency countries are more likely to invest abroad than those from weak-currency countries due to lower costs for borrowing and more favourable capitalisation of foreign earnings. Another economist, Caves (1988), claimed that currencies had a double impact on foreign direct investment. He argued that foreign direct investments are influenced by changes in the real exchange rate because they modify a firm's real cost and revenue flows. In addition, in his view expectations on exchange rate movements have an impact if future appreciations cause capital gains.

Capel (1993, Chapter 2) argues that the relation between exchange rates and foreign direct investment is highly complex. In her view the exposure to foreign exchange rate risk depends on the type of investment made. If the investment relates to a backward vertical linkage in a network, exposure can be different from the case of a forward vertical linkage. This is also the case for a horizontal investment *vis-à-vis* a vertical investment. Further, she indicates that the financing of the investment with internal or external funds and the risk attitude of a company's managers are important. Finally, she suggests that the market structure in which a firm operates is of major importance.

The views of Aliber, Caves and Capel advocate clearly that exchange rate fluctuations matter, but that their impact depends on many circumstances. Fluctuations influence the internalisation question via an impact on foreign revenues and costs. Also, the value of invested capital can be reduced when host currencies depreciate. On the other hand, exchange rate movements can create opportunities to purchase foreign assets cheaply. This depends on the direction in which the exchange rate moves and which risks exist for the future development of this rate.

Measuring risks from exchange rate fluctuations is not easy. Various methodological issues arise according to Stokman (1995, p. 45). A first issue is the difference between volatility and misalignment. Volatility refers to short-term movements in the exchange rate; misalignment is a long-term deviation from an equilibrium parity. Another issue is the effect of hedging activities. Hedging reduces risk, which implies that variations in the exchange rate may not be the same as risk. A third issue relates to the question whether variations should be derived from nominal exchange rates or real ones. Perée and Steinherr (1989) show that various measures are used to indicate exchange rate variability. There is no ideal concept because each concept can be used for specific analytical purposes only. Therefore, in this analysis a practical approach will be followed and particular specifications will be derived.

For analysing the relationship between foreign direct investment and the development of the exchange rate between currencies of home and host countries, it seems relevant to investigate:

- the direction in the development of the bilateral exchange rate, which relates to Stokman's misalignment issue; and
- the volatility in the development of the bilateral exchange rate, which relates to Stokman's hedging issue.

Before doing so, it is necessary to consider the third issue raised by Stokman: the use of nominal or real exchange rates. In his article, he studies the impact of nominal exchange rate changes on international trade. This seems appropriate because the nominal exchange rate gives some indication of competitive positions. For foreign direct investment, there is an inclination to follow Caves and use real exchange rates. In assessing foreign direct investment decisions a company evaluates real revenue and cost flows over a long time period. Further, a company pursuing a certain strategy is more likely to assess the real value of its assets in the long term, rather than their nominal value. Many currency movements are related to price movements and are therefore less relevant for such assessments.

The indicators that will be developed are based on the average monthly nominal bilateral exchange rates corrected with a monthly GDP deflator:

$$REX_{ij}^m = \frac{EX_{ij}^m \cdot P_j^m}{P_i^m}. \tag{3.13}$$

where:

EX_{ij}^m = average monthly nominal bilateral exchange rate of the home country's currency per unit of the host country's currency;

P^m = average monthly GDP deflator;

REX_{ij}^m = average monthly real bilateral exchange rate of the home country's currency per unit of the host country's currency.

However, if foreign direct investment is considered as a financial phenomenon instead of a real phenomenon, nominal exchange rate movements may be more relevant. The financing of a foreign direct investment is a highly complex question in which all kinds of domestic and foreign opportunities can play a role. In this study, foreign direct investment is considered more as a real phenomenon than as a financial phenomenon.

3.2.9.1 Exchange rate direction

The exchange rate may be at a level at which investors can purchase assets cheaply. This can be the case if investors consider a foreign currency to be undervalued. Equivocally, an overvalued foreign currency may block foreign direct investments. In fact, this relates to Stokman's misalignment problem.

Misalignment suggests that there is a difference between the actual exchange rate and a revealed or expected equilibrium exchange rate. Measuring such differences is difficult, but indications can be obtained if the direction of exchange rate movements is considered. Therefore, the relation between possible investment actions in view of the direction of exchange rate movements is assessed here.

Table 3.1   Home-country firms' investment actions in view of exchange rate movements towards third currencies

Home-country currency	Host-country currency	Bilateral exchange rate[a]	Home-country firms' view on host	Effect on FDI flow from home to host country
Stable	Stable	Stable	Single currency area	No major effect
Stable	Appreciating	Increasing	Expensive host	Friction
Stable	Depreciating	Decreasing	Attractive host	Stimulus
Appreciating	Stable	Decreasing	Attractive host	Stimulus
Appreciating	Appreciating	Indeterminate	Indeterminate	Indeterminate
Appreciating	Depreciating	Decreasing	Attractive host	Stimulus
Depreciating	Stable	Increasing	Expensive host	Friction
Depreciating	Appreciating	Increasing	Expensive host	Friction
Depreciating	Depreciating	Indeterminate	Indeterminate	Indeterminate

Note
a. Home country's currency per unit of the host country's currency.

Table 3.1 identifies possible foreign direct investment actions that companies may take when the exchange rate between home- and host-country currencies changes.[9] Three situations can occur. First, the bilateral exchange rate remains stable, which implies no major impact on foreign direct investment decisions. The company can consider the two currency areas as a single one. Second, the bilateral exchange rate increases. This makes the host country expensive for home-country investors because the investment cost in home-currency units will increase. This causes a friction to invest in the host country. Third, the bilateral exchange rate decreases. The host country becomes more attractive for home-country investors because total investment costs expressed in the home currency will decrease. The bilateral exchange rate changes cause a stimulus to invest abroad. If the development of the bilateral exchange rate is indeterminate, any of the three situations may arise.

According to Visser (1995, pp. 92–3), it should be noted that foreign direct investment itself has a long-term impact on the direction of exchange rate movements. In discussing a long-term portfolio model in which capital flows play a role, Visser argues that foreign direct investments in a host country may cause an appreciation in the host currency. The investments add to the stock of foreign capital in the host country, from which dividend and interest payments are made to the home country. In the long run, these payments may lead to a depreciation in the host currency and an appreciation in the home currency. In this study, these long-term effects are not taken into account.

In order to test the influence of the direction of exchange rate movements, it is necessary to develop indicators that can distinguish between an increasing and a decreasing bilateral exchange rate. If it increases, the indicator should have a positive value; if it decreases the value should be negative. The following indicators of exchange rate movements are derived from the average monthly real bilateral exchange rates.

The first exchange rate direction indicator (*REXDA*) measures the average (μ) relative changes of monthly real bilateral exchange rates during a period of M months:

$$REXDA_{ij} = \mathop{\mu}_{m=1}^{M} \left(\frac{REX_{ij}^{m} - REX_{ij}^{m-1}}{REX_{ij}^{m-1}} \right). \tag{3.14}$$

The second exchange rate direction indicator (*REXDQ*) measures the sum of changes in monthly real bilateral exchange rates during a period of M months divided by the average monthly real bilateral exchange rate (μ) during that period:

$$REXDQ_{ij} = \frac{\sum\limits_{m=1}^{M} \left(REX_{ij}^{m} - REX_{ij}^{m-1} \right)}{\mathop{\mu}\limits_{m=1}^{M} \left(REX_{ij}^{m} \right)}. \tag{3.15}$$

When the host country's currency is appreciating towards the home country's currency, *REX* has a tendency to increase. This implies that

REXDA and *REXDQ* are positive.[10] Such an appreciation makes an investment by an investor from a home country expensive: the value of the investment to be made in home-country currency units will increase. In the case of a depreciation, the situation is reversed: *REX* will decrease, *REXDA* and *REXDQ* are negative and the value of the envisaged investment will decrease.[11] Hence, there is likely to be a negative relation between the indicators of exchange rate direction (*REXD*) on one hand and foreign direct investment on the other:

$$\frac{\partial FDI_{ij}}{\partial REXD_{ij}} < 0. \tag{3.16}$$

3.2.9.2 Exchange rate volatility

So far, the volatility of the exchange rate has not been taken into account. Volatility is, however, also considered an important friction factor. Large fluctuations in the exchange rates of a host country's currency cause uncertainty about the value of the assets to be invested in. Although the movement of the exchange rate may then be favourable for foreign direct investments, the uncertainty of its future value may block the actual investment. Therefore, another set of exchange rate indicators is derived, which reflect the volatility of the real bilateral exchange rate.[12]

In view of Stokman's second issue on variability and risk, a distinction needs to be made between two categories of exchange rate variability:

- *expected variability*: the exchange rate follows expected tendencies. These can take various forms, such as a trend line or a seasonal pattern. Their consequences can be hedged on the futures markets for currencies, which more or less compensates for the exchange rate risk;
- *unexpected variability*: in general, there is a difference between the actual exchange rate and the expected exchange rate. These differences are of an erratic nature. This type of variability cannot be hedged.

In total, five alternative specifications are used in the analyses. Some specifications contain both types of variability. These are the unconditional specifications, which are based on the actual values of the real bilateral exchange rate. Other specifications try to eliminate expected variability. They are based either on the deviations of the actual exchange rates from its trend line value or on percentage changes in the exchange rate. These are referred to as the conditional specifications.[13]

$$REXVMM_{ij} = \frac{\max\limits_{m=1}^{M}\left(REX_{ij}^{m}\right) - \min\limits_{m=1}^{M}\left(REX_{ij}^{m}\right)}{\mu\limits_{m=1}^{M}\left(REX_{ij}^{m}\right)}. \tag{3.17}$$

The first specification is of the unconditional type. It is defined as the quotient of the difference between the maximum and the minimum value and the average value. Values are determined by the monthly real bilateral exchange rates during the period under consideration.

$$REXVSD_{ij} = \frac{\sigma\limits_{m=1}^{M}\left(REX_{ij}^{m}\right)}{\mu\limits_{m=1}^{M}\left(REX_{ij}^{m}\right)}. \tag{3.18}$$

The second specification is also unconditional in character. It is determined as the standard deviation divided by the average. Both are derived from the monthly real bilateral exchange rates during the observation period.

$$REXVTR_{ij} = \sigma\limits_{m=1}^{M}\left(REX_{ij}^{m} - \frac{\sum\limits_{m=m-5}^{m+6} REX_{ij}^{m}}{12}\right). \tag{3.19}$$

The third specification is a conditional one because it tries to eliminate the expected variability from the data. This is done by calculating a twelve-month moving average of the monthly real bilateral exchange rates and subtracting it from the actual values. Variability is then determined as the standard deviation of the resulting trend-line deviations.

$$REXVPK_{ij} = \sigma\limits_{m=1}^{M}\left\{\left(\frac{REX_{ij}^{m}}{REX_{ij}^{m-1}} - 1\right)\cdot 100\right\}. \tag{3.20}$$

Another conditional specification is the fourth indicator. For this indicator the expected variability is removed by calculating the month-to-month percentage change of the real bilateral exchange rate. This indicator can therefore be interpreted as a proxy for short-term variability.[14]

$$REXVPL_{ij} = \sum_{m=1}^{M} \left\{ \left(\frac{REX_{ij}^{m}}{REX_{ij}^{m-12}} - 1 \right) \cdot 100 \right\}. \tag{3.21}$$

The fifth specification resembles the previous one. It is also of the conditional type because it eliminates the trend line in a similar way. Expected variability is now removed by calculating the percentage change of the monthly real bilateral exchange rate versus its value in the same month in the previous year. To some extent a longer-term perspective is taken into account in this variability indicator.[15]

The relation between exchange rate volatility (*REXV*) and foreign direct investment seems obvious. Increasing volatility will discourage investors to transfer capital. The expected relation is therefore negative. This implies that investors will prefer to invest in host markets, where the volatility of the host currency's exchange rate *vis-à-vis* the home currency is lowest:

$$\frac{\partial FDI_{ij}}{\partial REXV_{ij}} < 0. \tag{3.22}$$

It must be noted, however, that the exchange rate volatility indicator represents only mutual variability of the currencies of home and host countries. It does not identify the stability of the home currency or the host currency *vis-à-vis* third currencies. If the home currency is stable and the host currency is not, one may expect that the host-currency instability leads to a disinclination to invest. In the case where the host currency is stable, but the home-country currency is not, there may be a situation in which investors try to find safe havens for their investment capital. Should this occur, the relation between the volatility indicator and foreign direct investment may become positive. The investment motive may then relate rather to a portfolio orientation, than to a corporate strategy orientation.

3.3 INVESTMENT DETERMINANTS AND CORPORATE STRATEGIES

In the previous chapter, three types of strategies identified by the United Nations were put forward: the stand-alone strategy, the simple affiliate integration strategy and the complex international production strategy. They were ranked in an increasing order of complexity in terms of network interlinkages and of coordination needs.

This section will discuss the relation between the empirical investment determinants in MOSAIC put forward in the previous section and the three types of corporate strategy. Each investment determinant will be discussed briefly with respect to its relevance for the three strategy types. Finally, for each strategy type a profile of relevant investment determinants will be derived.

Knowledge proxies the existence of certain ownership advantages that a company wants to combine with advantages available in foreign locations. This intention arises in any corporate strategy and is irrespective of the complexity of network linkages and coordination needs. This implies that knowledge transfer is a relevant push factor in all strategy types. However, as complex international production strategies seem to depend among others on technological developments, its relevance could be higher in such strategy types.

For market potential the relevance for corporate strategies differs. Market potential influences a company's revenue flows from output and therefore particularly determines the location of downstream economic activities in corporate networks. In stand-alone strategies, a foreign direct investment is particularly directed towards servicing the foreign market. Hence, in a stand-alone strategy, market size and per capita income are likely to be major pull factors. This may also be the case if simple affiliate integration strategies aim at downstream activities. In complex international production strategies, market potential is surely relevant, but in relation to other determinants not of major importance, whereas in simple affiliate integration strategies for upstream activities it seems a less obvious pull factor.

For labour costs, as a proxy for input orientation, the relevance in strategies also differs. Labour costs determine a company's production costs and therefore are likely to play an important role in locating upstream economic activities. For stand-alone strategies, labour costs are a less obvious determinant because such strategies are strongly market (downstream) orientated. In simple affiliate integration strategies for upstream activities, low labour costs in the host country could exert a major pull. The affiliate is then important for providing cheap inputs in subsequent stages of a corporate structure's network. In the case where the simple affiliate integration strategy is directed towards downstream activities, low labour costs may be a less obvious pull factor. If labour quality is identified as a determinant, a similar relevance can be expected. When complex international production strategies prevail, low labour costs or labour quality are a possible pull among other determinants.

Regarding return on investment differences and taxation differences, it can be expected that they are relevant stimulus or friction factors for any corporate strategy. Each investor evaluates the result of market revenues and production and transaction costs of the foreign direct investment, both before and after taxation, and puts it in the perspective of possible pre-tax and post-tax returns at home. However, differences can be more important in stand-alone and simple affiliate integration strategies. Complex international production strategies may emerge in reasonably well-integrated areas where differences may have become minor due to capital market integration and government policy coordination.

Transport costs also seem relevant for all corporate strategy types. The transport cost barrier continues to exist irrespective of the intensity of network linkages in the corporate structure. If transport costs can be considered a proxy for coordination costs, the relevance may be stronger in more complex strategies.

Cultural differences are an important barrier for adequate coordination between economic activities in corporate structures. It was shown that more complex corporate strategies require higher levels of coordination than strategies of a simpler nature. Therefore, if cultural differences are identified as a barrier to investments abroad, this may coincide with stand-alone and simple affiliate integration strategies. The lower level of coordination needed in such strategies may be a way for the investor to evade the friction from the cultural difference barrier. Because intensive coordination is a prerequisite of complex international production strategies, the cultural differences barrier may not exist on foreign direct investment relations where this strategy type prevails. Therefore, it is expected that cultural differences are a less obvious determinant for this strategy type.

The importance of trade intensity is expected to be high in all corporate strategy types because trade linkages reveal the potentials for other internationalisation modes. The direction of the relation between trade and foreign direct investment is likely to differ in the various strategy types. In a stand-alone strategy the investment may coincide with trade substitution. In such a strategy, a company may want to circumvent existing trade barriers by establishing a local subsidiary producing for the domestic market.[16] In other strategies, the relation between trade and foreign direct investment is likely to be complementary. The foreign affiliate belongs to a network of interlinked economic activities in a corporate structure. If the affiliate engages in an upstream activity, it exports to other activities in the network; if it is a downstream activity, it imports products from other activities in the network. In both cases trade intensity increases.

The direction of the exchange rate movement is a relevant stimulus or friction factor for each foreign direct investment decision. However, a clear linkage with corporate strategies does not seem obvious. In each strategy type, investors appraise the value of the foreign assets to be purchased.

The volatility of the exchange rate movement on the other hand seems more important. If foreign direct investments encounter barriers from exchange rate volatility, complex international production strategies are less obvious. If companies have to bother about exchange rate instability, the relations between economic activities in the corporate structure become seriously hampered. Therefore, it can be expected that complex international production strategies prevail on relations where exchange rate instability is not a major friction factor for foreign direct investments. In less complex strategies, however, the validity of this hypothesis continues to be relevant.

Table 3.2 Foreign direct investment determinant profiles of corporate strategies

Determinant	Stand-alone strategy	Simple affiliate integration strategy		Complex international production strategy
		Upstream	Downstream	
Knowledge transfer	Relevant push	Relevant push	Relevant push	Relevant push
Market size	Major pull	Less obvious pull	Major pull	Relevant pull
Per capita income	Major pull	Less obvious pull	Major pull	Relevant pull
Labour costs	Less obvious pull	Major pull	Less obvious pull	Possible pull
Return on investment differences	Possible determinant	Possible determinant	Possible determinant	Minor determinant
Taxation differences	Possible determinant	Possible determinant	Possible determinant	Minor determinant
Transport costs	Relevant friction	Relevant friction	Relevant friction	Relevant friction
Cultural differences	Relevant friction	Relevant friction	Relevant friction	Less obvious friction
Trade intensity	Major friction	Major stimulus	Major stimulus	Major stimulus
Exchange rate direction	Possible determinant	Possible determinant	Possible determinant	Possible determinant
Exchange rate volatility	Possible friction	Possible friction	Possible friction	Less obvious friction

The above can be summarized in profiles of relevant foreign direct investment determinants for the three strategy types. Table 3.2 shows these profiles with a qualitative indication of the expected relevancy of the investment determinants. Stand-alone strategies dominate when market orientation is strong enough to entail investments despite existing barriers. Generally, this coincides with trade substitution. Simple affiliate integration strategies prevail when investments relate to activities which have either a market or an input orientation. This depends on whether the activity is of a downstream or upstream nature. Barriers continue to exist, but the activity can play a role in a corporate structure's network of activities. This coincides with a complementary relation between investment and trade. Complex international production strategies arise on investment relations, where barriers in the field of cultural differences and exchange rate volatility have become less important for investing abroad. This enables close interlinkages among economic activities in the corporate structure's network.

3.4 MOSAIC ESTIMATIONS

In the previous sections the theoretical background for geographical patterns in foreign direct investments, developed in Chapter 2, has been translated into specific hypotheses to be incorporated into MOSAIC, the MOdel for Spatial Analysis of Investment Conditions. In summary, MOSAIC can be specified as the following gravity-type model:

$$FDI_{ij}^{t} = \begin{bmatrix} \alpha_0 \cdot (R\&D_i^{t})^{\alpha_1} \cdot (POP_j^{t})^{\alpha_2} \cdot (GCA_j^{t})^{\alpha_3} \cdot \\ (WAGE_j^{t})^{\alpha_4} \cdot (RLDIFF_{ij}^{t})^{\alpha_5} \cdot (TAXDIFF_{ij}^{t})^{\alpha_6} \cdot \\ (DISTANCE_{ij}^{t})^{\alpha_7} \cdot (CULTDIFF_{ij}^{t})^{\alpha_8} \cdot \\ (TRADE_{ij}^{t-1})^{\alpha_9} \cdot (REXD_{ij}^{t})^{\alpha_{10}} \cdot (REXV_{ij}^{t})^{\alpha_{11}} \end{bmatrix}. \tag{3.23}$$

where:

FDI	=	foreign direct investment;
R&D	=	knowledge transfer;
POP	=	market size (population);
GCA	=	per capita income (GDP per capita);
WAGE	=	labour costs;
RLDIFF	=	return on investment differences;
TAXDIFF	=	taxation differences;
DISTANCE	=	transport costs (physical distance);
CULTDIFF	=	cultural differences;

TRADE	= trade intensity;
REXD	= exchange rate direction;
REXV	= exchange rate volatility;
i	= home country *i*;
j	= host country *j*;
t	= year *t*.

Gravity-type models are by definition cross-section models, because they include spatial differences and not intertemporal differences. Hence, equation (3.23) applies for any year *t*.

MOSAIC estimations using ordinary least squares require two adaptations to equation (3.23). The first adaptation is that the dependent variable needs to be scaled. Trying to explain absolute levels of the dependent variable generally causes estimation problems due to intercorrelations with explanatory variables. The scaling of the dependent variable is done by dividing it by the total of all outward foreign direct investments in year *t*. This transforms the model into a spatial allocation model, because it tries to explain the relative share of a specific investment relation between the home and host countries in the investment total. The second adaptation is that the (scaled) dependent variable and the explanatory variables are transformed by taking their natural logarithms. This is necessary as ordinary least squares requires a linear model, whereas equation (3.23) is of a multiplicative nature. Hence, the model for any year *t* becomes:[17]

$$fdi_{ij}^{t} = \left[\begin{array}{l} \alpha_0' + \alpha_1 \cdot r\&d_i^{t} + \alpha_2 \cdot pop_j^{t} + \alpha_3 \cdot gca_j^{t} + \\ \alpha_4 \cdot wage_j^{t} + \alpha_5 \cdot rldiff_{ij}^{t} + \alpha_6 \cdot taxdiff_{ij}^{t} + \\ \alpha_7 \cdot distance_{ij}^{t} + \alpha_8 \cdot cultdiff_{ij}^{t} + \alpha_9 \cdot trade_{ij}^{t-1} + \\ \alpha_{10} \cdot rexd_{ij}^{t} + \alpha_{11} \cdot rexv_{ij}^{t} \end{array} \right]. \tag{3.24}$$

Initial attempts to estimate the thus specified model produced highly inconsistent results. Parameters that could be identified in one year appeared in other years with totally different values or had to be rejected. Also, the explanatory power of the model showed large differences from one year to another.

The inconsistency in the results was caused by two major problems. The first problem was the large fluctuations in the dependent variable, foreign direct investment shares, from one year to another. The value of the dependent variable in one year was totally different from the value of the dependent variable in another year. Consequently, regressing the model for year *t* gave completely different results compared to those from regressing the model for any other year. The second problem related to the number of observations and the number of degrees of freedom necessary for the regression. The number of observations was in some cases only marginally higher than the number of explanatory variables. In those cases, estimation of the model suffered from limited degrees of freedom.

A solution to the first problem is to moderate the year-to-year fluctuations in the dependent variable. In this case, the moderation is established by taking five-year totals of individual foreign direct investment flows and scaling these totals with the five-year total of all foreign direct investments abroad.[18] The summation over five years has the advantage that it circumvents statistical inconsistencies in data to some extent. This also leads to diminishing the number of flows on which disinvestments (negative flows) occur.[19] Another advantage is that the five-year sums of investments can be interpreted as some kind of investment stock variable, which proxies a level of foreign production. A consequence is that in order to be consistent, observations for five-year periods also have to be generated from annual data for the explanatory variables. This is done accordingly.

The second problem can be solved by pooling the cross-section data of individual five-year periods into one large data set.[20] This means the introduction of intertemporal variations in the five-year (moving) averages of the dependent variable and the explanatory variables in the cross-section analysis. The parameters of the explanatory variables are no longer estimated for different periods and cannot vary any more from one period to another. Their estimates are valid for all periods. The model now boils down to a 'generalised linear regression model' in which cross-section data and time-series data are combined (Kmenta 1971, p. 508). In such models, covariances among the residuals could disturb the regression results.

In order to meet with covariance problems, a so-called 'covariance model' can be used (Kmenta 1971, pp. 516–17). This model supposes that for each cross-sectional unit (the foreign direct investment relation between home and host countries) and for each temporal unit (the five-year period) a specific intercept can be determined. In order to test this, binary variables, or dummies, for both cross-sectional and temporal units are added to the generalised linear regression model except for the first cross-sectional and the first temporal units.[21] In regressing the model their estimated parameters become an approximation of the specific intercepts. In such a model the residuals for each cross-sectional unit over all time periods and for each time period over all investment relations obtain a zero mean and have a normal distribution.

However, inclusion of dummies for cross-sectional units may cause intercorrelation with the explanatory variables and give rise to multicollinearity problems. The dummies represent the same spatial differentiation that is already included in the explanatory variables. Therefore, in the model to be estimated, dummies for the foreign direct investment relations are not included. Hence, the following specification of MOSAIC is used in the estimations:

$$
fdi_{ij}^{t} = \begin{bmatrix} \alpha_{0}' + \alpha_{1} \cdot r\&d_{i}^{t} + \alpha_{2} \cdot pop_{j}^{t} + \alpha_{3} \cdot gca_{j}^{t} + \alpha_{4} \cdot wage_{j}^{t} + \\ \alpha_{5} \cdot rldiff_{ij}^{t} + \alpha_{6} \cdot taxdiff_{ij}^{t} + \alpha_{7} \cdot distance_{ij}^{t} + \\ \alpha_{8} \cdot cultdiff_{ij}^{t} + \alpha_{9} \cdot trade_{ij}^{t-1} + \alpha_{10} \cdot rexd_{ij}^{t} + \alpha_{11} \cdot rexv_{ij}^{t} + \\ \delta_{2} \cdot dum(2)^{t} + \delta_{p} \cdot dum(p)^{t} + \dots\dots + \delta_{P} \cdot dum(P)^{t} + \varepsilon_{ij}^{t} \end{bmatrix}.
\qquad (3.25)
$$

where:

fdi	=	foreign direct investment flow as a share of total flows;
r&d	=	knowledge transfer;
pop	=	market size (population);
gca	=	per capita income (GDP per capita);
wage	=	labour costs;
rldiff	=	return on investment differences;
taxdiff	=	taxation differences;
distance	=	transport costs (physical distance);
cultdiff	=	cultural differences;
trade	=	trade intensity;
rexd	=	exchange rate direction;
rexv	=	exchange rate volatility;
dum	=	period dummy (equals 1 for $p = t$, equals 0 for $p \neq t$; $p = 2, 3, \ldots, P$);
ϵ	=	residual;
i	=	home country *i*;
j	=	host country *j*;
t	=	five-year time period ($t = 1, 2, \ldots, T$; $T = P$).

In this model, the residuals of the individual foreign direct investment relations may not have a zero mean and may not be normally distributed over the time periods. Because the model is based on moving averages, the residuals may even follow an autoregressive scheme. This requires special attention in assessing the estimation results on the possible existence of strong covariances.

MOSAIC estimations are made for various data sets. The model will first be applied to a data set containing the geographical patterns in foreign direct investment flows within the European Union. Regressions will relate to the whole data set and to four subsets. Next, the model will be estimated for individual home countries: the data sets containing the geographical patterns of outward foreign direct investments from the United States, Japan, Germany and the Netherlands. For the former three countries, these analyses will consider flows to all host countries (the world) and host countries in three standard regions: Western Europe, South and Southeast Asia, and North and South America. It will be shown that these regions are generally the most important destinations of foreign direct investments from these home countries. For the Netherlands, data availability allows analyses only for some European countries plus the United States and Japan.

Data problems seriously hamper model testing and lead to choosing a flexible approach. Insufficient data on return on investment for host countries in Asia and Latin America forces us to refrain from testing these hypotheses in data (sub) sets containing investment flows destined for these countries. A similar problem exists for the taxation hypothesis. Data on taxation are available only for the countries of the European Union, the United States and Japan. Therefore, this hypothesis can only be tested in the intra-EU foreign direct investment data sets.[22] Further, when testing the model for data sets containing investment flows from individual home countries, the knowledge hypothesis has to be excluded from the regressions because the variables on knowledge start to behave as a constant. The variation in the knowledge variables relates only to changes in the home country over time. This variation is too low to contribute to the explanatory power of the regressions. A way to overcome this problem is to derive a knowledge indicator of the home country, which is in some way made relative to the host country. However, availability of knowledge data for host countries, particularly for non-OECD countries, is insufficient.[23]

The results of the model estimations will be presented in a standard table. First, some information on the regression will be mentioned: the five-year periods included and the countries involved. Then, some general statistics on the regression's quality will be presented. The R^2-statistic and the adjusted R^2-statistic will indicate which part of the dependent variable's variation is covered by the explanatory variables.[24] The F-statistic will test whether all estimated parameters are significantly different from zero. The Durbin–Watson (DW) statistic will test the existence of autocorrelations in the residuals for the whole model (not for the residuals of individual cross-sectional units or time periods). In addition, the number of cases included in the regression *vis-à-vis* the potential number of cases will be indicated.[25] Second, the table will show the estimated regression parameters for the independent variables in the model: for the hypothesised variables, the period dummies and the intercept. Together with the parameter, a T-value and a β-value will be presented. The T-value is a commonly known test statistic which identifies whether the parameter differs significantly from zero.[26] The β-value will give some indication of the relative importance of the determinant.[27]

The way in which model estimations for the various foreign direct investment relations are discussed is as follows. First, some expectations are expressed regarding the relevancy of the determinants in MOSAIC for the investment relation. This is derived from the profile of the expected prevailing corporate strategy. Then, the regression results are presented and assessed in view of the expectations. Finally, a conclusion is drawn on the main strategy type of the investment relation.

NOTES

1. Agarwal (1980, p. 744) refers to Markowitz and Tobin, who have formalised the theory of portfolio selection.
2. Capel (1993, Chapter 2) mentions 'foreign exchange transaction costs' as a relevant cost factor.
3. Caves (1982, p. 58) calls this the transactional approach.
4. For practical reasons, straight-line distances are used most often in gravity models. See Olsson (1965, p. 57).
5. Caves (1982, pp. 58–9) considers this the locational approach.
6. There could be a difference between formal control (equity ownership) and actual control (management style). The foreign entity, although fully owned, may have full or next to full autonomy. See the discussion on the definition of foreign direct investment in Appendix I.
7. For empirical testing, the culture barrier prevails for both the country i to country j and the country j to country i investments.
8. However, trade liberalisation has an impact on both the numerator and the denominator of the trade intensity variable in (3.11).
9. It is assumed that the volatility of the mutual exchange rate remains limited and, as a result, does not cause frictions in the investment action to be pursued.
10. *Ceteris paribus* the GDP deflators in home and host country.
11. The same applies to, respectively, a depreciation and an appreciation in the *home* country's currency.
12. These specifications have been used earlier in Morsink and Molle (1991a).
13. Others consider the unconditional specifications as 'volatility' and the conditional types as 'uncertainty'. See Martijn (1993, p. 136).
14. Weber (1991, p. 189) used a similar indicator based on nominal exchange rates to analyse asymmetries in nominal exchange rate shocks.
15. Weber (1991, p. 191) used a similar indicator for analysing asymmetries in real exchange rate shocks.
16. The local subsidiary could be interpreted as a more or less independent 'copy' of the corporate structure's network of activities.
17. The variables in lower-case letters should be considered as the natural logarithm of those in upper-case letters.
18. Effectively, this means the calculation of a five-year average of the relative share in total outward investments.
19. The foreign direct investment data relate to net investment flows. The gross investment flow made by investors from one country to another is corrected with the disinvestments made by these investors. It should be noted that these net investments do not relate to the balance of outward and inward (net) investment flows.

20. Pooling of annual observations solves the degrees of freedom problem, but not the large fluctuations in the dependent variable. Therefore, it is necessary to combine both solutions for model estimations.
21. Inclusion of dummies for these units would cause overdetermination of the model.
22. In principle, this hypothesis can also be tested in the data set for the Netherlands. However, severe intercorrelation problems led to excluding it from the model (see Chapter 8).
23. For the Netherlands, such data are available for all host countries in the data set, but the variables constructed along the lines presented here caused serious intercorrelations and led to excluding the knowledge hypothesis from the model (see Chapter 8).
24. $R_{adj}^2 = R^2 - \left(\dfrac{P(1-R^2)}{(N-P-1)} \right)$ in which P is the number of variables and N is the number of cases.
25. The potential number of cases is the number of possible investment relations times the number of five-year periods. The number of possible foreign investment relations is determined by the number of home and host countries.
26. It is possible that the T-value identifies the parameter not to be significantly different from zero and that the F-statistic suggests all estimated parameters in the regression to be indeed significantly different from zero. This implies that the separate contribution of a variable to the explanation of the dependent variable is weak, but its contribution in combination with other variables is quite strong. This joint contribution cannot be decomposed. See Kmenta (1971, p. 369).
27. The β-value is a re-estimate of the parameter based on standardised values of the dependent variable (y^r) predicted with the estimated model (y^p): $y^s = \left(\dfrac{y^p - \mu(y^p)}{\sigma(y^p)} \right)$.

4. Investments within the European Union

4.1 INTRODUCTION

Currently, in view of the subsequent stages of economic integration identified in Chapter 2, the European Union may be considered as a world region in which economic integration has reached a rather high level.[1] Its integration process started after the Second World War with the establishment of three treaties: the one on the European Coal and Steel Community in 1952, the one on the European Economic Community (the Treaty of Rome) in 1958, and the treaty on the European Atomic Energy Community, also in 1958. Over the years the number of member countries increased from six at the beginning to the current fifteen. The European integration process gained considerable momentum with the 1985 White Paper on Europe 1992 and the 1987 Single European Act to create a common market – the Internal Market – by 1992. With the conclusion of the Treaty of Maastricht in 1991, the initiatives were set to create the Economic and Monetary Union by the end of this decade. This Treaty also contained initiatives to establish a Political Union. With these initiatives and the revision of the Treaty during the Intergovernmental Conference in 1996–97, the European Union may move to a full economic union.

The subject of analysis in this chapter is intra-EU foreign direct investment during the 1980–92 period. The analysis is limited to the membership situation before 1 January 1995: the European Union of twelve countries. The accession into the Union of Austria, Finland and Sweden at that date is not taken into account. It must be noted that during the investigation period membership of the Union has changed twice. In 1981, Greece entered into the Union until then consisting of Germany, France, Italy, the United Kingdom, Denmark, Ireland and the Benelux countries; in 1986, Spain and Portugal became members.

This chapter will present the results of analysing the geographical dimension in intra-EU foreign direct investment patterns using MOSAIC. Data on these flows are derived from OECD and EUROSTAT statistics using a simple calibration method (see Appendix III). The next section will investigate the trends in investment patterns both spatially and sectorally. Spatial trends will be described, distinguishing between core and periphery countries. The subsequent section will deal with the results of MOSAIC estimations. Finally, the conclusions drawn from the model results will be summarised and evaluated.

4.2 INVESTMENT PATTERNS

4.2.1 Main Trends

Total intra-EU foreign direct investments increased from a mere ECU 4.1 billion in 1980 to a voluminous ECU 42.2 billion by 1992 (see also Figure 4.1). Between 1980 and 1982 there was a small decrease, but then, especially since 1984, a strong growth process evolved until 1990. In that year the EU total reached a record high of ECU 44.2 billion. This record was followed by a temporary drawback in 1991 and a modest recovery in 1992.

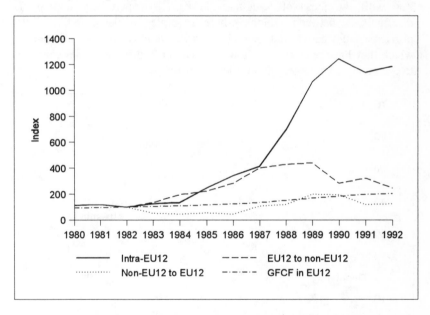

Figure 4.1   Development of EU foreign direct investment and gross fixed capital formation (1982 = 100; nominal)

The strong growth in intra-EU foreign direct investments coincides with a growing drive towards European integration (Somers 1991, p. 6). In particular, the initiation of the Internal Market programme with the Europe 1992 White Paper in 1985 and the acceptance of the Single European Act in 1987 must have stimulated foreign direct investment activity. This is particularly apparent after that year, as since then intra-EU investments started to grow much stronger than EU investments outside the Union. A large part of intra-EU investments relates to cross-border mergers and acquisitions among European companies.[2] Investments in the European Union by non-EU companies show an increasing trend between 1986 and 1989. This also coincides with the Internal Market programme. It seems, however, that these companies have not been as active in investing (via mergers and acquisitions or otherwise) in EU countries as companies located within the Union.

4.2.2   Identifying Core and Periphery Countries

A distinction is made between core and periphery countries. Although this distinction relates to countries and not to regions, this can be considered in line with the ideas of Krugman on core and periphery regions. He distinguishes between regions where synergies of labour skills, input provision, information and technology exchange have emerged and those in which they have not. As was shown in Chapter 2, these synergies contribute to ownership advantages and locational advantages.

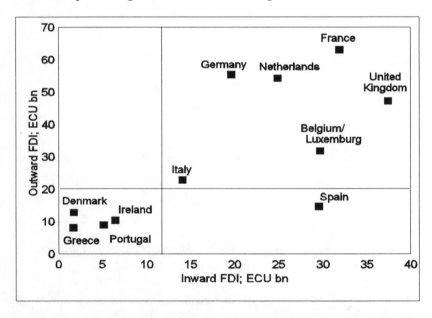

Figure 4.2   Foreign direct investment positions of EU countries, 1980–92

Sleuwaegen (1987, pp. 256–7) has developed a grid in which he assumes that outward foreign direct investment flows are an indication of a country's entrepreneurial competitiveness and inward investment flows indicate a country's locational competitiveness. The former reveals the existence of ownership advantages; the latter represents the availability of locational advantages. If a core region in the view of Krugman has high ownership and locational advantages, Sleuwaegen's grid can help to identify them.

Figure 4.2 shows the grid of intra-EU foreign direct investment flows. It identifies Germany, France, Italy, the Netherlands, the United Kingdom and Belgium/Luxemburg as core countries. These countries show considerable levels of outward and inward investment activity, which implies, following Krugman, high ownership and locational advantages.[3] For Denmark, Ireland, Portugal and Greece the opposite is the case, which qualifies them as periphery countries. Spain seems to have high locational advantages, but its ownership advantages are apparently not strong. Therefore, Spain can also be labelled as a periphery country.[4]

However, as every geographical distinction is based on arbitrary elements, the distinction between core and periphery may for some countries be questionable. In Italy, only the northern part of the country, in view of its economic importance, seems liable for a core qualification. The regions in the southern part can hardly be qualified as 'core'. Similar problems exist for other core countries: for example, for the northern part of the United Kingdom (Scotland and Northern Ireland). The identification of Denmark as a periphery country may also raise questions. In terms of GDP per capita, this country would rather qualify as a core country. Despite this, foreign direct investment activity in Denmark is quite low and to some extent atypical of core countries. Therefore, a periphery qualification seems more appropriate here.[5]

4.2.3 Outward Investment Flows

When looking at the outward flows of intra-EU foreign direct investments, various trends can be identified. Table 4.1 presents both structure and growth of outward flows.

For 1980–84, the table shows a large difference between core and periphery countries. Core countries obtain reasonably large shares in total investments. Germany is the most important investor country. France and the Netherlands compete for the second and third places. The United Kingdom takes the fourth position, followed by Italy and Belgium/Luxemburg. Countries in the periphery of the Union clearly obtain a marginal position with shares well below those of the core countries.

For all countries except Greece, the growth rates of outward foreign direct investment flows between 1980 and 1992 are very high. The strongest growth comes from countries in the periphery of the Union. Spain, with 56 per cent, is the fastest grower. Ireland and Portugal rank second. Spain's growth becomes stronger after its accession into the European Union in 1986.[6] The same appears to be true for Portugal.[7] The lowest growth rates show up for Germany and Italy, whereas investments from Greece, despite its membership of the European Union since 1981, do not seem to develop.[8] Other countries take an intermediate position.

Table 4.1   Geographical distribution and growth of intra-EU foreign direct investments by home country (1980–92; %)

Home country	1980–84	1984–88	1988–92	1980–92[a]
Germany	31.4	18.0	19.0	23.5
France	17.8	19.8	24.7	37.0
Italy	8.7	8.1	5.8	24.9
Netherlands	17.9	18.6	18.7	32.3
Belgium/Luxemburg	8.0	7.4	10.4	35.7
United Kingdom	13.1	23.7	14.8	33.4
Denmark	1.5	1.7	2.0	35.7
Ireland	0.4	0.8	1.0	46.4
Spain	0.8	1.7	3.1	56.0
Portugal	0.2	0.1	0.4	46.6
Greece	0.1	0.0	0.0	—
European Union (EU12)	100.0	100.0	100.0	31.5

Note
a.   Average nominal growth rate between first and last periods.

Source
Appendix III.

By 1988–92, despite the stronger growth in the periphery countries, the positions of the core and the periphery have not changed dramatically. The position of individual countries, however, has altered significantly. The low growth rate for Germany was mostly due to large reductions in investment flows at the beginning of the 1980s. This has led to a strong decline in Germany's share of the total until 1984–88. Since then, Germany's share stabilised just below 20 per cent. France has become the most important investor country.[9] The United Kingdom has maintained its position, but in the intermediate periods it has been far more dominant. In 1984–88, it ranked first.

Table 4.2 Sectoral distribution and growth of intra-EU foreign direct investments by investing industry (1984–92; %)

Investing industry	1984–88	1986–90	1988–92	1984–92[a]
Energy	5.7	1.5	2.7	12.7
Total manufacturing	34.9	34.0	32.8	33.7
Agriculture and food	4.1	7.6	7.1	56.0
Metallics	2.0	2.0	2.6[b]	53.8
Machinery	1.4	1.8	1.9[b]	55.7
Transport equipment	5.1	3.6	2.9	17.6
Electrical, electronics	8.2	7.8	6.8	29.4
Chemical industries	6.8	4.2	4.1	19.3
Other manufacturing	7.3	7.0	6.9[b]	38.0
Building and construction	0.4	0.9	0.8	60.6
Total commercial services	57.9	62.7	62.4	38.4
Finance and banking	22.0	25.9	25.5[b]	47.8
Insurance	8.6	10.8	10.9[b]	51.9
Trade, hotels and catering	17.1	12.2	10.5	20.1
Transport and communication	1.0	1.4	1.4	47.6
Real estate	3.8	4.6	4.5	41.9
Other commercial services	5.4	7.7	9.2[b]	68.6
Unallocated	1.1	0.9	1.3	44.0
Total	100.0	100.0	100.0	31.5

Notes
a. Average nominal growth rate between first and last periods.
b. 1987–91.

Source
EUROSTAT.

Although the periphery countries continue to have a marginal share in total outward foreign direct investments, the strong growth rates observed earlier have been translated into rapid increases of their shares. Spain has gained most. A similar trend can be observed for Ireland and Portugal. Denmark shows a moderate increase in its share.[10] Greece's share remains practically nil.

Table 4.2 shows that intra-EU foreign direct investments are made mostly by the service industries. About two-thirds of the total originates from these industries, of which finance and banking, insurance and trade, hotels and catering are the most important. Manufacturing has a share of about one-third. The agriculture and food and electrical and electronics industries are the most active in investing in other EU countries.

The share of service industries in total outward foreign direct investments shows an increase over the years, whereas manufacturing seems to lose ground. The growing importance of services originates particularly from financial services, transport and communication and other commercial services. The trade, hotels and catering group loses importance. The declining share in manufacturing is due to relatively low growth in the transport equipment and chemical industries. This is partly offset by rather strong growth in agriculture and food, and metallics.

4.2.4   Inward Investment Flows

An analysis similar to the one in the previous subsection can be made for inward intra-EU foreign direct investment flows. Table 4.3 presents their structure and growth trends.

In 1980–84, the most important core countries are Belgium/Luxemburg and France. Other core countries, such as Germany, Italy and the United Kingdom, obtain an intermediate ranking. Of the periphery countries, Spain has a considerable share and emerges as the third largest recipient of intra-EU investments. Another interesting, but still marginal, recipient in the periphery is Ireland.

As for outward investments, the average annual growth rates for inward foreign direct investments are very high. The highest growth rates can be observed for the United Kingdom, Spain and Portugal. The attractiveness of the United Kingdom may have been enhanced by the positive development in its economy following a severe recession. The popularity of Spain and Portugal for EU-investors has increased rapidly, which may coincide with their accession into the European Union in 1986 (Campa and Guillén 1996, p. 214). Other strong growers are Germany, Denmark and Ireland. The German position is particularly influenced by large investments from France, Italy, the Netherlands and the United Kingdom in 1989. In the following years the unification with the former German Democratic Republic (DDR) may have had a positive impact, with foreign investors taking over former DDR companies. The attractiveness of Denmark has clearly improved in the late 1980s and the beginning of the 1990s.[11] The growth rate for Ireland may reveal the success of policies in attracting foreign direct investments. The remaining countries, France, Italy,

Belgium/Luxemburg and Greece, have relatively low growth rates, indicating a limited popularity for these countries. On the whole, periphery countries show stronger growth rates for inward investments than do core countries.

Table 4.3 Geographical distribution and growth of intra-EU foreign direct investments by host country (1980–92; %)

Host country	1980–84	1984–88	1988–92	1980–92[a]
Germany	9.9	6.5	10.4	32.3
France	22.3	16.2	14.3	24.3
Italy	11.2	9.7	5.7	20.7
Netherlands[b]	1.0	15.9	13.0	80.5
Belgium/Luxemburg	24.3	12.7	14.9	23.7
United Kingdom	11.0	22.5	17.9	39.7
Denmark	1.0	0.2	1.0	31.7
Ireland	3.4	1.8	3.4	31.6
Spain	12.7	11.7	15.8	35.2
Portugal	2.1	1.7	2.7	36.1
Greece	1.1	0.7	0.7	24.9
European Union (EU12)	100.0	100.0	100.0	31.5

Notes
a. Average nominal growth rate between first and last periods.
b. Possible distortive effect from heavy disinvestments by UK investors during 1980–84.

Source
Appendix III.

The positions of EU countries in inward foreign direct investment flows have considerably changed by 1988–92. Investment activity among EU countries has dispersed more evenly over the Union. Although France and Belgium/Luxemburg still have dominant positions, they have not sustained their high shares. For France, the overall trend has been downward; for Belgium/Luxemburg, the development at the beginning of the 1980s has been far worse, as the share in 1988–92 has recovered slightly from the level in 1984–88. The United Kingdom has obtained the highest ranking in 1988–92. There is, however, a downward trend as the share in 1984–88 was higher. Germany shows a positive trend after a serious reduction at the beginning of the 1980s. For Italy, the share in inward investments is decreasing, which is also the case for the Netherlands. The periphery

Foreign Direct Investment and Corporate Networking

countries show a pattern similar to that of Germany: a downward trend at the beginning of the 1980s, but a recovery by the end of that decade.

The higher growth rates for periphery countries did not result in substantially higher shares of these countries in inward flows. The trend is, however, upward. This implies that the popularity of periphery countries for investors from inside the Union is increasing. This trend coincides with a restructuring of investment flows within the core region of the Union.

Table 4.4 Sectoral distribution and growth of intra-EU foreign direct investments by receiving industry (1984–92; %)

Receiving industry	1984–88	1986–90	1988–92	1984–92[a]
Energy	15.0	8.5	4.8	−3.1
Total manufacturing	23.7	24.6	28.7	34.9
Agriculture and food	5.0	6.2	7.4	41.8
Metallics	1.4	1.5	1.4[b]	33.9
Machinery	2.1	2.1	1.8[b]	27.3
Transport equipment	1.2	1.4	2.8	58.5
Electrical, electronics	3.7	2.8	4.3	33.8
Chemical industries	5.2	5.9	4.9	26.7
Other manufacturing	5.0	4.8	5.5[b]	38.8
Building and construction	2.9	1.6	0.8	−6.2
Total commercial services	57.6	64.0	64.2	32.1
Finance and banking	23.2	24.8	23.9[b]	35.4
Insurance	4.6	8.1	8.6[b]	64.9
Trade, hotels and catering	10.4	10.4	8.6	22.6
Transport and communication	0.9	0.5	0.9	28.6
Real estate	14.5	10.8	8.8	13.3
Other commercial services	3.9	9.3	10.5[b]	86.1
Unallocated	0.8	1.3	1.5	50.4
Total	100.0	100.0	100.0	31.5

Notes
a. Average nominal growth rate between first and last periods.
b. 1987–91.

Source
EUROSTAT.

The sectoral distribution of inward foreign direct investment flows among EU countries reveals that, as for outward investments, about two-thirds of the total relates to service industries. About one-quarter relates to manufacturing. In services, the scene is dominated by finance and banking; trade, hotels and catering; and real estate. For manufacturing, the agriculture and food industry and the chemical industries are most important.

Over the years an increasing share is shown for both services and manufacturing. This coincides with a strong decline in the share of energy and, to a lesser extent, in building and construction. In services, growth comes from strongly rising shares in insurance and other commercial services. Finance and banking, trade, hotel and catering, and real estate show declining shares. In manufacturing, transport equipment, and agriculture and food have strongly increasing shares. Chemicals and machinery have relatively low growth rates.

4.2.5 Interregional and Intra-regional Investment Relations

The analysis of outward and inward foreign direct investments within the Union revealed that they concentrate strongly in the core region. A stronger growth was signalled for the periphery. In view of the analyses to be made using MOSAIC, it is worth describing the importance of the investment interactions within the core and periphery regions and those between them.

Table 4.5 Geographical distribution and growth of interregional and intra-regional foreign direct investments within the EU (1980–92; %)

Investment relation	1980–84	1984–88	1988–92	1980–92[a]
Core to core	77.2	80.0	71.3	30.2
Core to periphery	19.8	15.8	22.2	33.3
Periphery to core	2.7	3.6	5.0	42.2
Periphery to periphery	0.4	0.6	1.5	55.7

Note
a. Average nominal growth rate between first and last periods.

Source
Appendix III.

In 1980–84, the bulk of intra-EU foreign direct investments takes place within the core region (see Table 4.5). More than three-quarters of investments are concentrated here. About another fifth of the investments are made from the core region to periphery countries.[12] With only 2.7 per cent, investments from periphery countries to the core are minor. Investments within the periphery are practically nil and may be of an incidental nature.

Between 1980–84 and 1984–88 the shares of interregional and intra-regional investments show diverging patterns. The share of core-to-core investments grows to 80 per cent. Also, the periphery-to-core investments and the intra-periphery investments show increasing, but still marginal, shares. The share of core-to-periphery investments compensates for these increases, because it declines substantially.

During the subsequent periods until 1988–92, investment attitudes seem to change. The attractiveness of the periphery countries must have risen substantially, because foreign direct investments in the periphery grow strongly. The share of core-to-periphery investments rises rapidly. Equivocally, although the share of intra-periphery investments remains marginal, it more than doubles between 1984–88 and 1988–92. This particularly relates to strong growth in investment flows between Spain and Portugal. The growing share of periphery investments has been detrimental to the share of investments within the core region: it has declined substantially with nearly 9 percentage points. The share of investments in the core from periphery countries has continued to grow.

These foreign direct investment patterns coincide with two different developments, which could explain the increased attractiveness of periphery countries. The first one is the accession of Spain and Portugal into the Union in 1986.[13] Before that year, companies apparently were reluctant to invest in these countries, although the relatively high share of Spain in total inward investments within the Union may suggest that some companies have considered it advantageous to invest there already before accession. The second development relates to the start of the Internal Market programme around 1985. This may have encouraged companies to seek new combinations of their ownership advantages with (new) locational advantages in periphery countries.

Sectoral data show that about two-thirds of total intra-EU foreign direct investments are made in service industries, particularly in finance and banking, insurance, trade, hotels and catering, and other commercial services.[14] Manufacturing is less important. The industry shares in total outward and inward investments reveal some imbalances, which suggests the existence of interindustry investments.

4.3 DETERMINANTS

This section will deal with the results of regressions using MOSAIC on the data sets for the European Union. First the results for all intra-EU foreign direct investment flows will be presented. Then, results will be discussed for subsets of these flows. The first subset contains investment flows among countries within the core region. The second relates to flows from countries in the core region to those in the periphery. In the third subset investment flows from the periphery region to countries in the core are included. Finally, the fourth subset deals with investments among countries in the periphery.

4.3.1 Intra-EU Foreign Direct Investments

Because the European Union is an integrating market area, European companies are likely to pursue corporate strategies of a more complex nature. Therefore, it is expected that MOSAIC will identify determinants of foreign direct investments that fit the strategy profile of complex international production systems. This implies that the hypotheses on knowledge transfer, market orientation and labour costs should obtain significant parameters. For trade, a complementary relation with investing abroad should prevail. Also, the barrier hypothesis on distance should be relevant. Physical distances throughout the Union do not change and continue to be a natural barrier.[15] Cultural differences may not be relevant any more, because integration causes growing interaction of people among countries.[16] Differences in return on investment and taxation should have significant influences, but may be less important in view of capital market integration and government policy coordination. Regarding exchange rates, the expectation is that support is found for the exchange rate direction hypothesis and that the volatility hypothesis is rejected. Exchange rate policies, such as the European Monetary System (EMS), must have achieved considerable stability among most European currencies, but may not have eliminated altogether the direction of exchange rate movements as a stimulus or friction factor.[17]

However, for the exchange rate hypotheses a different approach in estimating the model appeared to be necessary. In initial estimation attempts, the parameters for exchange rates were not significant. This was considered strange, because in earlier research a significant relation between exchange rate variability and foreign direct investment was found (Morsink and Molle 1991a and Molle and Morsink 1991).

Table 4.6   Intra-EU investments

Information:		Countries: 11		
Periods: 9 (1980–84 to 1988–92)		Belgium/Luxemburg, Denmark,		
No. of cases: 848 of 990 (85.6%)		France, Germany, Greece, Ireland,		
R^2: 0.668	F: 87.825	Italy, Netherlands, Portugal, Spain,		
R^2 (adjusted): 0.661	DW: 1.438	United Kingdom		
Determinant	Definition[a]	Parameter	T-value	β-value
Knowledge transfer	1	1.375	16.239	0.445
Market size	1	0.455	7.321	0.186
Per capita income	1b	0.416	3.303	0.109
Labour costs	1c	−0.379	−3.531	−0.087
ROI differences	1	0.531	2.574	0.061
Taxation differences	1	−1.125	−2.207	−0.052
Transport costs	1	−0.837	−10.820	−0.281
Cultural differences	1	−0.826	−5.217	−0.114
Trade intensity	1	0.547	7.301	0.224
Exchange rate direction	1[b]	−1.275	−5.132	−0.112
Exchange rate volatility	1[b]	−0.387	−2.419	−0.217
Dummy 1981–85		−0.295	−1.338	−0.037
Dummy 1982–86		−0.842	−3.570	−0.108
Dummy 1983–87		−0.988	−4.056	−0.126
Dummy 1984–88		0.054	0.108	0.007
Dummy 1985–89		0.364	0.714	0.047
Dummy 1986–90		0.353	0.704	0.046
Dummy 1987–91		0.544	1.105	0.072
Dummy 1988–92		0.661	1.364	0.088
Intercept		−4.442	−5.928	—

Notes
a. For variable definitions, see Appendix IV.
b. Influence limited to the 1980–84 to 1983–87 periods.

Analysis of the development of exchange rate variability over the time periods revealed that including shift dummies in MOSAIC is appropriate. Exchange rate variability diminished considerably from 1980 onwards and has become very low since the mid-80s. Stokman (1995, p. 50), when studying the relation between exchange rate movements and trade, found that the exchange rate risk during 1987–90 was only a third of the risk in the five years preceding the start of the EMS in 1979. In view of this, shift dummies have been introduced, which allow only influences of the exchange rate hypotheses during the first four periods in the analysis (1980–84 to 1983–87).

MOSAIC estimations for all intra-EU foreign direct investment flows lead to the observation that all hypothesized determinants seem to have a significant influence (see Table 4.6). Investors apparently want to use their knowledge in foreign locations and are probably attracted by high market potentials. Locations seem to be chosen for their low labour cost levels. Trade may lead to more investments, as the trade intensity parameter is significantly positive. Differences in return on investment and taxation also appear to determine foreign direct investments. Barriers seem to be encountered in terms of transport costs and cultural differences. Exchange rate movements may influence investments in the periods before 1984–88.

Most parameters obtain reasonable estimates. They reveal in general an inelastic relation with foreign direct investment. Only for knowledge transfer, taxation differences and exchange rate direction are elasticities above unity. For the latter variable, the relation disappears after the 1983–87 period.

The β-values of the parameters indicate a relatively strong influence from knowledge transfer. This may coincide with the large share of service industries in foreign direct investment, because knowledge is particularly important for some of these industries (for example, finance and banking, insurance and other commercial services). Although less than for knowledge transfer, the influence from market size, transport costs and exchange rate volatility are also relatively strong. The relevance of trade intensity may suggest a meaningful impact of economic integration processes such as the Internal Market programme. Of less importance are per capita income, cultural differences and exchange rate direction. The influences from labour costs and from differences in return on investment and taxation are relatively weak.

The relatively strong influence from transport costs supports the importance of transaction costs as a barrier to investment. This appears to be consistent with results found by Martin and Rogers (1995, p. 185). They find some evidence that the availability of infrastructure, which inevitably influences transport costs, is one of the main determinants for the location of industry throughout Europe.

The significant parameters for return on investment and taxation differences suggest that, depending on the flow's direction, these differences have either stimulated or blocked foreign investment. These results are supported by Mortensen (1992, p. 218), who concludes that foreign direct investment flows respond to differences in rates of return on capital. These results are also consistent with the results of Devereux and Freeman (1995, p. 97), who find significant parameters for the real rate of interest in the home country and the tax wedge between home and host countries. They conclude that taxation is a significant determinant for the allocation of foreign direct investment across alternative locations. Perhaps, there is a relation with tax incentive programmes for inward foreign direct investment by host countries. However, in reviewing some studies the OECD (1989a, pp. 44–5 and 54) concluded that the effect of international investment incentives is limited. This is in line with the observed minor influence in MOSAIC.

Interpreting the results on the exchange rate hypotheses leads to the observation that at the beginning of the 1980s, European investors apparently wanted to benefit from depreciations of host-country currencies or were blocked by appreciating host currencies *vis-à-vis* their home currencies. The elastic parameter suggests that investment flows were rather sensitive to this influence, but its β-value implies a limited impact. Regarding exchange rate risk it appears that fluctuations in exchange rates created barriers during the same period. These fluctuations presumably could not be hedged, because the exchange rate variable is of the unconditional type. Since the mid-1980s, influences from exchange rate changes seem to be no longer relevant for intra-EU investments.

The question can be raised whether the crisis in the EMS in 1990–92 has rendered the exchange rate hypotheses relevant again. Sapir, Sekkat and Weber (1994) identified a significantly negative impact of the EMS crisis on intra-European trade flows. Regressions were made for specifications of MOSAIC in which the shift dummy allowed reintroduction of the exchange rate variables for the 1988–92 period. These model estimates did not give support for the presumed reintroduction. However, it should be noted that our analysis is based on five-year averages, which may have caused an automatic levelling off of the EMS crisis in the exchange rate indicators.

The parameters of the period dummies and their β-values may reveal a growing influence from the Internal Market programme and may capture the steep rise in intra-EU foreign direct investments since its initiation. At the beginning of the 1980s, the pre-Internal Market programme period, parameters are negative. Since the mid-1980s, parameters have been positive and their values show an increasing trend. Another explanation for this shift could be the accession of Spain and Portugal in 1986. However, it must be noted that a relation could also exist with the introduction of the shift dummy for the exchange rate variables. The shift coincides with the sign change. Further, the parameters for 1987–91 and 1988–92 may capture the EMS crisis at the beginning of the 1990s. On the other hand, the β-values may indicate that period-specific influences are relatively less important.

The quality of the regression seems appropriate. The correlation coefficient reveals that about two-thirds of the variation in the dependent variable is explained by the model. Period dummies contribute little and leave the explanation to the explanatory variables. The Durbin–Watson statistic shows that there may be positive autocorrelation in the residuals. This may be caused by the residuals of some investment relations, which are relatively large and have rather high standard deviations. This is particularly the case for investment relations from the periphery to the core and for intra-periphery investments. In particular, investments from Portugal and Greece to Germany are badly predicted with a relatively large mean and standard deviation of the residuals. Also, the Greece-to-Italy, Ireland-to-Italy and Ireland-to-Denmark investment flows cause problems. The residuals for these investment relations show high covariances with the residuals of some other investment relations. In core-to-periphery investments the residuals for the flows from France and the United Kingdom to Denmark and from the Netherlands to Ireland reveal a less appropriate fit. For intra-core investment relations, residuals have means close to zero and low standard deviations. Intercorrelations among explanatory variables in the model are not high. Other specifications of MOSAIC, in which alternative definitions of the explanatory variables are used, give results similar to those presented here. This may suggest that the regression results are fairly stable. In addition, the *F*-statistic is sufficiently high, which implies that all estimated parameters are significantly different from zero.

The overall corporate strategy that emanates from the model results, seems to fit best with the expected profile of complex international production strategies. The strong influence from knowledge transfer and trade intensity complies particularly with this strategy's profile. The limited relevance of differences in culture, return on investment and taxation and the rejection of the exchange rate volatility hypothesis after 1983–87 may also be an indication for this strategy type. The less appropriate fit of the estimated model for periphery-to-core and intra-periphery investments may indicate that this strategy may not be pursued by investors from periphery countries.

4.3.2 Investments within the Core Region

As was shown in the previous section, intra-core investments constitute the bulk of intra-EU foreign direct investments. However, it was shown that after a small rise until the mid-1980s, its share in the total is declining in subsequent years due to a growing popularity of investment relations with periphery countries.

Table 4.7 Intra-EU investments within the core region

Information: Periods: 9 (1980–84 to 1988–92) No. of cases: 264 of 270 (97.8%) R^2: 0.308 F: 5.717 R^2 (adjusted): 0.254 DW: 2.034		Countries: 6 Belgium/Luxemburg, France, Germany, Italy, Netherlands, United Kingdom		
Determinant	Definition[a]	Parameter	T-value	β-value
Knowledge transfer	1	0.483	5.502	0.379
Market size	1	–0.082	–0.842	–0.079
Per capita income	1b	0.021	0.171	0.016
Labour costs	1c	0.125	1.398	0.105
ROI differences	1	–0.369	–0.684	–0.058
Taxation differences	1	–0.990	–1.221	–0.097
Transport costs	1	–0.194	–2.224	–0.196
Cultural differences	1	0.019	0.107	0.006
Trade intensity	1	0.262	2.383	0.164
Exchange rate direction	1[b]	–0.759	–2.829	–0.230
Exchange rate volatility	4[b]	–0.166	–1.236	–0.089
Dummy 1981–85		0.146	0.774	0.060
Dummy 1982–86		–0.027	–0.135	–0.011
Dummy 1983–87		–0.047	–0.221	–0.019
Dummy 1984–88		–0.022	–0.096	–0.009
Dummy 1985–89		0.179	0.748	0.073
Dummy 1986–90		0.093	0.394	0.038
Dummy 1987–91		0.014	0.065	0.006
Dummy 1988–92		–0.024	–0.118	–0.010
Intercept		1.828	1.325	—

Notes
a. For variable definitions, see Appendix IV.
b. Influence limited to the 1980–84 to 1983–87 periods.

Although there was some evidence for complex international production
strategies for all intra-EU investments, this strategy type more likely prevails
for intra-core investments. Hence, significant parameters are expected for
knowledge transfer, market potential, labour costs and differences in return
on investment and taxation. Support for barriers from cultural differences
and exchange rate volatility is less likely. Transport costs should remain as a

barrier and exchange rate direction should stimulate foreign direct investment decisions.

MOSAIC's regression results in Table 4.7 show the relevance of a limited set of determinants for intra-core investments. The hypotheses regarding knowledge transfer, transport costs, trade complementarity and exchange rate direction are accepted. The latter's influence is limited to the pre-1984–88 periods, as was also the case in the model for all intra-EU flows. β-values reveal that knowledge transfer is the most important determinant, which could mean an emphasis on knowledge-intensive (service) industries in intra-core investments. Transport costs, trade complementarity and exchange rate direction also have a relatively strong relevance. For trade, it seems that more trade leads to more investments between home and host countries, but the parameter suggests an inelastic relationship.

The hypotheses on market size and per capita income are not accepted. This is surprising in view of earlier results found by Culem (1988). Analysing foreign direct investment flows among the same countries as in our data set with the exception of Italy during the 1969–82 period, Culem found considerable support for market size (measured as the level of real GDP) and income growth (real GDP growth) in individual host countries as important explanatory variables. In principle, although other variables are used to indicate market size (population) and income growth (per capita GDP growth), our analysis should have given similar results. Possibly, the influence of economic integration may prevail here. Economic integration may have reached a stage in which companies invest without taking market size and per capita income of individual host countries into account. Instead of the size of the national market, the market size of the core region as a whole may have become the relevant determinant here. Regarding per capita income the spatial differences in purchasing power within the core may have become marginal rendering national per capita income irrelevant as a spatial allocation determinant within the core.[18] This seems logical in view of the large share of mergers and acquisitions in intra-EU foreign direct investments. Companies may have engaged in rationalising production processes in their activity networks throughout the core region in order to benefit from scale economies (United Nations 1996, p. 11).

The insignificance of cultural differences could also be explained by low spatial differences. Cultural differences among core countries are minor, possibly due to the increased interaction of people in the integrating core region.[19] This supports the notion of having reached a substantial level of integration in the core region.

Efforts have been made to test whether integration has rendered ineffective the influence from spatial differences in market size, per capita income and cultural differences. Shift dummies have been added to

MOSAIC to limit the influence of these variables to the periods prior to the Internal Market programme. However, the estimations have not supported any relevance for the shift dummies. This could imply that integration processes among core countries had already achieved substantial integration before the start of the Internal Market programme.

For labour costs a weakly significant positive parameter is found. This may suggest that investors accept high labour costs.[20] Possibly, they favour locations with more expensive, high-quality labour instead of low-cost labour. This could coincide with the large share of service industries in foreign direct investment. Some service industries, such as finance and banking, insurance and commercial services, may be more dependent on high-quality labour.

The hypotheses on return on investment and taxation differences obtain little support. The parameter of return on investment differences gets a theoretically unacceptable sign, but turns out to be insignificant. The hypothesis on taxation differences is accepted, but its significance is weak and its β-value suggests a low relevance. This implies little influence from attractive taxation policies by host countries in the core region.

For the exchange rate hypotheses the application of shift dummies, as for all intra-EU foreign direct investment flows, appears appropriate again. For all periods the hypotheses are not accepted, but when their influence is restricted to the beginning of the 1980s only, the direction variable gets a significant parameter. This indicates that investors in those years benefited from investment opportunities if host-country currencies were depreciating and encountered barriers from appreciating host currencies. The parameter's β-value indicates a substantial relevance, although the parameter is inelastic. Exchange rate volatility, here of the conditional type, apparently was considered less relevant. Its parameter is weakly significant and its β-value low. These results may show that exchange rate policies (such as the EMS) had already reduced exchange rate changes at the beginning of the 1980s to such an extent that for investments within the core region, exchange rate volatility was not really taken into account any more, but the direction of exchange rate movements still created barriers or opportunities. Since the mid-1980s their influence has apparently disappeared.

All period dummies obtain insignificant parameters and their β-values are relatively low. This implies that period-specific influences do not really exist. The observed trend in the dummy parameters of the model for all intra-EU foreign direct investment flows, which was attributed to growing economic integration, is not supported here. Possibly, this indicates little progress in the already achieved high level of integration within the core region.

Although the regression covers most cases, its explanatory power is limited. With only a third of the variance explained, the regression's fit is low. This is logical if for some explanatory variables geographical differentiation has become irrelevant due to (economic) integration. On the other hand, the irrelevance of all period dummies suggests that they leave variance coverage to the (remaining) explanatory variables. Further, the *F*-statistic suggests that the estimated model parameters do contribute to some extent to explaining the dependent variable, despite the insignificance of some individual parameters. Also, the Durbin–Watson statistic is satisfactory. In addition, for most foreign direct investment relations the residuals are minor. Covariances among these residuals and intercorrelations among explanatory variables seem to be absent. Using other definitions of explanatory variables in MOSAIC does not give better estimation results.

Comparing the results for intra-core investments with those for all intra-EU foreign direct investments leads to interesting observations. In both models, investments are rather strongly guided by knowledge transfer, but intra-core investments seem less sensitive to this determinant since its elasticity is lower than in the model for all flows. The same is true for transport costs and trade intensity. Spatial differences in national market potentials in the core region may have become so small, that they no longer guide investment flows, whereas for the Union as a whole they still do. Regarding cultural differences, a similar conclusion may be drawn. For labour costs, intra-core investors seem to take labour quality into consideration. In the model for all flows there was an indication that cheap labour is a relevant determinant. Return on investment differences are not accepted for intra-core investments, whereas they were significant, but not very relevant, for all investment flows. Taxation differences have an influence in both models, but for intra-core investments the influence seems less strong and less elastic. Further, exchange rate movements and exchange rate volatility appear in both models for the periods prior to 1984–88. However, it seems that exchange rate volatility in those years had already diminished to a large extent for intra-core currencies since its relevance for intra-core investments is substantially lower. Also, there is less influence from the period dummies and their parameters do not suggest influence from an integration trend. These results could mean that the core region has reached a higher level of integration than the Union as a whole. Possibly, foreign direct investments within the core may have started to behave like 'domestic' investments.

Although the identified determinants do not correspond completely with those in the profile of complex international production strategies, they could still point towards them. Indications for this are that exchange rate volatility has become irrelevant in the core region and trade intensity has a considerable influence. Further, differences in return on investment and taxation turn out to be of less importance. The labour cost parameter may indicate labour quality to be a relevant investment determinant. For geographical differences in market size, per capita income and cultural differences, the level of integration within the core may have rendered them ineffective as investment determinants. Because the set of home and host countries in which this strategy type prevails constitute a spatially identifiable area, one may speak of 'regional core networking' strategies.

4.3.3   Investments from the Core to the Periphery

Core-to-periphery investments have a share of about 20 per cent in total intra-EU foreign direct investments. These investment relations encountered a decline in relative terms until the mid-1980s. Since then, core investors seem to have regained interest in periphery locations for their investments.

For core-to-periphery investments, it appears likely to expect the simple affiliate integration strategy as the overall strategy type. Market potentials in periphery countries are lower than those in the core, which implies little market orientation. Most countries are relatively small. Also, GDP per capita is generally lower than in the core region. The lower standard of living may mean lower labour costs in the periphery. This could imply an emphasis of investments in activities with an upstream (input) orientation, for example in manufacturing. Differences in return on investment and taxation could also be of importance. Transport costs are a likely barrier in view of the generally large physical distances between core and periphery countries. Trade is expected to complement investments. Differences in culture between core and periphery should be relevant as they are likely to be higher than for intra-core relations. Further, support should be found for the exchange rate hypotheses, as the exchange rates of periphery country currencies *vis-à-vis* those in the core can be considered as less stable.

MOSAIC results for core-to-periphery investments are only to some extent in line with the expectations (see Table 4.8). Investments are made by transferring technology to periphery locations.[21] However, it seems that knowledge transfer is less important than other determinants. Perhaps, investments relate to less-knowledge-intensive activities, such as assembly in manufacturing or transportation and retailing services. Against the expectations, core investors are particularly attracted by market size, as the size hypothesis is accepted and its β-value is relatively high. This could be due to the emphasis of investments to Spain – the only large economy in the periphery – in the data set. Growth in per capita income, the purchasing power in periphery markets, seems of less relevance. This may reflect that investors appreciate market growth to some extent, but are aware of the lower income level in the periphery. Cheap labour costs are rejected as a determinant, but the significantly positive parameter may suggest that labour quality could be relevant.[22] However, estimating this parameter may be distorted by intercorrelation between return on investment differences and the labour cost variable. Return on investment and taxation differences are important determinants with rather high elasticities. Their β-values reveal an intermediate influence. Possibly, investments are sensitive to favourable taxation policies in periphery countries. The relation with trade is positive, which gives support to the expected complementarity between trade and investment. If trade intensity is an indication for economic integration one may expect a less-advanced economic integration process on core-to-periphery investment relations. Its β-value of intermediate size may indicate then that integration still contributes little. Transport costs are an important barrier. It obtains the strongest influence after market size, which is no surprise in view of the relatively large physical distances between home and host countries.[23] Cultural differences are a significant barrier to core-to-periphery investments, but its influence is not strong.

As in the cases for all intra-EU and for intra-core investment flows, in this model exchange rate hypotheses turn out to be irrelevant, too, when testing for all periods. Limiting the influence to the beginning of the 1980s leads to accepting both hypotheses. Hence, in those years core investors take advantage of depreciating periphery currencies, but exchange risk continues to be a major concern. The latter relates to erratic volatility only, because the indicator is of the conditional type. The regression does not identify unconditional volatility specifications, which suggests that hedging was at that time an effective risk-eliminating instrument. Exchange rate policies may have created sufficient stability in subsequent years to remove exchange rate volatility as an investment barrier. From this one may conclude that monetary integration gives a positive impulse to core-to-periphery investment. This is consistent with an earlier conclusion drawn concerning the positive effect that monetary integration would have on foreign direct investment from the richer to the poorer countries in the European Union (Molle and Morsink 1991, p. 98).

The period-dummy parameters show an interesting similarity with those in the model for all intra-EU flows. In the periods prior to the Internal Market programme the parameters have negative signs, whereas parameters obtain positive values in subsequent periods and reveal an increasing trend. Apparently, they capture the decline in the shares of core-to-periphery flows in total intra-EU foreign direct investments between 1980–84 and 1984–88 and their increase in later periods. This can coincide, as their β-values may indicate, with a growing economic integration effect. The accession of Spain and Portugal into the Union in 1986 may have contributed to this. However, the sign shift again coincides with the shift in the relevance of exchange rate variability in the model, but the β-values of the 1983–87 and 1984–88 period dummies suggest the sign shift to be of minor importance.

Table 4.8   Intra-EU investments from the core to the periphery

Information: Periods: 9 (1980–84 to 1988–92) No. of cases: 261 of 270 (96.7%) R^2: 0.772 F: 42.829 R^2 (adjusted): 0.753 DW: 1.867			Countries: 6 * 5 *from* Belgium/Luxemburg, France, Germany, Italy, Netherlands, United Kingdom *to* Denmark, Greece, Ireland, Portugal, Spain		
Determinant	Definition[a]	Parameter	T-value	β-value	
Knowledge transfer	1	0.550	4.649	0.206	
Market size	1	1.367	16.829	0.692	
Per capita income	1b	0.227	1.849	0.103	
Labour costs	1b	0.507	1.937	0.159	
ROI differences	1	1.477	2.618	0.226	
Taxation differences	1	−3.050	−4.826	−0.258	
Transport costs	1	−1.213	−7.846	−0.425	
Cultural differences	1	−0.543	−2.766	−0.109	
Trade intensity	1	0.347	3.994	0.158	
Exchange rate direction	1[b]	−0.782	−2.586	−0.103	
Exchange rate volatility	3[b]	−0.137	−4.010	−0.272	
Dummy 1981–85		−0.188	−0.856	−0.036	
Dummy 1982–86		−0.510	−2.109	−0.099	
Dummy 1983–87		−0.512	−2.023	−0.094	
Dummy 1984–88		0.114	0.375	0.022	
Dummy 1985–89		0.536	1.759	0.105	
Dummy 1986–90		0.634	2.106	0.125	
Dummy 1987–91		0.864	2.911	0.170	
Dummy 1988–92		1.064	3.597	0.209	
Intercept		−10.024	−6.698	—	

Notes
a. For variable definitions, see Appendix IV.
b. Influence limited to the 1980–84 to 1983–87 periods.

Although the MOSAIC results presented in Table 4.8 show considerable similarities with those for all intra-EU flows, some interesting differences can be noted. Market size and transport costs seem more important for core-to-periphery flows and their parameters suggest higher elasticities. Knowledge transfer appears to be less elastic and less important. For taxation differences both models identify elastic parameters, but the elasticity of this variable for core-to-periphery investments suggests a higher sensitivity. Also, this variable appears to be more relevant for core-to-periphery investments than for all flows. This implies a higher effectiveness for favourable taxation policies on core-to-periphery relations. Finally, in the periods prior to 1984–88, the significant parameters of the exchange rate variables reveal less sensitive elasticities for core-to-periphery investments than for all investment flows. This could be due to the relevance of hedging in core-to-periphery relations.

The model's results can be considered reasonable. The correlation coefficient indicates that more than three-quarters of the variance is explained by the model and the F-statistic allows acceptance of the hypothesis that all parameters are significantly different from zero. Although some period dummies have significant parameters, their β-values suggest low to intermediate contributions. The Durbin–Watson statistic shows little autocorrelation in the residuals. Further inspection of the residuals reveals that the fit for some investment relations is not strong, but this does not cause concern for the existence of large covariances. A less appropriate fit is observed for investments from France and the United Kingdom to Denmark and from the Netherlands to Ireland. These investment relations have the same problem in the model for all intra-EU foreign direct investment flows. Other specifications of MOSAIC for core-to-periphery investments do not reject the robustness of the results presented here. Including other definitions for the explanatory variables does not cause major changes in the relevance of determinants.

The determinants are consistent with the profile of simple affiliate integration strategies. Core investors seem interested in locational advantages in the periphery and do not appear to hesitate in making combinations with their ownership advantages. These strategies appear to have a downstream orientation and not, as expected, an upstream orientation. The locational advantages seem to come from existing market potentials rather than from low labour costs. The strong influence of market size supports this. However, the determinants may indicate a transition to complex international production strategies. This is particularly suggested by the rejection of exchange rate volatility after the 1983–87 period and the positive trend in the period-dummy parameters, which is attributed to an integration effect. Only the relevance of cultural differences argues against the transition, but its influence is not high. These results suggest that regional core networks, which already may have developed in the core region, extend their linkages to economic activities in the periphery. Such activities may be less knowledge intensive, for example assembling or retailing. This may give some indication that periphery countries are integrating with the core region. Possibly, in view of the considerable influence of taxation differences, favourable taxation policies by host countries in the periphery play a role here.

4.3.4   Investments from the Periphery to the Core

Given the still limited, but growing importance of periphery-to-core investments, less complex corporate strategies are likely to prevail. Possibly, simple affiliate integration strategies dominate: in an integrating Europe investors from periphery countries may see opportunities to engage more and more in activities in the core region. As market potentials in the core are higher than those in the periphery, there may be a downstream orientation. Cheap labour costs are a less obvious explanatory variable. In the core, wages tend to be higher than in the periphery, which renders the hypothesis on seeking cheap labour locations less logical. Instead, high labour costs in the core may be a barrier to invest there. As in core-to-periphery investments, periphery investors may encounter barriers from cultural differences and transport costs.

MOSAIC's regression results presented in Table 4.9 reveal that foreign direct investments from the periphery to the core are explained by knowledge transfer, cultural differences and the direction of the exchange rate. In particular, knowledge transfer is of major importance in view of its β-value and its elasticity turns out to be rather high. It must be noted, however, that this variable is correlated to return on investment differences, transport costs and cultural differences. The market potential hypotheses are rejected, which is strange in view of the expectations. Cheap labour costs seem less relevant. This variable may indicate the higher labour costs in the core region to be a barrier, but its β-value implies a low importance. Differences in return on investment do not obtain an acceptable parameter, but this may be due to intercorrelation problems. Cultural differences are identified as a relatively strong barrier with a high sensitivity to investments. Transport costs appear to be a relevant barrier, but the parameter – perhaps again due to intercorrelations – is not very significant and reveals an inelastic relationship.

Table 4.9 Intra-EU investments from the periphery to the core

Information:		Countries: 5 * 6		
Periods: 9 (1980–84 to 1988–92)		*from* Denmark, Greece, Ireland,		
No. of cases: 211 of 270 (78.1%)		Portugal, Spain *to* Belgium/		
R^2: 0.543	*F*: 11.962	Luxemburg, France, Germany, Italy,		
R^2 (adjusted): 0.498	*DW*: 2.152	Netherlands, United Kingdom		
Determinant	Definition[a]	Parameter	*T*-value	β-value
Knowledge transfer	2	2.840	9.472	1.145
Market size	1	0.033	0.115	0.011
Per capita income	1a	–0.087	–0.067	–0.008
Labour costs	1c	–0.228	–0.826	–0.053
ROI differences	1	–1.688	–2.818	–0.287
Taxation differences	1	–1.778	–0.948	–0.061
Transport costs	1	–0.348	–1.239	–0.090
Cultural differences	1	–1.966	–4.462	–0.340
Trade intensity	1	0.112	0.369	0.039
Exchange rate direction	2	–2.290	–2.208	–0.128
Exchange rate volatility	5	1.095	3.934	0.329
Dummy 1981–85		–0.480	–1.009	–0.065
Dummy 1982–86		–0.885	–1.805	–0.128
Dummy 1983–87		–1.193	–2.242	–0.173
Dummy 1984–88		–1.210	–2.139	–0.182
Dummy 1985–89		–1.210	–1.929	–0.175
Dummy 1986–90		–1.133	–1.637	–0.177
Dummy 1987–91		–0.882	–1.152	–0.140
Dummy 1988–92		–1.043	–1.263	–0.162
Intercept		2.754	0.676	—

Note
a. For variable definitions, see Appendix IV.

Regarding exchange rates an interesting observation can be made. The results reveal that the direction of the exchange rate movements is important: it gets an elastic and significant parameter for the whole observation period. Introducing shift dummies for particular periods, as in the analyses for investments originating from core countries, did not appear to be necessary. Hence, in contrast to the intra-core and the core-to-periphery investments, its influence seems to extend into the latter half of the 1980s and the 1990s. Because on the whole, core currencies appreciate towards periphery currencies, this can be interpreted as a barrier to periphery investors, which continues to persist over the years. For them, investments in the core become more expensive in terms of domestic currencies. However, exchange rate volatility shows a significantly positive parameter, indicating that exchange rate volatility stimulates investments abroad. Hedging is effective, because the volatility variable is of the conditional type. The β-value suggests that the influence from erratic exchange rate volatility is rather strong. One may wonder whether these results indicate a type of capital flight towards core countries. Although investing in strong-currency countries is more expensive, periphery investors may want to curb a further deterioration of their capital from uncertainty regarding the domestic currency. This could imply that volatility incites investors to make investments in the core in order to hedge their capital funds.[24] When selling their investment in the future, investors will make an exchange rate gain in terms of the domestic currency. Foreign direct investment then becomes a type of portfolio investment.

The period-dummy parameters reveal a substantial impact from period-specific influences. If, as in the core-to-periphery model, the period dummies capture economic integration, then the negative signs of their parameters may suggest a negative impact. The β-values suggest that this impact remains of intermediate importance. However, parameters seem to have moved from elastic to inelastic values since 1985–89, which may indicate a positive integration effect.

Apart from the differences in the observations regarding exchange rates, other differences with the model for all intra-EU foreign direct investments exist. The importance of knowledge transfer is stronger for periphery-to-core investments than for all flows, but its identification may be disturbed by intercorrelation problems. Market potentials do not seem to be relevant, whereas in the model for all intra-EU flows they were. Labour costs are also less relevant. Further, taxation differences seem to influence periphery-to-core flows less than all flows, but its parameter implies a higher sensitivity. Cultural differences appear to be a much stronger barrier here than for all flows, but the transport cost barrier seems less important. Again, intercorrelation may disturb this. Trade intensity reveals a complementary relationship as in the model for all flows, but its parameter is insignificant and its relevance is substantially lower.

Although the regression coefficient amounts to more than 50 per cent and the *F*-statistic accepts the parameters to be significantly different from zero, some doubts exist on the validity of the model. The Durbin–Watson statistic reveals the possibility that negative autocorrelation exists in the residuals. For some investment relations, the residuals are large and show considerable covariance with those of other relations. In general, these are the same relations that caused problems in the model for all intra-EU flows. This is particularly true for the investment flows from Portugal to Germany and from Ireland to Italy. Other indications that the regression results are not strong, arise from using MOSAIC estimations based on other definitions of the explanatory variables. These regressions give results deviating from those presented here. The intercorrelation problems noted earlier may cause this. In addition, the small size of the investment flows and the loss of more than 20 per cent of the number of cases may prevent us from reaching sustainable results.

There does not seem to be evidence that any of the corporate strategy types are relevant for periphery-to-core investments. None of the profiles for the three corporate strategy types match with the results obtained here. Whereas core investors try to make linkages with periphery region activities, periphery investors do not seem to create such linkages from a corporate strategy perspective. The results may rather point towards portfolio-orientated strategies. This conclusion is fed by the significantly positive parameter of exchange rate volatility and by the irrelevance of the market size and per capita income hypotheses.

4.3.5 Investments within the Periphery Region

It is not really clear what to expect for the determinants of foreign direct investments within the periphery region. Although the share of these investments in total intra-EU investments is rising, with only 1.5 per cent of the total in 1988–92 it still remains of marginal importance. Further, the type of countries in the periphery is less homogeneous than those in the core. Denmark and Ireland cannot really be considered equivalent to Spain, Portugal and Greece.

MOSAIC estimations for intra-periphery investment flows identify market size, taxation differences and transport costs as important determinants in view of their β-values (see Table 4.10). For market size, the dominant role of foreign direct investments to and from Spain in the data set could be an explanation. Per capita income is not accepted, as it obtains an incorrect parameter. The same is true for labour costs. Return on investment differences may play a substantial role, as its parameter is significant and its β-value suggests an intermediate importance. The support for the cultural differences hypothesis is weak. The high and significant value of the taxation differences parameter may indicate that investments are very sensitive to favourable taxation policies in the host country. The knowledge transfer hypothesis is accepted, but its β-value reveals an intermediate influence.

Table 4.10   Intra-EU investments within the periphery region

Information: Periods: 9 (1980–84 to 1988–92) No. of cases: 112 of 180 (62.2%) R^2: 0.742 F: 13.896 R^2 (adjusted): 0.688 DW: 2.210		Countries: 5 Denmark, Greece, Ireland, Portugal, Spain		
Determinant	Definition[a]	Parameter	*T*-value	β-value
Knowledge transfer	2	0.680	2.682	0.251
Market size	1	1.383	4.950	0.554
Per capita income	1b	−0.543	−1.330	−0.192
Labour costs	1c	0.227	0.522	0.057
ROI differences	1	1.898	3.022	0.309
Taxation differences	1	−8.256	−5.967	−0.610
Transport costs	1	−1.903	−4.519	−0.521
Cultural differences	3	−0.840	−1.472	−0.113
Trade intensity	1	−0.103	−0.381	−0.041
Exchange rate direction	1	−0.509	−1.308	−0.087
Exchange rate volatility	1	0.553	1.180	0.099
Dummy 1981–85		0.431	0.765	0.057
Dummy 1982–86		0.103	0.136	0.014
Dummy 1983–87		0.717	0.918	0.107
Dummy 1984–88		1.059	1.199	0.158
Dummy 1985–89		1.227	1.350	0.183
Dummy 1986–90		1.434	1.571	0.213
Dummy 1987–91		1.853	2.149	0.276
Dummy 1988–92		1.929	2.376	0.305
Intercept		−11.810	−3.532	—

Note
a. For variable definitions, see Appendix IV.

For trade a negative, but insignificant, relationship is found, which implies substitution between trade and foreign direct investment. This should be interpreted with care as the trade intensity variable is highly correlated with transport costs. The latter variable gets a rather high elasticity, implying a strong sensitivity between transport costs and investments. This may coincide with large distances on some of the intra-periphery investment relations. Perhaps, large distances also explain the negative parameter for trade intensity. The exchange rate direction hypothesis obtains a parameter with low significance. The parameter for exchange rate volatility is, as for the periphery-to-core investments, positive, but its significance is also low. Here, the variable is of the unconditional type, which implies that hedging is not taken into account. The identification of return on investment differences as a determinant of intermediate importance together with the positive parameter for exchange rate volatility may give support to the existence of portfolio-orientated motives for foreign direct investments.

Period dummies obtain parameters which show an increasing trend over time. Their β-values suggest a growing importance and their T-values imply a growing significance. This trend may coincide with the strong growth in intra-periphery investments. It may also indicate a positive impact from economic integration processes.

In comparison with the results for all intra-EU foreign direct investment flows, large differences emerge. For intra-periphery flows exchange rate movements may not have a large impact, but its influence extends to all observation periods. Knowledge transfer is less important, but its variable definition differs. Market size is much more important for intra-periphery flows. In this case, it obtains an elastic parameter, whereas for all flows it was inelastic. Per capita income growth is not accepted here. Another difference is the stronger emphasis in intra-periphery investments on influences from taxation differences and transport costs than in all investment flows. Their parameters also show a higher elasticity. Finally, although insignificant, an important difference is the substitutory relation between trade and foreign direct investments for intra-periphery flows.

Despite the high correlation coefficient and a sufficiently high F-statistic, some doubts exist about the validity of the model. First, some period dummies obtain significant parameters and their β-values suggest a sizeable contribution to explaining the dependent variable. Hence, the explanatory variables for the hypotheses in the model are not able to cover the movements in intra-periphery investments alone. Second, some of the parameters are questionable. In particular, the high values for the intercept and the taxation differences parameter suggest that there could be some misspecifications. Third, the Durbin–Watson statistic could indicate some negative autocorrelations. The residuals on many of the investment relations show relatively high standard deviations, causing some covariance problems. These are the same investment relations that have already caused problems in the model for all intra-EU foreign direct investment flows. Finally, the model does not hold if other variable definitions are included in the regressions. This may be due to considerable intercorrelation problems among some explanatory variables. The limited size of investment flows and the loss of nearly 40 per cent of the number of cases seem major problems.

As for periphery-to-core investments, the determinants for intra-periphery investments do not really allow the identification of an overall corporate strategy type. On one hand, one may interpret the strong influence from market size, the identification of transport costs as a strong barrier and the substitutory trade relation to be indications for a stand-alone strategy type. The high relevance of taxation differences suggests that favourable taxation in host countries plays a major role. On the other hand, the results may point towards portfolio-orientated strategies as for periphery-to-core investments. This is fed by an intermediate importance of return on investment differences and, although less significant, a positive influence from exchange rate volatility. In view of the incidental nature of intra-periphery investment flows, the latter type of strategies seems more likely.

4.4 CONCLUSION

The trends in intra-EU foreign direct investment flows reveal growing integration of economic activities throughout the Union. Strong growth rates are observed for the 1980–92 period, particularly after the mid-1980s. Growth rates are also stronger than those for outward and inward foreign direct investment flows with countries outside the Union. As this coincides with the Internal Market programme, this may suggest a relocation of production throughout the Union.

Another indication for growing integration can be derived from analysing the trends in foreign direct investment flows, distinguishing between core and periphery regions. Growth rates for intra-periphery investments and those for investments from periphery countries to the core of the Union are substantially higher than those for investments within the core. Also, investments by core investors to the periphery grow strongly. This suggests that companies in periphery countries become more involved in Union-wide corporate networks of economic activity.

However, the varying growth rates have not yet changed the dominance of investors from core countries in foreign direct investments within the European Union. Intra-core investments still constitute more than 70 per cent of total investments and investments from the core destined for periphery countries take another 20 per cent. The share of periphery investors, although growing, remains of marginal importance, both in terms of investing in core countries and in other periphery countries.

The sectoral distribution of intra-EU foreign direct investment flows shows a strong emphasis on investments in service industries. In particular, investment activity is high in finance and banking, insurance, trade, hotels and catering and other commercial services. In manufacturing, investments in agriculture and food and in chemicals prevail. Data also suggest that some interindustry investing takes place.

Table 4.11   *Summary of determinants for intra-EU foreign direct investments*

Determinant	All flows		Core to core		Core to periphery		Periphery to core		Periphery to periphery	
Knowledge transfer	✓	++	✓	++	✓	+	✓	++	✓	+
Market size	✓	++	X	−	✓	++	X	−	✓	++
Per capita income	✓	+	X	−	✓	−	X	−	X	+
Labour costs	✓	−	X	+	X	+	X	−	X	−
ROI differences	✓	−	X	−	✓	+	X	++	✓	+
Taxation differences	✓	−	O	−	✓	+	X	−	✓	++
Transport costs	✓	++	✓	++	✓	++	O	−	✓	++
Cultural differences	✓	+	X	−	✓	−	✓	++	O	+
Trade intensity	✓	++	✓	++	✓	+	X	−	X	−
Exchange rate direction	✓[a]	+	✓[a]	++	✓[a]	−	✓	+	O	−
Exchange rate volatility	✓[a]	++	O[a]	−	✓[a]	+	X	++	X	−

Note
a. Influence limited to the 1980–84 to 1983–87 periods.

Legend
✓ significant and theoretically correct parameter   ++ strong influence
O idem, but significance is weak   + intermediate influence
X not significant or theoretically incorrect parameter   − weak influence

MOSAIC's estimation results give reasonably clear views on the determinants of foreign direct investments throughout the European Union (see Table 4.11). Five models were tested: one on all intra-EU investment flows and four on subdivisions of these flows. Some interesting differences emerge for investment relations within and between the core and periphery regions.

The knowledge transfer hypothesis is accepted in all models and the extent of its influence varies from intermediate to strong. This means that companies in Europe are inclined to use their ownership advantages not only domestically, but also in other EU markets. Possibly, intra-core investments are more knowledge intensive than investments on other investment relations, as the knowledge variable seems to have a particularly strong influence in the model for intra-core investments. The model for all flows suggests an elastic relation with foreign direct investments, but the models for some subsets reveal in general an inelastic relationship. For periphery-to-core investments, knowledge transfer is elastic and highly important, but in that model estimation the knowledge variable turns out to be highly correlated with other variables.

The picture for market size is mixed. For intra-core investments and for investments from the periphery to the core, market size is not accepted as a relevant determinant. In the model for intra-core investments it is suspected that integration may have rendered the market size of individual countries irrelevant. Instead, the market size of the core region as a whole may have become the relevant determinant for these flows. For core-to-periphery and intra-periphery investments, market size is relevant as a locational advantage and obtains an elastic parameter.

The per capita income hypothesis turns out to be irrelevant for most subsets of foreign direct investment flows. Only for core-to-periphery investments is a significant parameter found for per capita income. Apparently, spatial differences in purchasing power are not a determining locational advantage. For the core region, an explanation could be that differences in purchasing power in national markets have become minor as a result of integration processes. For the periphery region, purchasing power is likely to be lower than in the core, and, as a result, a less obvious pull factor.

In the model for all intra-EU foreign direct investment flows cheap labour costs were identified as a relevant determinant, but this is not supported by the other models. Instead, for intra-core and core-to-periphery investments an inelastic positive influence is found. In particular, on the core-to-periphery relation this was considered strange, because some relevance of cheap labour costs was expected. If labour costs are considered a determinant for relocations of economic activities in an integrating market, this is not supported here. Rather, the positive parameters may be an indication that investors are interested in more expensive high-quality labour than in cheap labour even when seeking locations in periphery countries. In view of the growing complexity of networks of economic activity this may be logical. It may also coincide with the large share of service industries in foreign direct investment flows. For some service activities, high-quality labour could be more important than for other types of activity.

The hypothesis on return on investment differences is accepted in the models for all flows and those for core-to-periphery and intra-periphery investments. In the latter two models an elastic influence is found and its relevance seems to be of intermediate importance. For intra-core and periphery-to-core investments its influence is not supported.

For all intra-EU foreign direct investment flows and for most subsets, taxation differences are found to be of some relevance. Especially for investments in periphery countries, this variable seems to be of some importance and shows high elasticities. For investors from periphery countries undertaking activities in the core region of the Union, the hypothesis does not appear to be valid. For intra-core investments the influence is inelastic and of minor importance. This could imply that investors are led by favourable taxation policies for inward investments, particularly when investing in the periphery.

Transportation costs turn out to be relevant and of some importance for all investment relations. Companies investing in periphery countries consider transport costs a more important barrier than those investing in the core region. Further, the transport cost parameter for core-to-periphery investments and for intra-periphery investments reveals an elastic relationship, whereas for intra-core investments it is inelastic. Periphery investors in core countries seem to take transport costs for granted: although the distance parameter is theoretically correct, its significance is low. These results suggest a growing relevance of the transport cost barrier with increasing distances between home and host country.

Except for intra-core investments, cultural differences appear to be a relevant barrier. Core-to-periphery investments seem less sensitive to the culture barrier than periphery-to-core investments. In the latter group of foreign direct investments, the cultural differences parameter is elastic and has a considerable impact. For intra-periphery investments this barrier seems to be less important. Within the core region, cultural differences are not identified as an investment determinant. This may coincide with the integration process, which could have diminished cultural differences in the core substantially.

The relation between trade and foreign direct investment is positive for intra-core and core-to-periphery investments. This suggests that increasing trade relations and increasing economic integration lead to more foreign direct investments. The influence appears to be rather high for intra-core investments. For core-to-periphery investments the influence seems lower. The relation seems to be inelastic, as the parameter is less than unity in both models. For companies in periphery countries, the relation between trade and investment is not clear. Their investments in core countries show a complementary relation; those in other periphery countries seem to be substitutory. However, the parameter on both relations is insignificant and the influence appears to be weak.

The hypothesis on exchange rate direction is relevant for all intra-EU foreign direct investments. This implies that appreciating currencies in host countries appear to be a barrier to investment in those countries, whereas depreciating host currencies are a stimulus. For investments from core countries the influence is limited to the periods until 1983–87. In subsequent periods, the hypothesis has to be rejected. This suggests that exchange rate policies, such as the EMS, have rendered the bilateral movements in European currencies an ineffective determinant for core investors since the mid-1980s. For companies in the periphery, the hypothesis continues to prevail after 1983–87 on both periphery-to-core and intra-periphery relations, but its relevance is not large. Because periphery currencies have a tendency to depreciate versus core currencies, their movements *vis-à-vis* these currencies must be a barrier for periphery-to-core investments.

For exchange rate volatility the conclusion is different. For foreign direct investment relations within the core, the hypothesis obtains a parameter of weak significance for the periods prior to 1984–88. Apparently, the bilateral exchange rates among core-country currencies were already sufficiently stable at the beginning of the 1980s. For investments from the core to the periphery, the hypothesis is accepted in its conditional identity for the periods before 1984–88. This transforms exchange rate volatility on these investment relations into a barrier for those periods. This barrier seems to be of intermediate importance. Since 1984–88, the hypothesis is irrelevant. For periphery investors another result is found. In the models for intra-periphery and periphery-to-core investments, the influence of exchange rate volatility extends to the complete observation period, but the variable obtains positive parameters. This suggests a stimulus for investing abroad. For periphery-to-core investments the stimulus even appears to be of substantial importance. Because periphery currencies are in general less stable, this may indicate that periphery investors try to hedge their investment capital against a value loss from depreciating home currencies.

The above supports the idea that exchange rate stability has a positive effect on foreign direct investment (CEC 1990, p. 21).[25] Apparently, exchange rate policies have already achieved sufficient stability in mutual exchange rates to render adverse impacts on investment ineffective for intra-core and core-to-periphery investment relations. Therefore, the largest impact of the envisaged creation of a single currency on these foreign direct investment relations may not come from its introduction as such, but rather from the diminution of foreign exchange transaction costs.[26] For investments by companies located in the periphery, some more gains seem to be possible. Stability may eliminate the depreciation barrier for these investors. It will also take away the need for hedging investment capital against value losses from depreciating home currencies. This could allow a better allocation of investment capital and thus contribute to the integration of economic activities in periphery countries in Union-wide production networks.

Table 4.12   Summary of corporate strategies within the European Union

To → ↓ From	Core countries	Periphery countries
Core countries	Regional core networking	Downstream simple affiliate integration moving to regional core networking
Periphery countries	Portfolio ?	Portfolio ?

The overall picture which emerges from the MOSAIC regression results, is summarised in Table 4.12. It suggests a difference in corporate strategies on the four main investment relations within the European Union.

Core investors wanting to invest in the core region no longer appear to encounter barriers from cultural differences and exchange rate volatility. These barriers seem to have dissipated. Further, differences in national market potentials seem to have become less relevant, but these may not diverge very much any more within the core region due to economic integration processes. This may suggest that the core region is a reasonably well-integrated economic area in which foreign direct investments tend to behave as domestic investments. Taking this into account together with a relatively strong influence from knowledge transfer, there is an inclination to believe that the overall strategy pursued by companies in the core region is a regional core networking strategy.

For their investments in the periphery, core investors may pursue strategies which seem to shift from the downstream simple affiliate integration type to the regional core networking type. Core investors are influenced by the market size determinant, which is relevant for both strategy types. Labour costs seem to influence investment decisions, if they indicate the relevance of labour quality. The strategy shift is particularly supported by accepting the shift dummy for the exchange rate volatility barrier. After 1983–87, this barrier has become irrelevant. Support is given as well by a positive trend in the period-dummy parameters, which can be attributed to a growing importance of economic integration processes. Networking may relate particularly to less-knowledge-intensive activities, such as assembling or retailing, as knowledge transfer appears to be less relevant. However, although of limited importance, the relevance of the cultural differences barrier may still argue against the strategy shift. It seems that favourable taxation policies in the periphery are relevant.

Determinants for foreign direct investments made by companies from periphery countries do not clearly indicate any of the corporate strategy types. There is an inclination to believe that periphery investors have a portfolio orientation for their investments rather than an orientation based on a corporate strategy. Exchange rate volatility stimulates periphery companies to invest in the core region, which in view of the generally weaker currencies of their home countries could point towards a capital flight phenomenon. They apparently want to benefit from stable foreign currencies in the core region in order to maintain their asset values. This is supported to some extent by the irrelevance of the market potential hypotheses. For intra-periphery investments, the portfolio orientation can be derived not only from a positive parameter for exchange rate volatility, but also from the intermediate importance of return on investment differences. In addition, the existence of favourable taxation policies in the host country may play a role. However, it should be stressed that the model results for periphery investors are not strong.

The above results imply a reconsideration of the notion of the European Union to be a world region in which economic integration has reached a rather high level. Further, they may say something on the success of creating an Internal Market throughout the European Union. For the core countries, this process seems to be successful. Corporate structures in these countries pursue strategies in which the complex integration of economic activities has become possible.[27] They establish integrated networks of activities encompassing all core countries. For the periphery countries, the Internal Market may not have been realised yet. Investments still encounter problems with regard to exchange rate uncertainty and cultural barriers. Also, it appears that transport costs are an important barrier. However, as core-country companies are already incorporating periphery-country activities into their networks, a process of integration for periphery countries may have started.[28] These activities, though, may be less knowledge intensive. Apart from the Internal Market programme, other European policies may contribute to its realisation. Policies via the Structural Funds and via lending facilities of the European Investment Bank aim at improving locational advantages in terms of physical infrastructure (lower transport costs) and education and training (higher labour quality).[29] Further, the continuing efforts by the European Commission to achieve a full economic union by creating an Economic and Monetary Union and a European Political Union may be beneficial as well.

The results support the acceptance of the hypothesis that different countries give different opportunities for internalising optimal combinations of ownership and locational advantages in foreign direct investments. Spatial differences in various variables are accepted as investment determinants. They represent the varying opportunities that countries offer to foreign investors. It is also shown that opportunities vary from one region to the other depending on the state of integration that is achieved. Hence, the analysis in this chapter supports the theoretical framework for foreign direct investment.

NOTES

1. Molle (1994, p. 49) considers the European Union as a region where the velocity of integration exceeds the speed in other integration schemes.
2. According to Dunning (1997a, p. 28), intra-EU mergers and acquisitions and acquisitions of EU-firms by non-EU companies increased more than ten-fold between 1985–86 and 1989–90. According to the United Nations (1996, p. 10), the level of cross-border mergers and acquisitions in Western Europe is among the highest in the world, most of which appear within the European Union.
3. These are the same countries that Pelkmans (1983, pp. 43–6) included in his flow matrices of intra-EU foreign direct investments for 1966 and 1970. This may indicate that the founding members of the European Union plus the United Kingdom have a long tradition in investing in other core countries.
4. Recently, Dunning (1997a, p. 13) attributed the same countries to the core and the periphery.
5. This also seems to be the view of the OECD (1995e, p. 12).
6. According to Campa and Guillén (1996, p. 214), the integration into the European Union is very important for the rise in Spanish outward investments after 1986.
7. According to the OECD (1994g, p. 23), the share of investments from Portugal into the European Union has grown from 50.5 per cent of total outward flows in 1980–85 to 82.7 per cent around 1992.
8. In the period 1990–92, Greek outward investments amounted to about US$160 million. About 47 per cent was destined for the United States. Another 30 per cent went to EU member states. Further, 22 per cent of this total was headed for countries in Central and Eastern Europe, in particular Bulgaria, Albania and Romania. See OECD (1994h, p. 14).
9. See also United Nations (1994, p. 54).
10. The OECD (1995e, pp. 21–2) observed strong growth in outward foreign direct investments from Denmark from 1985 onwards, of which the European Union was the most important recipient. The share of EU countries in total outward investment flows has increased from 31.0 per cent in 1984 to 60.8 per cent during the period 1985–92.
11. For Denmark, inward investment flows started to rise considerably in 1987. See OECD (1995e, p. 12).
12. Appendix III shows that these investments are dominated by investments from Germany, France, the Netherlands and the United Kingdom to Spain, Portugal and Greece. See also Buckley and Artisien (1987, Chapter 3).
13. Buckley and Artisien (1987, p. 62) expected a major impact on inward investments in these countries.
14. See also Dunning, J.H. (1997a, pp. 20–21).
15. Transport costs can decrease due to new transportation technologies and the building of new and more efficient infrastructure. Further, in an integrating market transport can operate in a more competitive environment, which brings transport fares down. As was explained in Chapter 2, this can materialise in new ownership and locational advantages.
16. However, when countries or national identities in Europe perceive a diminishing attention for their cultural identities, they may pursue policies to preserve them.

17. The EMS does not apply to all EU currencies. The British pound had entered the EMS by the end of 1990, but had to leave the system in 1992. Also, in 1992 the Italian lira had to step out of the system. The Greek drachma has never been part of the EMS.
18. An indication for this may be that the standard deviation of the market size and per capita income variables are lower for intra-core investments than for all intra-EU foreign direct investments (7 per cent for market size; 32 per cent for per capita income).
19. The standard deviation of cultural differences on intra-core investment relations is 52 per cent lower than its standard deviation for all intra-EU foreign direct investment flows.
20. Culem (1988, p. 899) found support for a positive influence of unit labour costs in the host country relative to unit labour costs in the home country.
21. Technology transfer was identified as a major determinant of inward foreign direct investments into Spain. See Durán Herrera (1992, p. 250).
22. Buckley and Artisien (1987, p. 151) show that labour quality is a major determinant for north south direct investments. Bajo-Rubio and Sosvilla-Rivero (1994, p. 117) concluded that higher labour costs in Spain are not a serious threat to inward investments in Spain.
23. Martin and Rogers (1995, p. 185) consider the lower availability of infrastructure an important barrier for locating industry in periphery countries.
24. In this respect, the relatively large emphasis of finance and banking and insurance in intra-EU investments should be mentioned.
25. This notion was based on Morsink and Molle (1991a).
26. This may not relate to the costs of cross-border bank transfers, as banks themselves determine the charges for such transfers.
27. Cantwell (1992, p. 3) suggests that a shift towards regionally integrated corporate networks within Europe is found by Savary, van den Bulcke and de Lombaerde, Simões and Yannopoulos.
28. Cantwell (1992, pp. 9–10) suggests that a 'locational hierarchy' exists.
29. Martin and Rogers (1995, p. 185) consider the structural policies important for the location of industry in periphery countries, but suggest investments in telecommunication and education to be more effective.

5. Investments from the United States

5.1 INTRODUCTION

In this chapter the determinants of the outward foreign direct investment flows from the United States of America will be identified from estimations using MOSAIC. First, the geographical patterns in American foreign direct investments throughout the world will be described. Three geographical clusters can be identified in which investments concentrate. Next, the model estimates will be discussed. The model is first applied to all outgoing foreign direct investment flows. Then, the model is estimated for the three geographical clusters.

It is not possible to include all hypotheses in the model. The proxies for the knowledge hypothesis behave like constants in model estimations and therefore have to be excluded from the model. Also, the taxation differences hypothesis is excluded in view of data availability. Further, insufficient data for return on investment in countries in Asia and Latin America prohibit inclusion in model estimates for these regions.

5.2 INVESTMENT PATTERNS

Foreign direct investments from the United States show strong growth over the past decade (see Figure 5.1). For 1982, total outward investments amount to only US$1 billion, but this figure is distorted by large disinvestments in Latin America. Since 1982, outward investments increase substantially, reaching a high of US$29 billion in 1987. There is a temporary drop in 1988 followed by a major upsurge in 1989 to nearly US$38 billion. This is due to investments incurred by sustained economic growth overseas, particularly in Western Europe and East Asia (Scholl 1990, p. 60). For 1990, another temporary setback occurs, but in 1991 and 1992 the outflows increase again. According to the United Nations (1994, p. 52), US investors 'have been successful in finding some profitable investment opportunities abroad in spite of the recession at home and the prolonged economic slowdown in their host developed markets'. Scholl (1991, p. 28) considers this a reflection of US multinationals expanding their global operations.

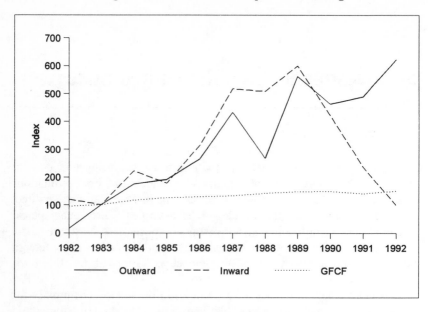

*Figure 5.1   Development of foreign direct investment from the USA and
gross fixed capital formation (1983 = 100; nominal)*

For inward foreign direct investments the trend is different. Investments
by foreigners in the United States increase particularly during 1985–89, but
decrease substantially in subsequent years. The level of domestic investments does not show major changes.

Table 5.1 reveals a strong clustering of US investments in three host
regions. Most American foreign direct investments are concentrated in
Western Europe: about half is destined for member countries of the
European Union and other West European countries. The second region is
North and South America, of which Canada, Brazil and Mexico are the most
important destinations. South and Southeast Asia, including Japan, is the
third largest region.

The dominant position of Western Europe coincides with American
foreign direct investments in specific host countries. Most investments in
Western Europe are destined for the United Kingdom. Other important host
countries are the Netherlands, Germany and France. Italy and Ireland are of
some interest. For the latter country, long-standing historical ties could
explain the relatively high share for such a small country (OECD 1994c, p.
15).

*Table 5.1 Geographical distribution and growth of total outward foreign
direct investments from the USA (1982–92; %)*

Host region	1982–86	1985–89	1988–92	1982–92[a]
Western Europe	58.3	50.1	47.1	16.3
European Union (EU12)	49.8	47.6	40.1	16.2
Germany	5.3	2.2	6.4	24.5
France	3.5	4.9	6.0	32.0
Italy	4.3	2.9	3.9	18.4
Netherlands	7.6	9.0	0.9	−16.3
United Kingdom	21.3	20.9	14.6	13.2
Ireland	4.9	3.2	2.6	8.5
Other Western Europe	8.5	2.5	7.1	16.9
South and Southeast Asia	15.2	6.8	10.5	13.3
Japan	3.5	2.8	2.2	11.2
Hong Kong	3.3	1.8	2.3	13.5
Singapore	0.9	0.3	1.8	35.9
Taiwan	0.6	0.7	0.8	24.1
Thailand	0.5	0.5	0.9	32.3
Indonesia	5.4	−0.2	1.1	−7.0
North and South America	20.5	41.2	37.4	33.2
Latin America	10.4	30.2	29.6	43.5
Brazil	3.6	5.7	6.1	31.7
Mexico	−1.5	2.0	5.1	—
Canada	10.1	11.0	7.7	15.3
Other regions	6.1	1.9	5.0	16.7
Central and Eastern Europe	0.0	0.0	0.5	—
Middle East	4.1	−0.4	1.0	−4.4
Australia and New Zealand	1.9	3.8	5.2	42.7
Africa	1.5	−1.0	−1.7	—
Other	−1.5	−0.4	0.0	—
Total	100.0	100.0	100.0	20.5

Note
a. Average nominal growth rate between first and last periods.

Source
OECD.

The trend for Western Europe and in particular the European Union is going down. This region's share in total US foreign direct investment decreases from nearly 50 per cent to some 40 per cent, with large differences from one country to another.[1] The shares of the United Kingdom and of the Netherlands, which are both of considerable importance as a host to American investments, decrease. The same is true for Ireland. Germany gains importance after a serious trough in the mid-1980s. France reveals an increasing trend. Italy's share remains fairly stable.

Countries in North and South America first encounter large dis-investment actions by Americans in 1982 and 1983. In subsequent years, investments in this region recover to a steady share of some 40 per cent in total US investments abroad. According to the United Nations (1994, p. 84), this is due to foreign direct investment related to debt–equity swaps until 1990 and privatisations since that year in South America. Also, reforms towards market-orientated economies in this region have initiated new foreign direct investments.

The most important host countries in North and South America are Canada, Brazil and Mexico. Canada, as a neighbouring country, reveals a downward trend since the mid-1980s. Brazil shows an upward trend, but this could be due to large disinvestments by Americans at the beginning of the 1980s. Mexico starts to become important after 1986, which is due to interesting debt–equity swaps for foreign investors and in later years the creation of the North American Free Trade Area (NAFTA; see Calderón, Mortimore and Peres 1996, p. 246). US investors may have wanted to benefit from the low wage costs in Mexico by creating *maquiladores* firms and from the expected abolition of trade barriers between both countries.

American foreign direct investments in South and Southeast Asia reveal at first instance a downward trend, but in the latter half of the 1980s and at the beginning of the 1990s this region's popularity to US investors increases again. This gives expression to the growing importance of the Pacific Rim region for the United States. However, there are diverging patterns. The share of investments in Japan continues its downward movement from the beginning of the 1980s. Apparently, this country has become less attractive in relative terms. On the other hand, investments in Hong Kong, Singapore, Thailand and Indonesia have grown strongly. The United Nations (1994, p. 53) indicates that this shift away from Japan also benefits some other countries such as Korea, Singapore and Taiwan.

Other world regions are of limited importance. Strong growth is shown for Australia and New Zealand, which also testifies to the increasing importance of the Pacific Rim to US investors. After the opening up of Central and Eastern Europe, Americans seem to have a growing interest in countries in this region, but the volume of investments still remains at a low level. For the Middle East the interest seems to decline and for Africa disinvestments prevail.

Table 5.2 Sectoral distribution and growth of total outward foreign direct investments from the USA (1982–92; %)

Investing industry	1982–86	1985–89	1988–92	1982–92[a]
Agriculture	–0.4	–0.2	0.1	—
Total manufacturing	56.2	35.6	42.9	16.2
Mining and quarrying	–6.5	–1.4	0.6	—
Oil and petroleum products	12.1	–5.9	–2.3	—
Food and beverages	8.8	2.6	7.4	18.1
Textiles and clothing	0.0	0.3	0.4	—
Paper, printing and publishing	2.1	5.5	5.3	41.6
Chemical products	11.1	11.6	12.3	23.7
Non-metallic products	2.6	2.3	1.7	13.7
Metal products	1.6	3.3	2.9	34.4
Mechanical equipment	12.8	6.3	2.3	–8.5
Electric and electronic equipment	2.0	2.6	3.6	34.9
Motor vehicles	3.4	5.8	5.1	29.7
Other transport equipment	0.2	0.2	0.1	16.3
Other manufacturing	6.1	2.3	3.3	9.6
Construction	0.7	0.2	0.3	5.5
Total commercial services	43.5	64.5	56.7	27.1
Wholesale and retail trade	11.9	12.0	13.5	24.1
Transport and storage	0.2	0.3	1.3	67.1
Finance, insurance and business services	29.8	49.5	35.0	24.9
Communication	0.3	0.2	3.2	79.1
Other commercial services	1.3	2.5	3.7	45.4
Total	100.0	100.0	100.0	20.5

Note
a. Average nominal growth rate between first and last periods.

Source
OECD.

The sectoral distribution of outward foreign direct investment (Table 5.2) shows an emphasis on services. Its share in total foreign investments rises from 43 per cent in 1982–86 to nearly 65 per cent in 1985–89, but then declines to some 57 per cent in 1988–92. The largest contribution to this share comes from investments by the group of finance, insurance and business services. These industries constitute more than one-third of total outward foreign direct investments. In the 1985–89 period it even amounted to half of total outward investment flows. Wholesale and retail trade is responsible for another 12 per cent.

The remainder of total foreign direct investments is mostly made in manufacturing. With a share of about 12 per cent, chemical products is the manufacturing industry with the largest involvement abroad. Other manufacturing industries of some importance are: food and beverages; mechanical equipment; motor vehicles; and paper, printing and publishing. The shares of these industries remain in general below 10 per cent of the total.

The shares of manufacturing and services change considerably over the years. Within manufacturing the share of chemical products remains stable. For motor vehicles, the share first increases, but later declines slightly. The food and beverages share strongly decreases, but recovers in the late 1980s. That for mechanical engineering also goes down strongly and does not recover. In service industries, the group of finance, insurance and business services first gains substantially, but later loses to other service industry groupings.

5.3 DETERMINANTS

5.3.1 Investments to the World

In view of the rather long international orientation of American investors, it seems logical to expect American corporate structures to pursue complex international production strategies. The profile of this strategy type contains market size, per capita income and the use of cheap labour inputs as relevant determinants. Also, a positive relation with trade is expected, allowing foreign locations to produce for both home and host markets with product shipments among affiliates. In principle, cultural differences and exchange rate volatility should not be major barriers, but for some regions these barriers may still exist.

Table 5.3 US investments throughout the world

Information: Periods: 7 (1982–86 to 1988–92) No. of cases: 213 of 245 (86.9%) R^2: 0.432 F: 10.767 R^2 (adjusted): 0.392 DW: 1.616		Countries: 35 Western Europe, South and Southeast Asia, North and South America plus Australia, Egypt, Finland, Israel, New Zealand and Turkey		
Determinant	Definition[a]	Parameter	T-value	β-value
Market size	1	0.008	0.119	0.007
Per capita income	2b	1.915	2.978	0.219
Labour costs	2b	−0.350	−0.414	−0.025
Transport costs	1	−0.592	−3.161	−0.207
Cultural differences	1	−2.051	−5.414	−0.335
Trade intensity	2a	0.934	7.320	0.426
Exchange rate direction	1	0.064	0.345	0.024
Exchange rate volatility	2	0.236	1.494	0.113
Dummy 1983–87		−0.316	−0.910	−0.065
Dummy 1984–88		−0.583	−1.715	−0.127
Dummy 1985–89		−0.733	−2.109	−0.159
Dummy 1986–90		−0.565	−1.609	−0.125
Dummy 1987–91		−0.140	−0.398	−0.031
Dummy 1988–92		−0.004	−0.010	0.000
Intercept		0.700	0.440	—

Note
a. For variable definitions, see Appendix IV.

MOSAIC results suggest that American investments abroad are guided by the host country's growth in per capita income, the trade relation and barriers coming from transport costs and cultural differences (see Table 5.3). The most important determinant for US investors seems to be the trade relation, as its β-value is highest. The relation with trade appears to be positive with an elasticity close to unity.[2] This may indicate that trade liberalisation is highly important to US investors. Elasticities reveal that investments are sensitive to per capita income and cultural differences as their parameters are elastic. Barriers from cultural differences have a considerable impact as their parameter's β-value ranks second. Apparently, American investors favour an 'American friendly' climate. This may explain the large shares in total investments of countries such as the United Kingdom, Canada and Australia. The use of cheap labour in the host country does not seem to be a strong determinant. The parameter is theoretically correct, but its significance is low. Possibly, this coincides with the relatively strong growth in foreign direct investments in some capital-intensive manufacturing industries and some human capital-intensive service industries, which may favour high-quality labour instead of low-cost labour. Market size and exchange rate movements are not relevant determinants. Neither hypothesis on exchange rates is accepted. The stature of the US dollar as an international currency could play a role here.

The negative period-dummy parameters may reflect changing influences from existing investment barriers. For some periods in the mid-1980s significant parameters are observed. Their β-values suggest an intermediate importance from such barriers, but in later periods their influence seems to fade.

The regression's quality is not high. The explanatory power is low. Some period dummies get significant parameters, which implies that the explanatory variables cannot fully cover the variance in the dependent variable. The Durbin–Watson statistic could suggest that some positive autocorrelation exists in the residuals of the estimated model. In particular, the residuals for US investments to Greece, Norway and New Zealand cause major covariance problems. To a lesser extent, this is also the case for the Netherlands, Finland, Egypt and Indonesia. In addition, the results are sensitive to alternative model specifications. Including other variable definitions in the regression provokes substantial changes in the set of significant parameters. Intercorrelations do not seem to be the major trouble here. Possibly, the heterogeneity of host countries in the data set causes the limited explanatory power of the model.

Although the model estimates are doubtful, the results may give some support to the existence of complex international production strategies. Investors appear to be strongly led by market orientation and existing complementary trade relations. Further, the exchange rate hypotheses are not accepted. The high relevance of cultural differences could mean that strategies may still be of a less complex nature, for example the downstream simple affiliate integration type. This may be the case for less American-orientated host countries.

5.3.2   Investments to Western Europe

In the previous section it was shown that although there is a declining trend, about half of US investments abroad are destined for Western Europe. American investors are particularly active in the core region of the European Union. Important host countries are the United Kingdom, the Netherlands,

Germany, France and Italy. In the periphery of the Union, Ireland seems to be an interesting destination for American investors.

US investments in Western Europe have a long tradition.[3] This may imply that complex international production strategies could prevail here. Market potential and cheap input provision must be of considerable importance. Return on investment differences may not have a major influence. A complementary trade relation should exist, but in view of the fear of creating a Fortress Europe, investments may have a tariff-jumping character. This could imply trade substitution instead of trade complementarity. Cultural differences and exchange rate changes should not be strong barriers.

MOSAIC's estimation results (see Table 5.4) indicate that market size, per capita income and a complementary trade relation are significant determinants. Their β-values suggest that trade intensity and market orientation are dominant influences. Per capita income is even more important than market size, which makes the purchasing power influence stronger than the volume of potential customers. The trade parameter does not support the tariff-jumping character of investments, which renders the Fortress Europe fear obsolete. A relevant barrier is transport costs. A barrier from cultural differences is not really encountered, because the parameter is insignificant and its β-value reveals a low influence.[4] American investors are indifferent about the direction in which exchange rates move. The exchange rate direction parameter is insignificant and the variable contributes little to the model. The positive parameter of exchange rate volatility may reflect an incentive for US investors to invest in Europe from substantial fluctuations of the US dollar *vis-à-vis* European currencies throughout the 1980s.

The strong market orientation and the irrelevance of trade barriers were also conclusions of economists studying the pre-1980 US investments in Europe. Scaperlanda and Mauer (1969, p. 566) stressed the importance of the EU market and advocated doubts about the relevance of trade barriers. Later, Scaperlanda and Balough (1983, p. 389) reaffirmed market size to be a major determinant. However, the irrelevance of trade barriers was not identified by Schmitz (1970, p. 731), Schmitz and Bieri (1972, p. 268) and Lunn (1980, p. 99). Since the analysis presented here is based on more recent data, the results seem to indicate that those of Scaperlanda and Mauer are still valid.

The labour cost variable obtains a positive parameter, which is theoretically incorrect. Maybe this is an indication of Krugman's synergy effect in terms of labour quality. The rather high value of the parameter even suggests a considerable sensitivity. American investors probably seek high-quality labour for their affiliate activities and, in view of its elasticity and β-value, are inclined to settle in countries where such labour is available.

Table 5.4   US investments to Western Europe

Information: Periods: 7 (1982–86 to 1988–92) No. of cases: 83 of 98 (84.7%) R^2: 0.816 F: 19.846 R^2 (adjusted): 0.775 DW: 2.429		Countries: 14 Austria, Belgium/Luxemburg, Denmark, France, Germany, Greece, Ireland, Italy, Netherlands, Norway, Portugal, Spain, Sweden, United Kingdom		
Determinant	Definition[a]	Parameter	T-value	β-value
Market size	1	0.429	2.985	0.243
Per capita income	2a	1.135	3.104	0.331
Labour costs	2c	2.477	1.780	0.161
ROI differences	1	–0.017	–0.066	–0.006
Transport costs	1	–4.073	–2.138	–0.211
Cultural differences	2	–0.702	–1.011	–0.091
Trade intensity	1	1.873	5.345	0.471
Exchange rate direction	2	2.382	0.670	0.099
Exchange rate volatility	1	2.159	1.592	0.154
Dummy 1983–87		–0.325	–0.566	–0.057
Dummy 1984–88		–0.734	–1.101	–0.138
Dummy 1985–89		–1.068	–1.351	–0.202
Dummy 1986–90		–1.077	–1.244	–0.204
Dummy 1987–91		–0.801	–1.240	–0.157
Dummy 1988–92		–0.619	–1.269	–0.121
Intercept		9.255	1.935	—

Note
a. For variable definitions, see Appendix IV.

Milner and Pentecost (1994, pp. 99–100) give further support for the model results. They have investigated whether US investments in manufacturing in the United Kingdom are related to cheap (manual) labour. Further, they have tested the relevance of the EU market for these investments. Their conclusion is that US investments are indeed guided by the large potentials of the EU market, but that cheap labour is not really a determinant. Earlier, Culem (1988, p. 897) observed that the low labour cost motive was already absent as a determinant to US investments in Europe in the 1969–82 period. Rather, investments are related to relatively capital-intensive and non-manual labour-(skill-)intensive activities. The sectoral composition of US investments abroad presented earlier may be consistent with this observation, as relatively strong growth is signalled in industries such as paper, printing and publishing, metal products, and electric and electronic components. This could also coincide with the high share of investments in service industries, in particular finance, insurance and business services, communication and other commercial services. Such industries may favour labour quality instead of its low price.

The results of recent research by Aristotelous and Fountas (1996) seem to be consistent with our results as well. They analyse US investments in nine EU countries during the 1980–92 period and find a significant influence of market orientation measured in terms of the real GDP level in the host country and its growth rate. Further, little support is given in their analysis to the existence of trade barriers. They find little evidence for an influence from the direction in which real exchange rates move.

Research by the (Dutch) Economic Institute for Small and Medium-sized Enterprises (EIM) on some case studies also supports our observations to some extent.[5] Most subsidiaries of US corporate structures have the sales function as their main type of economic activity. In addition, the provision of (customer) services is important. Only in a few cases is production mentioned, but mostly in combination with sales and service activities. This is an indication that most subsidiaries are established from a market-orientation point of view.

The parameters for the period dummies may mirror the overall downward trend in the share of US investments in Europe in total US investments. Especially between 1982–86 and 1985–89, this share and these periods' parameters decline substantially.

The estimated model has a high explanatory power. This is particularly due to the explanatory variables, since the period dummies show low to intermediate influences. The Durbin–Watson statistic suggests that negative autocorrelation could exist in the model's residuals. In particular, the residuals for US investments in Greece and Norway, as in the world model, cause covariance problems with residuals of investment relations elsewhere in Europe. Although some intercorrelation among explanatory variables exists, other model specifications do not result in substantially different estimation results.

MOSAIC results for Western Europe have some similarities with those for world investments. Per capita income, complementary trade relations and a barrier from transport costs were also identified as relevant determinants for world investments. Here, foreign direct investments seem to be more sensitive to transport costs in view of the rather high parameter. Further, cultural barriers may be less important than in the world model. Also, the exchange rate hypotheses are rejected in both regressions. An important difference is the labour cost parameter. For Western Europe it appears that it is not the level of labour costs which is taken into consideration, but rather labour quality. The overall similarity is not a surprise, as foreign direct investments in Western Europe constitute about half of world foreign direct investments. However, variable specifications for the various determinants used in the regressions differ. On the whole, it seems that the model results for this region appear to be more sustainable than in the world model.

The prevailing corporate strategy can indeed be identified as the regional core networking type of complex international production strategies. This is supported by the strong influence from trade complementarity and a considerable influence from market orientation. Support may also come from a labour-quality orientation of investors and the low relevance of cultural differences. This may mean that network linkages develop between the United States and Western Europe. As a result, US–European core networks may have developed.

5.3.3   Investments to South and Southeast Asia

US investments in South and Southeast Asia are identified in the previous section as the third largest destination cluster. At the beginning of the 1980s, foreign direct investments to this region show a decline in relative terms, but in subsequent years this trend seems to be curbed by investments in newly industrialising countries in this region.

In view of the above, it seems likely that strategies may not be as complex as those for Europe. Simple affiliate integration strategies may prevail here. A market (downstream) orientation seems relevant, as some Asian markets have developed strongly. Input (upstream) orientation can also be expected. Most countries in this region have substantially lower labour costs than in the United States, which renders the labour cost hypothesis relevant. Regarding trade, a complementary relationship fits in this strategy type, but for some markets, for example Japan, trade barriers could exist. This would imply a substitutory trade relation. Further, as some Asian currencies have not been very stable over the years, the exchange rate hypotheses are expected to be valid here. Finally, support is also expected for the barriers from transport costs and cultural differences, in view of the large distances, both physically and culturally, between the United States and the Asian region.

MOSAIC results support the hypotheses on the substitutory relation with trade and on barriers from transport costs, cultural differences and (conditional) exchange rate volatility, as is shown in Table 5.5. In particular, transport costs and trade intensity are important, as is shown by their parameters' β-values. Both parameters also suggest elastic relationships. Apparently, US investors favour the foreign direct investment mode of internationalisation in view of large geographical distances and existing trade barriers. However, the transport cost and trade intensity variables are rather strongly correlated, which may have distorted the estimation.

Table 5.5   US investments to South and Southeast Asia

Information: Periods: 7 (1982–86 to 1988–92) No. of cases: 61 of 70 (87.1%) R^2: 0.674 F: 6.788 R^2 (adjusted): 0.575 DW: 1.728		Countries: 10 China, Hong Kong, India, Indonesia, Japan, Korea, Malaysia, Philippines, Singapore, Thailand		
Determinant	Definition[a]	Parameter	*T*-value	β-value
Market size	1	–0.355	–4.736	–0.653
Per capita income	2b	0.994	1.412	0.155
Labour costs	2c	–0.443	–0.746	–0.075
Transport costs	1	–9.479	–5.888	–1.008
Cultural differences	3	–1.039	–2.555	–0.403
Trade intensity	2a	–1.892	–4.151	–0.716
Exchange rate direction	1	–0.564	–1.353	–0.222
Exchange rate volatility	3	–0.125	–2.345	–0.276
Dummy 1983–87		–0.374	–1.024	–0.121
Dummy 1984–88		–0.502	–1.298	–0.162
Dummy 1985–89		–0.822	–2.063	–0.266
Dummy 1986–90		–0.816	–2.162	–0.289
Dummy 1987–91		–0.525	–1.361	–0.186
Dummy 1988–92		–0.406	–1.076	–0.138
Intercept		23.939	4.903	—

Note
a. For variable definitions, see Appendix IV.

Other hypotheses are not accepted. Market size obtains a significant, but theoretically incorrect parameter. Possibly the large size of the domestic US market makes the size of foreign markets less attractive and could even become a barrier to investments abroad. Per capita income has a parameter which reveals a weak significance. Apparently, American investors consider purchasing power in Asian markets of minor importance or not sufficiently developed, possibly again in view of their strong home market. This could coincide with the relatively low growth of US investments to this region. Labour costs do not seem to be a consideration, either. Although its parameter is theoretically correct, its significance is low and its β-value reveals minor influence. These results imply investments to be neither strongly market orientated nor considerably input orientated.

Regarding the exchange rate hypotheses, the results are to some extent surprising. The direction hypothesis is accepted, but the parameter's significance is weak. The volatility hypothesis is accepted for a volatility variable of the conditional type. The above implies that American investors may try to benefit from depreciating host currencies by using some kind of hedging facility. Remaining exchange rate volatility continues to be a barrier. Possibly, this indicates that US investors favour countries where currencies are pegged to the US dollar, such as Singapore and Thailand. The strength of the Japanese yen *vis-à-vis* the US dollar may be a barrier for US investments in Japan and may explain the continuous decline in the share of US investments in this country.

As for US investments to Western Europe, the period dummies of US investments in Asia may indicate the trend of their shares in total US investments abroad.[6] At the beginning of the 1980s the trend is downward, which may be reflected in the decreasing parameter values. After the 1985–89 period shares recover, which may explain the positive turn in the (still negative) parameter values for subsequent periods. β-values indicate these influences to be of limited importance.

Because of the significant influence from the period dummies, the explanatory variables are not able to cover all variance in US investments into South and Southeast Asia. The Durbin–Watson statistic may indicate limited positive autocorrelation in the residuals of the regression, but the residuals do not have alarming values. Concern arises from the high value of the intercept, which may be related to the high parameter of transport costs. Other model specifications with different definitions for the explanatory variables do not improve the results presented here.

The results for investments in Asia differ considerably from those for world investments. Market orientation is of less importance here, whereas a sizeable number of barriers seem more relevant. In particular, the transport cost barrier reveals a stronger influence than in the model for world investments, but this may be due to intercorrelation problems. Another major difference is the substitutory relation with trade. In the world model a complementary relation was identified. Further, the exchange rate hypotheses are relevant for investments in Asia, whereas in the results from using MOSAIC for world investments they were not.

The corporate strategy which emanates from these results can, against expectations, best be qualified as a stand-alone strategy. The high relevance of the substitutory trade relation points towards this strategy's profile. Also, the importance of barriers from transport costs, cultural differences and exchange rate volatility support this. On the other hand, the limited relevance of market orientation is a counter indication. The state of development of host countries in Asia in combination with high transport costs and trade barriers may force US investors to engage in such strategies.

5.3.4   Investments to North and South America

North and South America is the second largest destination region for US investments abroad. After heavy disinvestments at the beginning of the 1980s, this region's share in the total rapidly recovers to a substantial 40 per cent of the total. In particular, foreign direct investments in South America are important. Investments in Mexico seem to increase in the latter half of the 1980s. For Canada's share in the total, a downward trend is observed.

Since the United States themselves belong to the North and South American region, one may expect determinants which could point towards complex international production strategies. Market potentials, especially in North America, are strong. Input (upstream) orientation could be relevant for South American countries, since labour costs in these countries are substantially lower than in the United States. Cultural differences may be large, because cultural traditions in Latin American countries are notably different from those in North America. Because of NAFTA a complementary trade relation is likely for Canadian and Mexican investments. The same could be true for non-NAFTA countries in the region if input orientation is relevant. Finally, exchange rate volatility may not be a barrier for North America, but for South America, where currencies have been rather unstable throughout the 1980s, this is less obvious.

The regression results from MOSAIC estimations (Table 5.6) identify market size, cultural differences and exchange rate volatility as major determinants in view of their β-values. Per capita income is also important since its parameter is significant. The parameters of both market potential hypotheses suggest an elastic relationship. This may show that all markets are attractive to US investors: the Canadian and Mexican markets because of NAFTA; the other Latin American markets as newly industrialising countries.[7] Cultural differences appear as a major barrier. Exchange rate volatility is also a serious barrier. This variable is of the conditional type, implying that hedging facilities can be used. It may be the case that US investors favour countries with currencies pegged to the US dollar.

Other parameters' β-values show less important determinants. The parameter of the labour cost hypothesis is not acceptable. Apparently, the cheap labour motive is not important to US investors. For Mexico, this is surprising in view of the location of assembly plants in this country by US companies incurred by the creation of NAFTA. Perhaps the emphasis on finance, insurance and business service investments, for which cheap labour could be less important than for manufacturing, could be an explanation for this.[8] The transport cost hypothesis is rejected, which implies that transport costs are not a serious barrier. The trade relation appears to be complementary. However, its parameter is not significant and its β-value suggests a marginal importance. For the direction of exchange rate movements a significant inelastic parameter is found, which suggests that American investors want to benefit cautiously from depreciating host-country currencies.

Table 5.6   US investments to North and South America

Information: Periods: 7 (1982–86 to 1988–92) No. of cases: 30 of 35 (85.7%) R^2: 0.966 F: 30.396 R^2 (adjusted): 0.934 DW: 2.226	Countries: 5 Argentina, Brazil, Canada, Chile, Mexico		
Determinant	Definition[a]	Parameter T-value β-value	
Market size	1	1.895 3.280 1.318	
Per capita income	2b	1.022 1.731 0.173	
Labour costs	2b	0.523 0.416 0.036	
Transport costs	1	0.514 0.700 0.331	
Cultural differences	1	−4.946 −3.147 −0.997	
Trade intensity	2c	0.205 0.735 0.076	
Exchange rate direction	2	−0.591 −1.963 −0.233	
Exchange rate volatility	4	−0.861 −2.126 −1.107	
Dummy 1983–87		−0.238 −0.756 −0.058	
Dummy 1984–88		−0.046 −0.143 −0.014	
Dummy 1985–89		0.096 0.268 0.029	
Dummy 1986–90		0.257 0.711 0.079	
Dummy 1987–91		0.196 0.510 0.060	
Dummy 1988–92		0.162 0.402 0.049	
Intercept		−7.999 −3.760 —	

Note
a. For variable definitions, see Appendix IV.

The parameters of the period dummies may capture the trend in the share of foreign direct investments to North and South America in total US investments abroad. The negative, but insignificant, parameters for the

1983–87 and 1984–88 period dummies may still reflect the disinvestments in Latin America at the beginning of the 1980s. In later periods, the positive parameters are consistent with the observed recovery of this region's share.

Although the model is fairly well able to explain the variation in US investments, some doubts exist on its sustainability. The high correlation coefficient should be put in the perspective of the small data set, which contains only data for Canada and four Latin American countries. The small data set causes high intercorrelations among some variables, particularly between market size and exchange rate direction and between transport costs and exchange rate volatility. Using alternative definitions does not solve these problems. Further, the Durbin–Watson statistic could indicate that some negative autocorrelation exists. However, residuals for all investment relations are low and do not cause covariances. Further, all period dummies have insignificant parameters, which implies that the explanatory variables are mostly responsible for explaining the variance in the dependent variable.

More clarification could be obtained if a distinction were possible between data for NAFTA countries and non-NAFTA countries. However, a data set for NAFTA would contain data only for Canada and Mexico, whereas the one for non-NAFTA countries would be limited to Argentina, Brazil and Chile. These data sets are too small for a proper testing of MOSAIC.

In comparison to the world model, the strong emphasis on market size, cultural barriers and exchange rate volatility is striking. Market size was not relevant in the world model. Instead, per capita income was more important there. Cultural differences were identified as a barrier to world investments, but not as strongly as for investments in the Americas. The world model did not identify exchange rate volatility as a barrier. Further, the absence of transport costs and trade intensity as relevant investment determinants in America is a remarkable difference.

In view of the doubts on the model results, conclusions on the overall corporate strategy need to be drawn carefully. The model results seem to fit best with the profile for stand-alone strategies. In particular, the strong emphasis of market size, cultural differences and exchange rate volatility is an indication for this. The relevant parameters for per capita income and exchange rate direction give additional support. Possibly, this strategy prevails for South American countries, because the barriers from cultural differences and exchange rate volatility seem particularly valid for these countries. The state of development of these countries would justify such a strategy. For Canada and Mexico – countries signatory to the NAFTA agreement – regional core networking strategies would comply more with expectations.[9] However, in view of the model's results, any conclusions on this are speculative.

5.4 CONCLUSION

Foreign direct investment from the United States has known a strong upward trend throughout the 1982–92 period. Although in 1988 and 1990 temporary troughs can be noted, the upward trend seems to continue into the 1990s.

US investments tend to cluster particularly in Western Europe and North and South America. The share of Western Europe in total foreign direct investments declines, whereas Latin America's share increases. The diminishing European share can be attributed to a strong decrease in the share of the United Kingdom. Growth of the share for Latin America comes from large investments in Brazil and Mexico.

The importance of South and Southeast Asia is limited. At first, there is a declining share for this region, but by the end of the 1980s and at the beginning of the 1990s its popularity is growing. Also, Australia and New Zealand are important. Their share is modest, but increasing. Apparently, American investors are discovering the growth potentials of the whole of the Pacific region encompassing both South and Southeast Asia and host countries on the southern hemisphere across the Pacific.

The bulk of US investments abroad is made by the group of finance, insurance and business service industries. Other important industries are wholesale and retail sales and chemical products. Industries with an increasing involvement abroad are communication, food and beverages and paper, printing and publishing, whereas mechanical equipment is losing its share in the total.

MOSAIC results are summarised in Table 5.7. They give differing views on the determinants of American foreign direct investments. Given the large share of European investments in the total, determinants of world investments are dominated by those for Europe. Some interesting differences emerge for investments in Asia and America.

American investors apparently consider market potential highly important for investing abroad. It is identified as a major determinant for investments in Europe and America, particularly in terms of market size. For Europe an inelastic relation is found, whereas for America the parameter is elastic. Per capita income appears to play a role in all regions, but its influence is strongest only in Europe. In this region, per capita income obtains an elastic parameter, whereas for Asia and America inelastic parameters are found. However, for Europe another variable specification is used.

The cheap labour cost hypothesis, or more broadly the input orientation hypothesis, is not supported, either for world investment flows, or for flows to the individual regions. Only for Asia is the labour cost parameter theoretically correct, but it is insignificant. For Europe, a significantly positive parameter is found. There is an inclination to consider this as an indication for a need for more expensive high-quality labour in foreign direct investments by (human) capital-intensive industries, particularly in services.

Table 5.7 Summary of determinants for foreign direct investments from the USA

Determinant	World		Europe		Asia		America	
Market size	✗	–	✓	+	✗	++	✓	++
Per capita income	✓	+	✓	++	○	–	○	+
Labour costs	✗	–	✗	–	✗	–	✗	–
ROI differences	n.a.	n.a.	✗	–	n.a.	n.a.	n.a.	n.a.
Transport costs	✓	+	✓	+	✓	++	✗	+
Cultural differences	✓	++	✗	–	✓	+	✓	++
Trade intensity	✓	++	✓	++	✗	++	✗	–
Exchange rate direction	✗	–	✗	–	○	+	✓	+
Exchange rate volatility	✗	–	✗	–	✓	+	✓	++

Legend
✓ significant   ++ strong influence
○ weakly significant   + intermediate influence
✗ not significant or theoretically incorrect parameter   – weak influence

Two barriers are important for US investments abroad. Transport costs are a significant barrier for American investments in Europe and Asia. For both regions, a very high elasticity is found for this determinant. For America, transport costs seem less relevant. The second barrier relates to cultural differences. They create barriers for US investments in Europe, Asia and America. In Europe, this barrier is insignificant and of minor importance. The inelastic parameter value suggests a low sensitivity. For Asia, the relevance is higher and the parameter is just above unity, implying a higher sensitivity. Cultural differences show up as a major barrier for investments in America. In addition, the elastic parameter reveals a high sensitivity.

For trade relations a mixed picture emerges. Foreign direct investments in Europe tend to complement trade flows, as the trade parameter for this region is significantly positive. Trade relations also appear to have a strong influence on investments in Europe. This renders obsolete a fear of a

Fortress Europe. A substitutory trade relation is found for investments in Asia. Again, the trade variable is rather important, but may reveal this time the existence of substantial trade barriers. For both regions, the relation is elastic, implying a relatively high sensitivity. In the model estimations for North and South America, trade intensity is not identified as a significant determinant.

The results reveal varying influences for the exchange rate hypotheses. They are irrelevant for investments in Europe, but the positive parameter for exchange rate volatility may reflect a stimulus from considerable fluctuations in the US dollar exchange rate *vis-à-vis* European currencies. For foreign direct investments in Asia and America, the volatility hypothesis is accepted. However, the variable used in the regressions suggests that only unexpected movements are relevant. This could relate to the pegging of some host-country currencies to the US dollar.

Table 5.8   Summary of overall strategies of corporate structures from the USA

Region	Corporate strategy
Western Europe	Regional core networking
South and Southeast Asia	Stand alone
North and South America	Stand alone (regional core networking for NAFTA countries?)

To some extent and with sufficient caution for their interpretation, the results could indicate that US corporate structures pursue in general a regional core networking strategy encompassing the United States and Western Europe (see Table 5.8). Indications for this could be the market orientation and the irrelevance of exchange rate volatility in Europe. Other indications are that trade relations with Europe are complementary and rather important. Further support is given by the significant positive parameter for labour costs, indicating a search for high-quality employment and the low relevance of cultural differences in the European model.

For South and Southeast Asia and North and South America, an overall stand-alone strategy seems to emanate from the results. The substitutory trade relation for Asia, the strong market orientation for America and barriers from cultural differences and conditional exchange rate volatility are indications of this strategy type. However, it could be the case that for Canada and Mexico, strategies are aimed at linking activities to US–European regional core networks as a result of integration processes incurred by NAFTA.

The results on American foreign direct investments give support to accepting the general hypothesis formulated at the end of Chapter 2. Spatial differences create different locational advantages in different host countries. US investors want to combine their ownership advantages with these locational advantages. It is also clear that differences exist in the opportunities offered by various world regions.

NOTES

1. In terms of foreign direct investment stock in European countries, the picture is different. According to the OECD (1995f, p. 27), Europe's share in this stock increases from 35 per cent in 1983 to 41 per cent in 1992. The OECD attributes this trend to the liberalisation processes in Europe.
2. This seems to be consistent with results found by Lipsey (1994, p. 23) by assessing various empirical studies. He concludes that production outside the United States has little effect on exports, which is more likely to be positive than negative.
3. According to Dunning and Cantwell (1991, p. 168), US firms have been producing in EU markets for more than half a century.
4. This barrier may have disappeared, since Culem (1988, p. 887) found a significant 'cultural proximity dummy' for US investments in the United Kingdom during 1969–82.
5. This institute has investigated the growth in employment and the type of activities of foreign subsidiaries of American corporate structures established in Denmark, Netherlands, Sweden and Switzerland (EIM 1993). For Germany, the Bundesland Nordrhein-Westfalia has been included in the analysis.
6. The trend coincides with the trend in some manufacturing industries, namely mining and quarrying, food and beverages, and other manufacturing. Possibly, if these industries dominate in US investments in Asia, the dummies capture specific sectoral characteristics.
7. Calderón, Mortimore and Peres (1996, p. 253) suggest that the size of the domestic market is an important determinant for investments into Mexico.
8. Debt–equity swaps for foreign investors may be particularly interesting for these service industries.
9. According to Calderón, Mortimore and Peres (1996, p. 273), the integration of Mexico into the North American cluster has intensified sharply in the last decade.

6. Investments from Japan

6.1 INTRODUCTION

This chapter deals with the identification of determinants for geographical patterns in foreign direct investment flows originating from Japan. First, a description is made of trends in Japanese foreign direct investments throughout the world and those to some major clusters of countries. Then, the estimates from model regressions are discussed. Regressions are made on all outgoing foreign direct investment flows and on subsets of data for three geographical clusters.

As in the case of US investments, for Japanese foreign direct investments it is not possible to include all hypotheses in MOSAIC. The knowledge hypothesis has to be excluded.[1] Similarly, the taxation difference hypothesis has to be skipped and the return on investment differences hypothesis can be included only for West European countries.

6.2 INVESTMENT PATTERNS

Japanese outward foreign direct investments show a strongly increasing trend. From 1982 to 1989 outward investments grew from US$7.7 billion to US$67.5 billion (see also Figure 6.1). This implies an annual average growth rate of over 36 per cent.

The rapid increase in outward foreign direct investments starts in 1985. According to Kume (1993), this coincides with sharp appreciations of the Japanese yen in 1985 and 1986.

After 1989, foreign direct investments abroad decrease considerably, to US$34.1 billion in 1992. This rupture in the trend is caused not only by recessionary tendencies in those years, but also, according to the United Nations (1994, pp. 41–2), by some particular forces. One explanation is that large losses sustained by Japanese multinational companies made them reconsider or postpone foreign direct investments. Another factor is the restrictive lending policies of Japanese banks, which had encountered some bad loan problems. Other forces come from dropping asset prices and some poorly performing investments in the United States and Europe. Further, investments decline because of the completion of production facilities in the United States and in Europe.

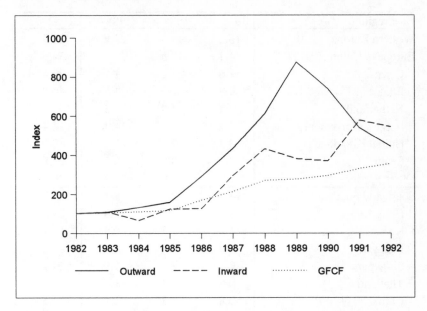

Figure 6.1   Development of foreign direct investment from Japan and gross fixed capital formation (1982 = 100; nominal)

The development of inward foreign direct investments shows a pattern which is different from the outward investment trend. Before 1988, the pattern is strongly upward, just as for outward investments. In 1989 and 1990, the level of foreign direct investments in Japan goes down slightly. The following year reveals a strong recovery, whereas Japanese investments abroad decline. In 1992, however, inward investments again show a moderate decrease.

Four major investment clusters can be identified from the geographical distribution of Japanese investments abroad (see Table 6.1). The largest cluster concerns the investments in North America. The share of this cluster rises from more than 40 per cent at the beginning of the 1980s to nearly half of the total by the end of the 1980s and the beginning of the 1990s. The investments are nearly all destined for the United States. Another important cluster is found for Western Europe, particularly the European Union: the investment share for this cluster shows a steady growth over the years. The third largest host region is the one closest to Japan: the countries in South and Southeast Asia.[2] This region's share in the total is more or less stable.

*Table 6.1   Geographical distribution and growth of total outward foreign
direct investments from Japan (1982–92; %)*

Host region	1982–86	1985–89	1988–92	1982–92[a]
Western Europe	15.1	19.5	21.8	34.4
European Union (EU12)	14.1	18.5	20.7	34.7
Germany	1.6	1.2	1.9	30.4
France	0.9	1.2	1.7	40.8
Netherlands	3.1	4.9	5.3	37.9
Belgium/Luxemburg	4.1	2.8	1.3	4.4
United Kingdom	3.3	7.1	9.1	49.7
Spain	0.6	0.6	0.7	27.8
Other Western Europe	1.0	1.0	1.2	28.8
South and Southeast Asia	14.2	12.3	13.4	25.2
Hong Kong	3.3	2.9	2.8	23.2
Korea	1.5	1.3	0.8	12.7
Malaysia	1.0	0.8	1.4	33.2
Singapore	2.3	2.1	1.9	23.2
Thailand	0.8	1.4	1.9	47.7
China	0.8	1.3	1.1	34.5
Indonesia	3.0	1.3	2.1	19.1
Philippines	0.4	0.3	0.4	27.1
North and South America	63.0	61.1	55.9	23.9
North America	41.5	48.0	47.3	29.2
United States of America	40.0	46.3	45.4	29.1
Latin America	21.5	13.1	8.6	8.6
Brazil	2.7	0.9	0.9	4.3
Mexico	1.1	0.3	0.2	–2.8
Other regions	7.6	7.1	8.8	29.6
Central and Eastern Europe	0.0	0.0	0.2	—
Australia and New Zealand	3.6	5.3	6.4	39.3
Middle East	1.1	0.3	0.5	9.7
Africa	2.7	1.1	1.2	9.5
Other	0.2	0.4	0.7	53.4
Total	100.0	100.0	100.0	26.4

Note
a.   Average nominal growth rate between first and last periods.

Source
OECD.

By the end of the 1980s and the beginning of the 1990s, there seems to be a slight upward trend. Concerning the fourth cluster, Latin America, a strong downward trend is shown with relatively low growth rates. In our analysis this cluster has to be combined with the North American region.

Trends in Japanese foreign direct investments to the European Union vary from one country to another. Most investments are destined for the United Kingdom and the Netherlands.[3] For the United Kingdom, investments develop very fast until 1988–92; for the Netherlands, the development is less strong.[4] Other countries in the Union do not show major shares. Germany's share first decreases slightly, but then recovers. For France a continuous, but slow upward trend is shown. Belgium/Luxemburg reveals a relatively strong downward trend.

According to the United Nations (1994, p. 71), Japan is the principal source country for foreign direct investments in South and Southeast Asia. However, the shares in the total reveal a rather scattered picture. Shares of individual countries do not go beyond 3.5 per cent. The most important host countries in this region, with shares ranging from 2 to 3 per cent, are Hong Kong and Singapore. In these countries, investments relate particularly to service industries (Kume 1993, p. 56). Indonesia and Thailand are also major hosts, where investments tend to concentrate in manufacturing.[5]

A distinction can be made between 'traditional' and 'second-tier' newly industrialising countries. Hong Kong, Singapore and Korea belong to the group of traditional countries in which Japanese foreign direct investments seem to have reached a state of maturity. Although growth rates are still substantial, investment shares of these countries tend to stabilise or decline. For the second-tier group of countries, Indonesia, Malaysia, Thailand and China, Japanese investments seem to start gaining momentum. Indonesia's share reveals a slight downward trend at first, but in later periods it rises again. The share for Thailand shows an increasing trend. Malaysia tends to follow Indonesia's trend. China shows a strong increase at first, but later the share decreases. The Philippines and Taiwan (not included in Table 6.1) do not seem to have a major share of Japanese investments.

For Japanese foreign direct investments in Latin America, only limited information exists. Investments in Brazil have a downward tendency. A similar trend exists for Mexico. The shares of Argentina and Chile (not included in Table 6.1) are marginal and do not show major changes. The trends for the countries mentioned here cannot explain fully the substantial decrease in this region's share in Japanese investments. In relative terms, it seems that the Japanese invested heavily in other countries in Latin America in the early 1980s, but became cautious about further extensions of their involvement in later years.

Table 6.2 Sectoral distribution and growth of total outward foreign direct investments from Japan (1982–92; %)

Investing industry	1982–86	1985–89	1988–92	1982–92[a]
Agriculture	0.4	0.4	0.4	26.4
Total manufacturing	26.7	26.4	29.9	28.8
Mining and quarrying	4.7	2.2	2.4	13.0
Food, beverages and tobacco	0.8	1.2	1.5	40.0
Textiles, leather and clothing	0.7	0.6	1.1	36.4
Paper, printing and publishing	0.4	0.5	0.7	35.3
Chemical products	2.4	2.6	3.8	35.8
Metal products	3.9	2.4	2.3	15.8
Mechanical equipment	2.5	2.7	2.8	29.4
Electric and electronic equipment	4.4	6.3	7.0	36.5
Motor vehicles and other transport equipment	4.7	3.4	3.4	19.9
Other manufacturing	2.2	4.3	4.9	45.1
Construction	0.9	0.8	0.9	26.0
Total commercial services	69.6	71.0	67.6	25.8
Wholesale and retail trade	13.1	7.7	9.5	19.8
Transport and storage	11.7	5.8	4.7	8.6
Finance, insurance and business services	24.5	27.5	18.6	20.8
Other commercial services	20.2	30.0	34.7	38.4
Unallocated	2.4	1.5	1.2	12.4
Total	100.0	100.0	100.0	26.4

Note
a. Average nominal growth rate between first and last periods.

Source
OECD.

For the remaining host regions some changes occur. For Australia and New Zealand the share nearly doubles. Apparently, these countries have increasingly become part of the South and Southeast Asian region: the Pacific Rim. Central and Eastern Europe do not seem to be important yet, although some investments were made after the opening up of countries in this region in 1989. The importance of the Middle East and Africa remains at a marginal level.

Table 6.2 shows that more than two-thirds of Japanese foreign direct investments abroad relate to investments made by service industries.[6] Within services, the group of finance, insurance and business services and the group of other commercial services are responsible for the bulk of these investments. Wholesale and retail trade and transport and storage have a relatively low share. The complement of the large services share in the total lies with manufacturing industries, which are less active in investing abroad than service industries. The largest share in manufacturing is with electric and electronic equipment. Other manufacturing industries of some interest are chemical products, metal products, mechanical equipment and motor vehicles.[7]

The trends in the industry shares reveal that the service industry is losing and manufacturing is gaining importance. In services, the loss concentrates in the group of finance, insurance and business service industries and transport and storage. This loss is partly compensated by increasing shares of wholesale and retail sales and of other commercial services. The gain in manufacturing comes not only from electric and electronic equipment, but also from chemical products. These trends suggest a concentration of the observed decline in total outward foreign direct investments in some service industries.

6.3 DETERMINANTS

6.3.1 Investments to the World

For Japanese foreign direct investments throughout the world, complex international production strategies may be relevant. Like American multinationals, Japanese corporate structures have a commonly known internationalisation perspective. The profile of complex international production strategies suggests that Japanese investors are likely to be interested in strong market potentials and cheap inputs. Support for these hypotheses is therefore expected. In principle, a complementary trade relation should appear. However, Japanese exports seem to coincide with considerable discussions on trade barriers. This may have moved them to engage in tariff jumping, or as Bhagwati has called them, *quid pro quo* investments.[8] Further, although less obvious in this strategy's profile, Japanese investors probably encounter considerable barriers from cultural differences, as language, business practices and management styles differ substantially from those elsewhere. Concerning exchange rates, Japanese investors may be influenced by the strength of the Japanese yen. This may give them opportunities to purchase foreign assets cheaply. Volatility of host currencies could be a valid, but less important, barrier in this strategy type.

Table 6.3   Japanese investments throughout the world

Information: Periods: 7 (1982–86 to 1988–92) No. of cases: 227 of 231 (98.3%) R^2: 0.514 F: 16.036 R^2 (adjusted): 0.482 DW: 2.075		Countries: 33 Western Europe, South and Southeast Asia, North and South America plus Australia, Finland, New Zealand and Turkey		
Determinant	Definition[a]	Parameter	*T*-value	β-value
Market size	1	0.506	4.853	0.328
Per capita income	2a	0.939	6.755	0.507
Labour costs	2b	−1.682	−1.456	−0.074
Transport costs	1	0.400	1.509	0.106
Cultural differences	1	−1.367	−3.565	−0.190
Trade intensity	2a	1.644	8.521	0.613
Exchange rate direction	1	−0.196	−0.622	−0.044
Exchange rate volatility	1	−0.004	−0.013	−0.000
Dummy 1983–87		−0.179	−0.427	−0.027
Dummy 1984–88		−0.332	−0.789	−0.051
Dummy 1985–89		−0.248	−0.580	−0.038
Dummy 1986–90		−0.163	−0.372	−0.025
Dummy 1987–91		−0.150	−0.329	−0.023
Dummy 1988–92		−0.034	−0.075	−0.005
Intercept		3.187	2.199	—

Note
a. For variable definitions, see Appendix IV.

MOSAIC estimations for Japanese world investments show diverging results *vis-à-vis* the expectations (see Table 6.3). Market size and per capita income show up as relevant and substantially important determinants. The latter seems more important than the former in view of their β-values. The parameter for labour costs has a weak significance and contributes little to the regression. This may coincide with the large emphasis of investments abroad by service industries, for which labour costs may be less important than for manufacturing. For transport costs, a weakly significant positive parameter is found. This is inconsistent with our hypothesis, but this may be an indication that physical distance prohibits the trade alternative for internationalisation. Cultural differences are identified as a friction factor with an elastic relation with the dependent variable, but its relevance appears to be of limited importance. Regarding the trade hypothesis, an elastic complementary relation is found, which does not support tariff jumping. Its β-value makes this variable the most dominant one in explaining world investments. Exchange rate direction and volatility are not major concerns for Japanese investors in view of their insignificant parameters.

The negative period-dummy parameters may capture the existence of political investment barriers, as in the model for US investments to the world. The influence of these barriers appears to be minor in view of the insignificant inelastic parameter values and their low β-values. The parameters may reveal a declining trend in the already low importance of such barriers.

· The model is able to explain about half of the variation in the data set. The explanatory variables take care of most of the variance, as the period dummies obtain insignificant parameters. The Durbin–Watson statistic shows that no autocorrelation in the residuals exists. Further analysis shows that for most investment relations the residuals do not cause concern. Only for Japanese foreign direct investments in Norway and Turkey is the model less able to fit actual data. However, no large covariances for the residuals on these relations with those of others can be observed. Other specifications of MOSAIC using different definitions of the explanatory variables do not cause major changes in the results. In particular, a specification is tested without the transport cost variable, as it appears to have some intercorrelation with the trade intensity variable. Estimating this specification of MOSAIC leads to accepting the same hypotheses.

The model results give some support for the expected complex international production strategies. This can be derived from accepting the hypotheses regarding market size and per capita income and trade intensity. In particular, the rather strong and positive influence of trade intensity supports this. Also, the rejection of the exchange rate volatility hypothesis complies with this strategy type. Another indication is that labour costs are relevant with a less strong influence. The only counter indication is the validity of the cultural differences hypothesis, but its importance seems limited.

6.3.2 Investments to Western Europe

Western Europe was identified as the second largest geographical cluster in Japanese foreign direct investments abroad. These investments are particularly destined to some specific countries in the European Union: the United Kingdom and the Netherlands. Investments within this cluster to non-EU countries are of marginal size.

For foreign direct investments to Western Europe, the complex international production strategy type is likely to prevail. Japanese investors must consider Europe to be an important market area for their products. Also, the labour cost hypothesis can be relevant, as the labour costs in Japan are considerably high. The trade relation must be complementary. However, the creation of the Internal Market may coincide with a fear of a Fortress Europe. Therefore, tariff-jumping motives can prevail, which would imply substitution between trade and foreign direct investment. For differences in return on investment a positive relation is likely to be valid. Further, although the strategy's profile suggests otherwise, the Japanese may have to cope with large differences between Japanese and European cultures. Regarding exchange rates, it can be expected in this strategy type that the direction hypothesis is accepted, whereas for exchange rate volatility this is less likely.

MOSAIC estimations for Japanese investments to West European countries (Table 6.4) suggest a strong influence from the per capita income hypothesis. Its β-value is among the highest and its elasticity suggests a high sensitivity. However, this variable suffers from some intercorrelation with return on investment differences and transport costs. Market size is rejected because of a theoretically incorrect parameter. Perhaps, Japanese investors are guided by the size of the European market as a whole instead of differences in national market sizes. As most Japanese investments to Western Europe relate to EU countries, this may be true for the EU market. This could explain the relatively large share of the Netherlands, a country with a small national market, but a large hinterland.

Support is also found for the hypothesis on cultural differences, which seems to be of major importance. This supports the idea that Japanese investors want to benefit from strong market potentials in Europe, but encounter some problems with cultural differences. Possibly, this could explain the emphasis of the United Kingdom and the Netherlands in the distribution of Japanese foreign direct investments in Western Europe. These countries may be more open to Japanese culture than other European countries.

For labour costs, the hypothesis on cheap labour is not rejected, but the parameter is insignificant. Its β-value reveals a low influence. In this respect, it is interesting to note that Balasubramanyam and Greenaway (1994, p. 106) mention the relatively low labour costs in the United Kingdom as an important determinant for Japanese investments in this country. On the whole, however, since most Japanese investments concentrate in Europe's core region, cheap labour does not appear to be a relevant determinant. This seems logical in view of the large share of investments in some service industries, which may favour good-quality labour. Ozawa indicates that this is also the case for manufacturing.[9]

Return on investment does not seem to be a relevant determinant either, but this could be due to the observed intercorrelation problem with per capita income.

Table 6.4 Japanese investments to Western Europe

Information:		Countries: 14		
Periods: 7 (1982–86 to 1988–92)		Austria, Belgium/Luxemburg,		
No. of cases: 96 of 98 (98.0%)		Denmark, France, Germany,		
R^2: 0.839	F: 27.780	Greece, Ireland, Italy, Netherlands,		
R^2 (adjusted): 0.801	DW: 1.747	Norway, Portugal, Spain, Sweden,		
		United Kingdom		
Determinant	Definition[a]	Parameter	T-value	β-value
Market size	1	–0.854	–3.430	–0.373
Per capita income	2a	5.972	10.073	1.205
Labour costs	2c	–1.625	–1.097	–0.080
ROI differences	1	0.198	0.497	0.041
Transport costs	1	21.780	11.136	1.202
Cultural differences	1	–3.044	–7.141	–0.530
Trade intensity	1	2.085	5.826	0.369
Exchange rate direction	1	4.147	1.733	0.252
Exchange rate volatility	4	0.743	0.384	0.034
Dummy 1983–87		0.231	0.522	0.033
Dummy 1984–88		–0.140	–0.303	–0.021
Dummy 1985–89		–0.736	–1.118	–0.109
Dummy 1986–90		–1.418	–1.564	–0.209
Dummy 1987–91		–1.606	–1.901	–0.237
Dummy 1988–92		–1.788	–2.111	–0.264
Intercept		–44.548	–9.629	—

Note
a. For variable definitions, see Appendix IV.

The trade intensity parameter shows that investments have a complementary orientation with trade, which may indicate that a number of Japanese investments relate to assembly plants manufacturing products for the European markets using Japanese components. This may relate to electric and electronic equipment, and motor vehicles.

Concerning exchange rate movements, no acceptance is obtained for either hypothesis. The positive parameter for exchange rate direction is theoretically unacceptable, but its significance is not strong. The parameter for exchange rate volatility is insignificant. It seems that Japanese investors do not use the strength of the yen for purchasing assets cheaply and do not really consider movements of European currencies towards the yen to be a threat to their investments. Probably, differences in exchange rate movements and volatility have become small enough to be of importance to Japanese investors. As most Japanese investments concentrate in Europe's core region, this may be due to effective exchange rate stabilisation policies, such as the EMS, among core countries.

For the transport cost barrier, a strange result is obtained. Its proxy, the distance variable, gets a significantly positive parameter of a very high level. This suggests that the estimation of this variable's parameter is distorted in some way. The parameter seems to be compensated by the regression's intercept, which is also significant and extremely high. Possibly, this is due to intercorrelations with the per capita income variable. On the other hand, the result may indicate that physical distance prohibits the use of the trade mode and stimulates the choice of the foreign direct investment mode.

The importance of various determinants for Japanese foreign direct investments is supported by EIM research on foreign subsidiaries in Europe (EIM 1993). The most common economic activity of Japanese subsidiaries appears to be sales activities, sometimes combined with (customer) services. This seems consistent with accepting the per capita income hypothesis in MOSAIC.

Regarding trade, the observation meets with conclusions drawn by Belderbos (1994, pp. 236–7) on foreign direct investment in Europe in the electronics industry. Belderbos indicates that investments in distribution subsidiaries in the European Union coincide with higher exports than for other investment types. In addition, subcontractor firms in a vertical *keiretsu*, or network in this study's terminology, continue to export to Europe. Belderbos claims that a substitutory relation also exists in the electronics industry.[10] For some final products the relation between trade and foreign direct investment is indeed substitutory when investments relate to assembly in Europe. However, this phenomenon is compensated by intensified trade in components and more trade in other final products to European distribution activities in the networks. Investment causes a change in the composition of trade, rather than a reduction.

To some extent the results qualify the fear of a Fortress Europe.[11] Japanese investors may indeed have feared this and thus may have engaged in establishing affiliates in Europe. Possibly, the positive parameter for transport costs is an indication. However, this fear seems less obvious when trade and investments have a complementary relationship, as is supported by the significantly positive trade parameter. In view of this, Japanese investments in Europe may be of Bhagwati's *quid pro quo* type, as this type of foreign investment complements trade (Balasubramanyam and Greenaway 1994, pp. 118–19). Maybe, as Ozawa (1991, p. 145) suggests, the term Fortress Europe applies to some manufacturing industries, which have a relatively low share in total investments.

Recent research by Aristotelous and Fountas (1996, p. 579) may give support to our results. Market orientation in terms of total GDP is identified in their model as a relevant determinant. They also find a market integration dummy, which would support our explanation of rejecting the market size hypothesis in MOSAIC. Further, their weak significance for trade tariffs seems to be consistent with our observation on the existence of complementary trade relations. However, they consider their results to be not very strong.

The period dummies show mostly negative parameters, which reveal growing elasticities and growing β-values. An explanation could be that they capture an increasing Fortress Europe effect. However, this was already considered less obvious. It seems more likely that the dummy parameters are related to the declining growth rate in the increasing share of investments in Europe and the strong decline in total outward investments since 1989.

Although doubts exist about the level of the estimated parameters, the model may give a reasonable explanation of Japanese foreign direct investments in Europe. The correlation coefficient is well above 80 per cent and most period dummies have a minor influence. Some concern exists regarding the Durbin–Watson statistic, as it suggests positive autocorrelation in the residuals. This may be related to the peculiar parameters for the transport cost hypothesis and the intercept. Model estimations without the transport cost hypothesis give no other results, but do show an improvement in the Durbin–Watson statistic. Another explanation may be the rather bad fit of MOSAIC for investments in Norway, which causes some covariance problems with residuals of other investment relations. This was also the case in the world model.

In comparison with the MOSAIC specification for world investments, the model for European investments is influenced by more or less the same determinants: per capita income, cultural differences and complementary trade relations. As in the world model, per capita income has a rather strong influence. Cultural barriers seem more important for investments in Europe than for world investments. For trade intensity it is the other way around. In the European model the labour cost hypothesis obtains less support and market size is rejected. Exchange rate direction and exchange rate volatility are not accepted in any of the two models.

The results give some support for complex international production strategies. Indications for this are that the Japanese invest in Europe for market potential reasons. Although the market size of individual countries is rejected, the size of the European core region may be more relevant. The complementary trade relation suggests the creation of network linkages between Japanese and European activities, but this variable's influence is only intermediate. Further, the Japanese do not really take exchange rate changes into account. However, cultural differences continue to be a significant and rather important barrier. This does not fit in this type of strategy, but may not be strange in view of the large differences between European and Japanese cultures. All in all, it seems that some evidence exists for regional core networking strategies integrating Japanese and European economic activities.

6.3.3   Investments to South and Southeast Asia

South and Southeast Asia constitutes the third largest geographical cluster of host countries for Japanese investments abroad. It seems that two groups of countries can be distinguished: traditional newly industrialising countries and second-tier newly industrialising countries. Foreign direct investment shares for the former group seem to stabilise or even decline, whereas those for the latter group tend to increase. It also appears that investments to this region, particularly to second-tier newly industrialising countries, are dominated by investments in manufacturing industries.

Belderbos and Sleuwaegen (1996a) have found evidence that Japanese investors develop regional core networks in Asia. They show that companies in the Japanese electronics and precision machinery industry establish manufacturing plants throughout the Southeast Asian region which are closely connected to their parents in terms of knowledge transfer (R&D, marketing) and liquidity provision. In their view, inter-firm linkages, which they proxied by the number of manufacturing subsidiaries belonging to a horizontal *keiretsu*, lower barriers for Japanese foreign direct investments.

In view of the above, it seems appropriate to expect determinants that fit into the complex international production strategy type for Japanese foreign direct investments in Asia. Investors may try to benefit from emerging markets, where products made by local subsidiaries can be traded. This can be the case particularly for investments in the traditional newly industrialising countries in this region. On the other hand, they can try to lower their production costs by locating parts of their production systems in economies with low labour costs. This may prevail for investments in the second-tier newly industrialising countries. Especially in the latter case, intensified trade in components and final products between home and host markets is expected. This implies a complementary relation between trade and foreign direct investment. Cultural differences may not be a barrier, because the difference between cultural traditions in Japan and in other parts of Asia may not be as large as for countries outside Asia. The exchange rate direction hypothesis can play a role. The Japanese yen is generally considered as a strong currency, which implies depreciating host currencies *vis-à-vis* the yen. This creates cheap investment opportunities abroad for Japanese corporate structures. Volatility of such currencies may not prevent them from purchasing such assets, when regional core networking strategies prevail.

Table 6.5   Japanese investments to South and Southeast Asia

Information: Periods: 7 (1982–86 to 1988–92) No. of cases: 62 of 63 (98.4%) R^2: 0.944 F: 57.010 R^2 (adjusted): 0.928 DW: 2.546		Countries: 9 China, Hong Kong, India, Indonesia, Korea, Malaysia, Philippines, Singapore, Thailand	
Determinant	Definition[a]	Parameter T-value	β-value
Market size	1	−0.426 −11.612	−0.646
Per capita income	2b	1.967 6.278	0.327
Labour costs	2a	−1.547 −7.396	−0.324
Transport costs	1	0.965 6.244	0.383
Cultural differences	4	−1.442 −3.655	−0.213
Trade intensity	2a	3.472 11.877	0.790
Exchange rate direction	1	−0.582 −3.082	−0.230
Exchange rate volatility	3	−0.078 −2.923	−0.138
Dummy 1983–87		−0.218 −1.219	−0.061
Dummy 1984–88		−0.176 −1.069	−0.049
Dummy 1985–89		−0.039 −0.230	−0.011
Dummy 1986–90		−0.017 −0.095	−0.005
Dummy 1987–91		0.170 0.839	0.048
Dummy 1988–92		0.552 2.499	0.147
Intercept		8.162 6.940	—

Note
a. For variable definitions, see Appendix IV.

Not all expected relations are accepted in MOSAIC's results, as is shown in Table 6.5. Per capita income, in terms of GDP per capita growth, and labour costs are indeed important determinants. Market size is not supported. This suggests that it is not the volume of the markets in Asian countries that is interesting, but rather their growth in purchasing power. This seems logical in view of the small size of traditional newly industrialising countries and the strong growth in GDP per capita in the second-tier group of countries. Perhaps, the large domestic market for Japanese investors also plays a role. The importance of low labour costs is consistent with the view that Japanese investors seek cheap production locations for their manufacturing activities, particularly in the second-tier group of countries. Cultural differences emerge as a significant friction factor, which indicates that these differences are more prominent than is expected initially. However, its β-value shows a minor importance and the variable suffers from some intercorrelation with per capita income and trade intensity. The relation between trade and investment is complementary, as was expected. This variable contributes most as its β-value is highest. Further, its elasticity reveals a strong sensitivity, but again intercorrelations may disturb this result. For the exchange rate direction hypothesis the expectation is accepted: investors indeed want to benefit from the appreciation of the yen, but its importance does not appear to be large. However, although of less importance, exchange rate uncertainty is taken into account. The uncertainty variable is conditional, which implies that Japanese investors are able to hedge expected exchange rate movements. The transport cost hypothesis again obtains a positive parameter, which supports the inclination of Japanese companies to choose the investment mode of internationalisation in favour of the trade mode.

Some support for MOSAIC's estimation results is given by Chen (1993, pp. 33–6). He states that Japan started to invest in Asia in the early 1970s for the purpose of finding low-cost production locations and expanding markets.[12] Further, according to Chen, the sharp revaluation of the yen in 1986–87 stimulated Japanese companies to invest in Asia.[13] In addition, Chen advocates that Japanese investments have a strong trade orientation. These observations also arise from the MOSAIC estimations presented here.

The period-dummy parameters may represent the observed transition in foreign direct investment shares from traditional newly industrialising countries to the second-tier group of countries in South and Southeast Asia. This may coincide with the slight decrease in the share of investments in services, which seem to dominate in countries of the former group, and the modest increase in the share of manufacturing investments. The latter could relate to foreign direct investments in the second-tier group of countries. However, the β-values of the dummy variables reveal a low influence.

The regression is fairly well able to explain Japanese foreign direct investments in Asia. The correlation coefficient is sufficiently high. The period dummies suggest minor period-specific influences. The Durbin–Watson statistic implies that some negative autocorrelation in the residuals could exist, but covariances among residuals of individual investment relations are small and do not raise concern. However, the high *T*-values of market size and trade intensity cast some doubts on the model's specification, but the model results are sustained when alternative definitions of variables are used.

Compared with using MOSAIC for Japanese world investments, the Asia model seems to deviate to the extent that the exchange rate hypotheses are accepted here and not in the world model. In both models trade complementarity is an important determinant, but in the Asian model the elasticity is higher. Per capita income is also identified in both models, but again the elasticity in the Asian model is higher. Another common determinant is the barrier from cultural differences. However, in both models, the influence is not large. The market size hypothesis is rejected in the Asian model, whereas in the world model it was accepted. Finally, the cheap labour cost hypothesis is now a significant determinant of intermediate importance, whereas in the world model it was weakly supported.

The model results give some evidence for the existence of regional core networking strategies for Japanese foreign direct investments in Asia and therefore support the conclusions drawn by Belderbos and Sleuwaegen. The relevance of the per capita income hypothesis and the labour cost hypothesis together with the rather strong influence of the complementary trade relation comply with this strategy's profile. On the other hand, the barriers from cultural differences and exchange rate volatility do not fit, but their β-values reveal a minor influence.

6.3.4 Investments to North and South America

When discussing the geographical structure of Japanese investments abroad, North America was identified as the most important region, whereas South America appeared to be of limited importance. In particular, the United States were found to absorb nearly half of Japanese investments abroad. The relevance of South America showed a strong decline. As these regions include only a limited number of countries, they have to be combined in order to get an acceptable number of cases in the data set for testing MOSAIC.

In view of the dominance of North America in the data set, it appears likely that complex international production strategies prevail. The market size and per capita income hypotheses seem to be relevant for both the large US market and the emerging markets in South America. Also, Japanese investors may want to benefit from cheap production locations in view of high labour costs in the home economy, particularly for investments in South America. Regarding trade, a complementary relation is expected. However, there are indications that Japanese investors have been afraid that certain trade measures might block exports from Japan to the United States. This may mean that the trade relation is substitutory. In principle, according to the profile of the expected strategy type, Japanese investors should not encounter barriers in terms of cultural differences and exchange rate volatility. However, cultural differences may be large in view of language barriers and differences in business practice and management style. Also, the volatility of the US dollar and particularly South American currencies *vis-à-vis* the Japanese yen may invoke a considerable barrier.

MOSAIC estimations for Japanese investments in the Americas show that Japanese investors are guided by market size, labour costs and exchange rate volatility (Table 6.6). The parameter of market size reveals an elasticity well above unity, suggesting a high sensitivity. Its β-value implies a major influence. This is no surprise given the large potential of the US market and the large share of US investments in total Japanese investments abroad. The exchange rate volatility hypothesis is supported for a conditional specification of the variable. Its importance is even relatively high as shown by its β-value. Possibly, in view of unstable currencies in South America, this implies that Japanese investors have favoured investments in the United States instead of in South American countries. This could further explain the strong dominance of US investments in total foreign investments from Japan. Labour costs obtain a significant and highly elastic parameter. This gives support to the cheap labour cost hypothesis, but its importance in the model is not as high as for market size and exchange rate volatility. This result may coincide with a growing share of manufacturing investments in the latter part of the 1980s. Such investments may favour locations with relatively cheap labour.

Hypotheses on other determinants are not accepted. Per capita income has a positive parameter, but it is insignificant. The same is true for transport costs. The positive parameter is consistent with the results of the models for all Japanese foreign direct investments and for those in Europe and Asia. This may again indicate that Japanese investors favour the investment mode of internationalisation. Cultural differences obtain an adequate parameter, but its insignificance renders this barrier to be irrelevant. Perhaps, in view of the heavy emphasis of investments in the United States, the Japanese are well able to cope with differences between Japanese and American cultures. Finally, the exchange rate direction parameter is not supported.

Table 6.6 Japanese investments to North and South America

Information: Periods: 7 (1982–86 to 1988–92) No. of cases: 42 of 42 (100.0%) R^2: 0.846 F: 10.608 R^2 (adjusted): 0.766 DW: 1.908		Countries: 6 Argentina, Brazil, Canada, Chile, Mexico, United States		
Determinant	Definition[a]	Parameter	T-value	β-value
Market size	1	1.734	6.082	0.805
Per capita income	2b	0.844	0.430	0.063
Labour costs	2a	−7.996	−2.683	−0.297
Transport costs	1	2.218	0.461	0.136
Cultural differences	4	−0.441	−0.287	−0.058
Trade intensity	2c	−0.263	−0.626	−0.068
Exchange rate direction	2	−0.082	−0.106	−0.012
Exchange rate volatility	4	−1.579	−2.692	−0.688
Dummy 1983–87		−0.596	−0.879	−0.094
Dummy 1984–88		−0.404	−0.546	−0.064
Dummy 1985–89		−0.458	−0.620	−0.073
Dummy 1986–90		−0.391	−0.560	−0.062
Dummy 1987–91		−0.573	−0.794	−0.091
Dummy 1988–92		−0.679	−0.965	−0.108
Intercept		25.649	1.224	—

Note
a. For variable definitions, see Appendix IV.

The negative parameter for trade may reveal that foreign direct investments substitute the export of products from Japan to the markets in North and South America. This may relate particularly to trade barriers for the US market. De Melo and Tarr (1995, pp. 5–6) argue that during the 1980s, voluntary export restraints for Japanese exports to the United States led to strong growth in Japanese investments in car manufacturing in this country.[14] Therefore, these investments can be considered as tariff jumping. Drake and Caves (1992, p. 243) find a highly significant influence from trade protection measures against Japanese imports. The substitutory relation with trade was also found by Sleuwaegen and Yamawaki (1990, p. 21). They found that intra-firm trade between Japanese parents and their US subsidiaries reduced in magnitude and was replaced by local manufacturing. However, it should be noted that the MOSAIC results relate to investment flows by all industries and not just to those of manufacturing. It was shown that the bulk of Japanese investments abroad is made in services, which may cause the trade parameter to be insignificant here.

The parameters of the period dummies are all negative and seem to remain in the same order of magnitude. Possibly they capture the downward trend in the share of North and South America in total foreign direct investments. This could relate particularly to Latin America. Another possibility is that they represent the threat of trade measures against Japanese imports (into the United States). However, their β-values reveal minor influence.

The model has a high explanatory power with a correlation coefficient above 80 per cent and insignificant parameters for all period dummies. This implies that the explanatory variables support most of the variance in the dependent variable. However, it should be noted that the number of observations in the data set is fairly limited. The Durbin–Watson statistic could indicate some minor negative autocorrelations in the residuals. This could be due to a less appropriate fit of the model for Japanese investments in Mexico. Further, the labour cost parameter and the intercept raise concern about their validity. The model is also sensitive to including other variable definitions. An explanation can be found with relatively high intercorrelations among the explanatory variables, which is due to the limited number of cases.

Some differences exist between the American model presented here and the world model. Market size is accepted in both models, but for North and South America the influence is stronger and more elastic. Per capita income is not supported for America. The strong influence of this determinant in the world model may coincide with foreign direct investments in Western Europe and South and Southeast Asia. Labour costs are considerably relevant for investments in America. They were less important in the world model. Transport costs have a positive parameter in both models, but in the American model their parameter is insignificant. Cultural barriers are not accepted here. The same is true for trade intensity and exchange rate direction. Exchange rate volatility is important in the American model, but not in the world model.

The model results seem to fit best in the simple affiliate integration strategy profile and not in the expected profile of complex international production strategies. The results reveal a strong market (downstream) orientation, but also a convincing input (upstream) orientation. The important contribution of the exchange rate volatility barrier particularly argues against the existence of complex strategies. On the other hand, the rejection of the cultural differences barrier argues in favour of such strategies. The negative parameter for trade intensity could suggest a stand-alone strategy, but the parameter's insignificance, together with accepting the labour cost hypothesis, raises doubts about this.

A possibility is that the combination of foreign direct investments to two different geographical clusters disturbs the estimation results. There is an inclination to assume that Japanese investors create regional core networks in North America. This is supported by accepting market size and labour costs as relevant determinants. The insignificance of cultural barriers may be another indication of this. If a substitutory trade relation exists, this may indicate that these networks are transplants of Japanese production systems. It is possible that this is the case in manufacturing. The substitutory trade relation may also relate to investments in South America and give support to the existence of stand-alone strategies there. This is consistent with the major influence from market size. Such strategies seem logical in view of the relatively limited size of foreign direct investments in South America.

6.4 CONCLUSION

Japanese foreign direct investments grow particularly strong between 1985 and 1989. Before 1985, hardly any increases emerge; after 1989 a strong decline occurs. Explanations of the post-1989 decline come from recessionary tendencies in the 1990s, large losses with Japanese multinational companies and restrictive lending policies by Japanese banks. Other factors are a deterioration of asset prices and poor performances of investments in Europe and the United States in previous years.

The geographical distribution of Japanese foreign direct investments throughout the world shows a clustering in four world regions. North America emerges as a very important region, with about half of total Japanese investments abroad. This share remains fairly stable over the years. Western Europe is the second largest region, and its importance is increasing. The third cluster in the ranking is South and Southeast Asia, which constitutes more than 10 per cent of total Japanese foreign direct investments. Were Australia and New Zealand to be included, this region would become as important as Western Europe. Within the Asian cluster a difference seems to exist between traditional newly industrialising countries and second-tier industrialising countries. Investment shares of the former tend to stabilise, whereas those of the latter reveal an upward tendency. The fourth cluster is Latin America. This region is becoming less important as its share in the total deteriorates.

The sectoral distribution of Japanese investments abroad shows a heavy emphasis on service industry investments. More than two-thirds of total investments is made by various service industries, of which the group of finance, insurance and business services is the largest. Manufacturing is responsible for the remainder. In manufacturing the largest foreign direct investments are made by electric and electronic equipment. Trends in the shares show that service investments are decreasing, whereas those in manufacturing are gaining, in importance.

Table 6.7 Summary of determinants for foreign direct investments from Japan

Determinant	World		Europe		Asia		America	
Market size	✓	++	✗	+	✗	++	✓	++
Per capita income	✓	++	✓	++	✓	+	✗	–
Labour costs	O	–	✗	–	✓	+	✓	+
ROI differences	n.a.	n.a.	✗	–	n.a.	n.a.	n.a.	n.a.
Transport costs	✗	–	✗	++	✗	+	✗	+
Cultural differences	✓	+	✓	+	✓	–	✗	–
Trade intensity	✓	++	✓	+	✓	++	✗	–
Exchange rate direction	✗	–	✗	+	✓	–	✗	–
Exchange rate volatility	✗	–	✗	–	✓	–	✓	++

Legend
✓ significant
O weakly significant
✗ not significant or theoretically incorrect parameter

++ strong influence
+ intermediate influence
– weak influence

The results from the MOSAIC estimations vary from one world region to another (Table 6.7). Except for the exchange rate hypotheses, similarities exist for Western Europe and South and Southeast Asia. For North and South America the picture deviates substantially from the other two regions.

The hypotheses on market potential are accepted in all regions. It appears that market size is important for foreign direct investments in North and South America and not per capita income. For Western Europe and South and Southeast Asia, market potential is determined by per capita income and not market size. In Europe, per capita income is more important than in Asia and the elasticity for Europe reveals a higher sensitivity than for Asia.

Cheap labour costs appear to be relevant, with an elastic parameter for all three world regions. However, for Europe the parameter is insignificant. Elasticity is highest for America, but some doubts exist on its correctness. For Asia and America, labour costs appear to be of intermediate importance to Japanese investors.

The transport cost hypothesis obtains a strange parameter for all regions, as it is consistently positive. This suggests that distance is rather a stimulus for Japanese companies to invest abroad. Maybe this indicates that Japanese investors have an inclination to choose in favour of the foreign direct investment mode of internationalisation rather than other modes. Transport costs seem to be highly relevant, especially for Europe, but the value of its parameter is extremely high and seems to be misspecified.

Japanese investors encounter significant barriers from cultural differences in Europe and Asia. In Europe, cultural differences are a barrier of intermediate importance for which Japanese investments are highly sensitive. For Asia the significant influence is surprising, because the differences between Japanese and other Asian cultures do not seem to be large, but their influence is low. For North and South America, no barrier from culture could be observed, which is also surprising. However, the dominance of foreign direct investments in the United States may show that the Japanese are able to cope adequately with cultural traditions in the US market.

The relation between trade and foreign direct investment is positive for South and Southeast Asia, and Western Europe. This determinant is highly important for investments in Asia. Its parameter for this region reveals a high elasticity. For Europe, the importance is less, but the parameter again indicates an elastic relationship. This is not consistent with a possible threat from a Fortress Europe. For North and South America a negative parameter is found. There, trade barriers may cause this substitutory relationship, but uncertainty exists on the validity of this estimation result.

The exchange rate hypotheses do not seem relevant for Western Europe, whereas for South and Southeast Asia and North and South America they do. In Europe, exchange rate policies may have created sufficient stability for Japanese investors. In Asia, both exchange rate hypotheses are identified as relevant, but of low influence. Accepting the direction hypothesis implies that Japanese investors may have purchased assets in Asia relatively cheaply in yen terms, using the relative strength of the yen. The significance of the exchange rate volatility hypothesis, which is of the conditional type, reveals that erratic exchange rate movements could still be a barrier. For America, the volatility hypothesis is strongly supported. This makes exchange rate volatility, again of the conditional type, an important barrier for Japanese investments to these regions. However, doubts about the validity of the American model may qualify this result.

In assessing all Japanese investments abroad throughout the world, there was an indication that complex international production strategies would exist (see Table 6.8). Market potential, input orientation and complementary trade relations were identified as significant determinants. The exchange rate volatility hypothesis was rejected. The only counter indication was acceptance of the cultural differences hypothesis, but its importance was low. Regional specifications of MOSAIC qualified these observations.

Table 6.8   Summary of overall strategies of corporate structures from Japan

Region	Corporate strategy
Western Europe	Regional core networking
South and Southeast Asia	Regional core networking
North and South America	Simple affiliate integration (trade substituting regional core networking in North America?; stand alone in South America?)

In Western Europe, Japanese investors indeed seem to pursue complex international production strategies. MOSAIC results indicate regional core networking strategies to prevail. Activities in Europe appear to integrate with those in Japan, creating Japanese–European corporate networks. Indications are that foreign direct investments are market orientated, trade relations are complementary and exchange rate movements are irrelevant. However, as for world investments, cultural differences continue to be a barrier and their importance appears to be considerable.

For Japanese investments in South and Southeast Asia, complex international production strategies also seem to emerge from the results. Although cultural differences and exchange rate volatility are significant barriers for investments in this region, their influence is outnumbered by trade complementarity and market potential. In particular, the strong influence from trade relations is considered an important indication for the creation of regional core networks throughout Asia. Japanese investors want to benefit from growing market potentials in some countries. Further, the significant labour cost variable suggests that they engage in outsourcing by using cheap production opportunities, possibly in the region's second-tier newly industrialising countries.

In North and South America a simple affiliate integration strategy may prevail. The acceptance of both market potential and input orientation as major determinants and the identification of exchange rate volatility as a major barrier fit this strategy's profile. However, although other determinants are insignificant, other strategies may also prevail. The theoretically correct, but insignificant parameter for cultural differences could imply the existence of regional core networking strategies. The negative, but also insignificant parameter for trade suggests a substitutory trade relation, which is relevant for stand-alone strategies. Possibly, strategies differ for North and South America. For North America the regional core networking strategy is more likely, but the substitutory trade relation could imply transplanting Japanese networks of economic activities to this region. This could particularly be the case for manufacturing investments in the United States, where voluntary export restraints and local content requirements seem to have incited such behaviour. For South America a stand-alone strategy is more likely in view of the limited size of foreign direct investments in this region. Further analysis for both subregions seems advisable.

The results for Japanese investments presented here may support the acceptance of the hypothesis put forward in the theoretical part of this study. Japanese investors use different opportunities offered in different host countries throughout the world. They seek combinations of their ownership advantages with different locational advantages and internalise them. This also supports the theoretical framework on foreign direct investment.

NOTES

1. Others show that knowledge is indeed positively related to Japanese outward foreign direct investment flows. See, for example, Caves (1993), Drake and Caves (1992).
2. See also Balasubramanyam and Greenaway (1992, p. 177).
3. See also Balasubramanyam and Greenaway (1994, p. 105).
4. Dunning and Cantwell (1991, pp. 155–6) analyse the stock of Japanese foreign direct investments in Europe and come to similar conclusions.
5. According to Garnaut (1996, p. 24), Japanese foreign direct investments in China and ASEAN countries concentrated in manufacturing.
6. Dunning and Cantwell (1991, pp. 155–7) give a similar picture for the stock of Japanese investments in Europe.
7. Ozawa (1991, p. 135) argues that assembly-based, mass-market-orientated manufacturing industries, notably automobiles and consumer electronics, are particularly attracted to Europe.
8. Foreign direct investments which try to defuse a tariff threat. See Bhagwati (1987, p. 11).
9. Ozawa (1991, p. 149) claims that Japanese affiliates help local suppliers to rationalise and raise productivity instead of shifting parts production to low-wage countries.
10. See also Belderbos and Sleuwaegen (1996b).
11. Balasubramanyam and Greenaway (1992, p. 186) suggest that 'these fears are probably exaggerated'.
12. A survey in 1989 among Japanese firms with overseas investments reveals low labour costs, cheap materials and strong market potentials to be important motives for moving to Asian countries. See Takeuchi (1991, pp. 65–7).
13. Dicken (1988, p. 646) had already announced this reaction to the yen revaluation.
14. For more indications, see OECD (1995f, p. 16).

7. Investments from Germany

7.1 INTRODUCTION

The determinants that can be identified from MOSAIC estimations for the foreign direct investment flows originating from Germany will be described in this chapter. As for US and Japanese investments, this chapter will start with the trends in German foreign direct investments throughout the world and in three geographical clusters. Next, MOSAIC results will be discussed for all outgoing investment flows and for the flows to countries in the geographical clusters.

As for the United States and Japan, not all hypotheses are included in the model estimations for Germany. This applies to the knowledge hypothesis, the taxation differences hypothesis and, for non-European countries, the return on investment differences hypothesis.

7.2 INVESTMENT PATTERNS

The trend in outward foreign direct investments from Germany shows a steady growth from DM 6.0 billion in 1982 to DM 21.9 billion in 1986 (see also Figure 7.1). In 1987, there is a reduction, but this is only temporary. In subsequent years, growth in foreign direct investments accelerates again until 1990. For 1991, a considerable slowdown in growth occurs, but the level of foreign direct investment still increases to a high of DM 39.3 billion. In 1992, however, a firm reduction appears. The levelling off in 1991 and the reduction in 1992 coincide with an economic slowdown in Europe (United Nations 1994, p. 54).

Inward foreign direct investments follow an erratic pattern. In some years, the level of investments increases. In other years, it goes down. In particular, in 1989, inward investments were very high.[1] On the whole, however, the trend is less steep than for outward investments.

In Table 7.1 two major clusters appear in German foreign direct investments abroad. The first cluster relates to countries in Western Europe. The second cluster contains the investments in North and South America. Investments in other parts of the world, including the South and Southeast Asian region, remain of limited importance.

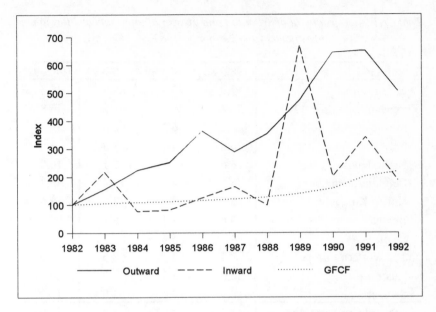

*Figure 7.1   Development of foreign direct investment from Germany and
gross fixed capital formation (1982 = 100; nominal)*

The cluster of European countries becomes more and more important over
the years. The share of investments within the European Union rises from
about a third at the beginning of the 1980s to about two-thirds in the last
period. Investments in other European countries tend to increase also, but
less prominently than for the Union. This reveals the continued adaptation
of corporate strategies and structures to the ongoing economic integration
process in the European market (United Nations 1994, p. 55).

Some countries in Europe have increased their popularity for German
investors more than others. Upward trends in the share of foreign direct
investments can be found for France, Belgium/Luxemburg, the United
Kingdom and Ireland with an emphasis on the latter three countries.[2] Trends
for the Netherlands, Spain, Austria and Switzerland show a stable share. A
strong downward trend can be observed for Italy.

Table 7.1   Geographical distribution and growth of total outward foreign direct investments from Germany (1982–92; %)

Host region	1982–86	1985–89	1988–92	1982–92[a]
Western Europe	42.9	47.9	69.7	25.4
European Union (EU12)	35.2	40.9	61.2	26.8
France	5.6	6.3	9.0	25.3
Italy	6.6	4.4	3.8	5.5
Netherlands	6.6	6.2	7.1	16.9
Belgium/Luxemburg	4.6	6.1	13.4	38.3
United Kingdom	5.5	9.8	12.5	32.6
Ireland	0.4	1.4	8.2	92.2
Spain	4.7	5.4	5.5	18.8
Other Western Europe	7.7	7.1	8.5	17.5
Austria	2.0	2.5	2.7	20.9
Switzerland	4.9	2.9	4.0	12.1
South and Southeast Asia	3.1	2.7	3.0	14.9
Japan	1.0	1.1	1.4	21.1
North and South America	50.9	47.0	23.5	1.6
North America	45.7	44.8	21.4	1.9
United States of America	41.6	41.9	18.7	1.2
Latin America	5.2	2.1	2.1	–0.8
Brazil	3.0	1.1	0.8	–7.8
Mexico	0.6	0.5	0.6	13.0
Other regions	3.2	2.4	3.9	19.5
Central and Eastern Europe	0.1	0.3	2.3	83.1
Australia and New Zealand	1.2	1.0	0.5	0.3
Middle East	1.0	1.3	0.7	8.2
Africa	0.9	0.0	0.4	2.7
Other	–0.0	–0.3	–0.1	50.6
Total	100.0	100.0	100.0	15.6

Note
a. Average nominal growth rate between first and last periods.

Source
OECD.

Table 7.2 Sectoral distribution and growth of total outward foreign direct investments from Germany (1986–92; %)

Investing industry	1986–90	1987–91	1988–92	1986–92[a]
Agriculture	0.0	0.0	0.0	–18.4
Total manufacturing	45.5	42.4	41.7	9.6
Mining and quarrying	1.7	1.9	1.2	–2.5
Oil	0.2	0.2	0.1	–8.6
Food, beverages and tobacco	1.8	2.0	1.9	19.8
Textiles, leather and clothing	0.7	0.7	0.8	29.1
Paper, printing and publishing	1.4	1.6	1.7	26.2
Chemical products	12.3	9.0	8.3	–5.7
Coal and petroleum products	0.9	2.6	2.6	99.1
Non-metallic products	2.7	2.5	1.8	–7.5
Metal products	2.8	2.8	2.5	7.1
Mechanical equipment	4.2	4.4	4.7	21.7
Electric and electronic equipment	10.4	8.2	7.9	–0.3
Motor vehicles	5.9	5.2	6.5	19.7
Other transport equipment	0.1	0.6	0.6	181.0
Other manufacturing	0.4	0.6	1.0	74.8
Construction	0.5	0.5	0.4	10.2
Total commercial services	39.3	40.7	41.8	18.2
Wholesale and retail trade	2.3	2.2	2.7	25.0
Transport, storage and communication	0.6	0.6	0.8	39.8
Finance, insurance and business services	27.4	30.6	33.4	26.3
Other commercial services	9.0	7.2	4.8	–15.9
Unallocated	14.8	16.4	16.1	19.7
Total	100.0	100.0	100.0	15.6

Note
a. Average nominal growth rate between first and last periods.

Source
OECD.

The cluster of foreign direct investments in North and South America shows a declining trend in the latter part of the 1980s and at the beginning of the 1990s. The share decreases from less than half of total German investments abroad to less than a quarter. The bulk of investments in this region is destined for the United States and it is for this country in particular that the decline in investment flows is shown. Except for Mexico, the trend for South America is also downward. Already, at the beginning of the 1980s, German involvement in this region was modest. In subsequent years the foreign direct investments to this region go down to relatively marginal shares. It seems that German investors have replaced their investment involvements in the Americas with those in Europe, in particular in the European Union.

South and Southeast Asia can hardly be identified as a separate cluster of German investments abroad. The share of this region, some 3 per cent of the total, is really low. Investments in Japan are most important and the importance of this country increases relatively strongly as its share in Asian investments increases from about a third in 1982–86 to about half in 1988–92. For other countries in this region shares are less than one per cent of total foreign direct investments. The growth rate for this region amounts to some 15 per cent annually, which is lower than average growth in some other regions. This implies a declining German involvement in Asia in relative terms and, in view of its increasing share, a concentration in Japan.

Foreign direct investments in other parts of the world are marginal and show different patterns. The rapid increase in the share of Central and Eastern Europe at the beginning of the 1990s of course coincides with the fall of the Berlin Wall. Countries in this region, in particular Hungary and the Czech Republic, have attracted the interest of German investors (United Nations 1994, p. 54). Investments in Australia and New Zealand show a declining share and those in the Middle East and Africa fluctuate.

The sectoral composition of foreign direct investment from Germany, as shown in Table 7.2, reveals major shares of three industries. The group of finance, insurance and business services constitutes about a third of the total. Chemical products, and electric and electronic equipment each take another 10 per cent in the total. Shares of intermediate size can be noted for mechanical equipment and motor vehicles. Their shares in total foreign direct investments amount to some 5 per cent. The shares of other industries are only marginal.

Trends in the shares of the various industries show different developments. In general, a substitution is visible from manufacturing to services. In particular, in manufacturing a decreasing trend is shown for chemical products, and electric and electronic equipment. This trend is partly offset by an increase in the shares of other transport equipment; coal and petroleum products; textiles, leather and clothing; paper, printing and publishing; and other manufacturing. The group of finance, insurance and business services is particularly responsible for the increasing share of commercial services.

7.3 DETERMINANTS

7.3.1 Investments to the World

In view of the large emphasis on European and American host countries, German foreign direct investments may be the result of complex international production strategies. Market size and per capita income, together with input orientation seem logical determinants. For trade, a complementary relation is likely to prevail. German investors may also want to benefit from the relative strength of the German mark *vis-à-vis* other currencies. The exchange rate direction hypothesis may therefore be appropriate, but exchange rate volatility should not be a barrier. Cultural differences are not expected to be a major barrier, whereas transport costs are likely to remain a friction factor.

The empirical analysis with MOSAIC shows five relevant determinants of German investments abroad (see Table 7.3). Investors from Germany are led primarily by the host country's market potential in terms of market size and per capita income. This is shown by the relatively high β-values of these determinants. Their elasticities indicate that sensitivity is not large. There is an indication that German investors also consider input orientations, as the labour cost parameter is weakly significant. Perhaps, this is an explanation for the relatively strong growth in the shares of some manufacturing industries in total investments abroad for which low labour costs could be more relevant. However, its influence is low. Germans encounter relatively serious barriers from transport costs and cultural differences, as their β-values show, but sensitivity is low as their elasticities remain below unity.

The hypotheses on trade relations and exchange rate changes are not supported. For trade the relation is negative, but insignificant and contributes little to the explanatory power of the model. Both exchange rate hypotheses obtain a negative parameter, but they are also insignificant and of marginal importance.

The results are in line with those found by Moore (1993, p. 128). He concludes that German investments abroad are sensitive to the size of the host market and to labour costs. He also identifies geographical proximity to be of relevance, which supports the acceptance of our transport cost hypothesis. Regarding exchange rates, as in the results presented here, he finds no evidence that German investors favour investment relations with countries with stable currencies.

Table 7.3   German investments throughout the world

Information: Periods: 7 (1982–86 to 1988–92) No. of cases: 197 of 203 (97.0%) R^2: 0.702 F: 30.612 R^2 (adjusted): 0.679 DW: 2.064		Countries: 29 Western Europe, South and Southeast Asia plus Australia, Canada, Finland, Israel, Mexico, Turkey, United States		
Determinant	Definition[a]	Parameter	*T*-value	β-value
Market size	1	0.663	11.020	0.567
Per capita income	2a	1.071	14.388	0.830
Labour costs	2c	−0.447	−1.600	−0.069
Transport costs	1	−0.582	−7.290	−0.377
Cultural differences	4	−0.759	−5.988	−0.266
Trade intensity	2c	−0.096	−0.374	−0.020
Exchange rate direction	1	−0.199	−0.932	−0.044
Exchange rate volatility	3	−0.007	−0.233	−0.010
Dummy 1983–87		0.238	0.808	0.046
Dummy 1984–88		0.184	0.593	0.036
Dummy 1985–89		0.159	0.505	0.032
Dummy 1986–90		0.218	0.675	0.043
Dummy 1987–91		0.827	2.415	0.161
Dummy 1988–92		1.934	5.776	0.376
Intercept		−3.893	−3.945	—

Note
a. For variable definitions, see Appendix IV.

Apart from those for 1987–91 and 1988–92, period dummies do not seem to have a major influence in the model. The dummies for 1987–91 and 1988–92 may be related to the observed slowdown in foreign direct investment activity in 1991 and the reduction in 1992. However, this trend would imply negative parameters for these dummies instead of significantly positive ones.

With a correlation coefficient of about 70 per cent, the regression's quality is reasonable. Except for 1987–91 and 1988–92, period dummies are insignificant. Further, the Durbin–Watson statistic suggests absence of autocorrelations in the residuals. Intercorrelations among explanatory variables do not seem to exist. Including other variable definitions in the model does not cause major changes in the results. The regression is therefore reasonably sustainable. However, for some investment relations the model's fit is not high. This is the case for German investments in Ireland, Malaysia, Singapore and Thailand. In addition, some host countries in Latin America had to be eliminated from the data set in order to obtain a reasonable fit.

The MOSAIC results suggest that German corporate structures pursue stand-alone or downstream simple affiliate integration strategies instead of the expected complex international production strategies. The strong market orientation testifies to this. Additional support comes from identifying cultural differences as a relatively serious barrier. Although not significant, the negative parameter for trade intensity could point to the existence of stand-alone strategies as the prevailing type.

7.3.2 Investments to Western Europe

Western Europe was identified as the largest geographical cluster in German investments abroad. Within this cluster the European Union turned out to be a subregion of considerable importance, in which the growth in relative shares was largest.

The determinants of German foreign direct investments in Western Europe are expected to be in line with those of intra-EU investments. In Chapter 4, German investments belong to the investments originating from the core region. For those investments, regional core networking strategies were identified as particularly relevant. It is therefore obvious to expect such strategies for German investments in Europe as well. Hence, market orientation and input orientation are likely determinants. Trade relations should be complementary. Cultural differences fit less into this strategy's profile, but they can be relevant for non-core countries. The same can be true for exchange rate influences. Transport cost barriers are likely to persist.

The regression results using MOSAIC are to some extent surprising (see Table 7.4). The surprise is with a number of hypotheses. Labour costs in Western European host countries are not relevant to German investors, which gives an indication that input orientation is not really a motive to invest abroad. This may coincide with the large and rising share of finance, insurance and business services for which low labour costs may be less relevant. Cultural differences are accepted as a barrier of intermediate importance. Particularly surprising is the significant substitutory trade relation, which suggests that Germans want to service other European markets by transferring activities to those markets. However, some correlation of the trade intensity variable and the distance variable could disturb this result. Another surprise is that, although its elasticity is low, the hypothesis on conditional exchange rate volatility is accepted. Its β-value reveals an intermediate influence. This may imply that German companies prefer to invest in countries which in some way have pegged their currency to the German mark in order to minimise erratic exchange rate movements. However, the parameter shows a low elasticity and thus a minor sensitivity. Not surprising is that the results support the market potential hypotheses. In particular, the market size variable is highly relevant as is shown by its β-value, but its elasticity is low. Per capita income, in terms of purchasing power growth, obtains a significant and elastic parameter, but its relevance is not large. The transport cost barrier is accepted and identified as very important.

Accepting the cultural differences barrier is consistent with the identification of cultural differences as a significant barrier in the model for all intra-EU investments and in the model for core-to-periphery investments within the European Union (see Chapter 4). The result for German investments in Western Europe suggests that Germans are inclined to prefer investments in countries with little differences *vis-à-vis* the German culture. This could explain why about half of German investments in Western Europe is destined for German-orientated countries. These countries may also be the countries with stable currencies *vis-à-vis* the German mark.

EIM research on some case studies shows that subsidiaries of German origin tend to engage mostly in sales and service activities (EIM 1993, Section 2.2). This gives some support for the presented model results, as market potential is particularly relevant for these activities. Also, EIM shows that production activities are transferred, which is in line with the identified substitutory trade relation.

The period dummies may capture an economic integration effect. Parameter values increase over the time periods. Their significance and their relevance also appear to rise over time. This coincides with the strong upward trend in the share of intra-EU investments in total investments abroad.

The model is fairly well able to explain the variance in German foreign direct investments throughout Western Europe. The correlation coefficient amounts to more than 80 per cent. Most period dummies do not contribute strongly to the regression. The Durbin–Watson statistic could suggest that some positive autocorrelation in the residuals exists. Again, the model's fit for investments in Ireland seems to cause some trouble, but covariances with the residuals of other investment relations remain low. The rather high intercept could give rise to some concern as well. Using other variable definitions in MOSAIC estimations gives no other results. In particular, other definitions of the trade variable were tested, but these estimations did not lead to adaptations in the obtained results.

Table 7.4   German investments to Western Europe

Information: Periods: 7 (1982–86 to 1988–92) No. of cases: 91 of 91 (100.0%) R^2: 0.879 F: 36.239 R^2 (adjusted): 0.855 DW: 1.848		Countries: 13 Austria, Belgium/Luxemburg, Denmark, France, Greece, Ireland, Italy, Netherlands, Norway, Portugal, Spain, Sweden, United Kingdom		
Determinant	Definition[a]	Parameter	T-value	β-value
Market size	1	0.756	11.135	0.566
Per capita income	2b	2.008	3.474	0.170
Labour costs	2c	0.114	0.170	0.010
ROI differences	1	0.114	0.741	0.042
Transport costs	1	−1.650	−9.549	−0.757
Cultural differences	2	−1.145	−4.047	−0.237
Trade intensity	2a	−0.981	−4.405	−0.338
Exchange rate direction	1	−0.466	−0.594	−0.031
Exchange rate volatility	3	−0.079	−1.719	−0.142
Dummy 1983–87		−0.014	−0.072	−0.004
Dummy 1984–88		−0.030	−0.145	−0.008
Dummy 1985–89		0.194	0.926	0.052
Dummy 1986–90		0.365	1.625	0.099
Dummy 1987–91		0.556	2.297	0.150
Dummy 1988–92		0.709	3.162	0.192
Intercept		−9.238	−4.615	—

Note
a. For variable definitions, see Appendix IV.

Comparing the European model with the world model reveals some interesting differences. Per capita income is less important than in the world model, but the more elastic parameter suggests a higher sensitivity. Transport costs are a much stronger barrier for European investments and the elasticity is higher. European investments also seem to be more sensitive to cultural differences, as this variable's parameter is higher than in the world model. For trade the European model identifies a substitutory relation with investments. This was also the case in the world model, but the parameter was insignificant there. Finally, an interesting difference is the significant parameter for conditional exchange rate volatility for European investments.

The identified determinants comply with the profile of stand-alone strategies, rather than with the expected regional core networking strategies. This is supported by the substitutory trade relation and the strong market orientation. Also, rejection of the labour cost hypothesis and acceptance of the cultural differences and exchange rate volatility hypotheses testify to this. Another indication is the high importance of the transport cost barrier. Possibly, German investors have a strong orientation towards German-orientated countries. This may imply that strategies differ between German-orientated countries on the one hand and less German-orientated countries on the other hand. For the former group of countries one may speculate that a regional core networking strategy could prevail, as transport distances, cultural differences and exchange rate volatility may be minor for these relations. For the latter group stand-alone strategies could be relevant due to important barriers from transport costs, cultural differences and exchange rate volatility. This speculation may be justified in view of earlier conclusions on strategies of investors from the core region within Europe.

7.3.3   Investments to South and Southeast Asia

Although foreign direct investment flows to Asian countries are marginal, data availability for these countries allows MOSAIC testing. The marginal character of these investments may suggest that corporate strategies for German investments in this region are of a stand-alone nature. In such strategies, a strong market orientation will prevail in which investments are likely to replace exports from home production facilities. Investors will encounter barriers from cultural differences and high transport costs in view of the large distances. Further, exchange rate volatility will be of relevance.

MOSAIC results more or less support the expectations (see Table 7.5). In particular, the market potential hypothesis is accepted, as both market size and per capita income are significant. In particular, the β-value of the per capita income determinant contributes strongly to the explanation of investment flows. This may coincide with relatively strong growth in foreign direct investments to Japan. Transport costs also seem to be a determinant, but the significance of this barrier is not high. Labour cost obtains a theoretically acceptable parameter, but it is insignificant. The same is true for cultural differences and exchange rate direction. For cultural differences this result is surprising in view of the significant parameter for this variable in both models for the world and for Western Europe. For trade intensity a negative parameter is found, implying substitution between trade and foreign direct investment, but the parameter appears to be insignificant and its contribution to the regression does not seem to be very important. Because of its positive parameter, conditional exchange rate volatility is rejected as a relevant hypothesis. This suggests that German investors may have a capital flight motive, which in view of the stability of the German mark is not very likely. It is possible that this variable suffers from some correlation with the transport cost variable.

Table 7.5   German investments to South and Southeast Asia

Information:	Countries: 9		
Periods: 7 (1982–86 to 1988–92)	China, Hong Kong, India,		
No. of cases: 57 of 63 (90.5%)	Indonesia, Japan, Korea, Malaysia,		
R^2: 0.675 F: 6.224	Singapore, Thailand		
R^2 (adjusted): 0.566 DW: 2.477			
Determinant	Definition[a]	Parameter	T-value	β-value
---	---	---	---	---
Market size	1	0.337	3.290	0.575
Per capita income	2a	0.929	6.224	1.312
Labour costs	2b	−0.531	−0.570	−0.058
Transport costs	1	−1.738	−1.817	−0.263
Cultural differences	1	−0.239	−0.238	−0.037
Trade intensity	2c	−0.174	−0.507	−0.067
Exchange rate direction	1	−0.208	−1.017	−0.119
Exchange rate volatility	5	1.337	2.302	0.317
Dummy 1983–87		0.321	0.723	0.092
Dummy 1984–88		0.199	0.442	0.060
Dummy 1985–89		−0.227	−0.496	−0.072
Dummy 1986–90		0.109	0.238	0.035
Dummy 1987–91		1.342	2.377	0.407
Dummy 1988–92		1.436	2.588	0.436
Intercept		−2.148	−0.703	—

Note
a. For variable definitions, see Appendix IV.

The period dummies apparently represent the trend in shares of Asian investments in the total. At the beginning of the 1980s there is a weak decline in shares for this region, which is reflected in a downward trend in parameter values. In later years, shares show modest increases. The same happens with the period-dummy parameters. The period dummies for

1987–91 and 1988–92 seem to indicate a period-specific influence, which is of considerable relevance to the model. This was also the case in the model for world investments.

The explanatory power of the model can be considered adequate. Apart from the 1987–91 and 1988–92 period dummies, period-specific influences seem to be marginal. The Durbin–Watson statistic may indicate that the model tested here suffers from negative autocorrelation in the residuals. This is probably caused by the residuals for foreign direct investments in Malaysia and Thailand. Testing other specifications of MOSAIC reveals that the model results are not very sustainable, which qualifies the conclusions drawn from the model results presented here. The strength of market orientation is, however, accepted in those tests.

Except for cultural differences and exchange rate volatility, the Asian model resembles the world model. The relative importance of variables is more or less the same and parameters are in the same order of magnitude. Only for per capita income is a stronger emphasis found, and for transport costs the elasticity is higher.

Despite the doubts on the sustainability of the results, there is an inclination to believe that stand-alone strategies prevail in Asia. The clearest indication is given by accepting the market potential hypotheses. Although the significance of other parameters is not strong, this strategy type seems appropriate in view of the marginal size of foreign direct investments in this region.

7.3.4   Investments to North and South America

As was shown earlier, German investors are particularly active in the United States. However, a strong decline was observed in the latter periods included in the analysis. Possibly, German investors have replaced investments in America with investments in Europe in view of the integration process in the latter region.

The observed decline may not fit into complex international production strategies. Maintaining network linkages implies increased investments rather than a decline. Therefore, one may expect the simple affiliate integration strategy type. For North America a strong market orientation seems likely, whereas for South America an input orientation could prevail. Cultural differences, in particular those for Latin America, are expected to be large. They may thus mean a serious barrier to foreign investments. For trade the relation should be complementary. However, markets in America are at some distance from the home country, which, as for Japanese investments in this region, may cause the relation to be substitutory. The strength of the German mark may make the exchange rate direction hypothesis relevant, as it allows German investors to purchase foreign assets relatively cheaply. Exchange rate volatility will cause German investors to refrain from engaging in foreign assets.

Table 7.6 German investments to North and South America

Information:		Countries: 5		
Periods: 7 (1982–86 to 1988–92)		Argentina, Brazil, Canada, Mexico,		
No. of cases: 35 of 35 (100.0%)		United States		
R^2: 0.981	F: 72.884			
R^2 (adjusted): 0.967	DW: 2.296			
Determinant	Definition[a]	Parameter	T-value	β-value
Market size	1	0.308	2.100	0.167
Per capita income	2b	−0.753	−1.377	−0.092
Labour costs	2a	−4.807	−4.263	−0.254
Transport costs	1	−6.954	−7.808	−0.987
Cultural differences	4	−2.046	−1.622	−0.126
Trade intensity	2a	0.987	2.798	0.352
Exchange rate direction	2[b]	0.518	2.517	0.150
Exchange rate volatility	1[b]	−0.573	−1.502	−0.200
Dummy 1983–87		0.146	0.755	0.032
Dummy 1984–88		−0.082	−0.423	−0.018
Dummy 1985–89		−0.232	−1.239	−0.051
Dummy 1986–90		−0.443	−2.357	−0.097
Dummy 1987–91		−0.571	−2.837	−0.126
Dummy 1988–92		−0.705	−3.512	−0.155
Intercept		41.020	4.773	—

Notes
a. For variable definitions, see Appendix IV.
b. Influence limited to South American countries only.

For the exchange rate hypotheses an adaptation had to be made. Intercorrelations with other variables and strange results from other model specifications lead us to consider these hypotheses irrelevant for investments in the United States and Canada. This can be justified by considering that although the exchange rates *vis-à-vis* the US and Canadian dollar alternate, the fluctuations of South American currencies are much larger. Further, convertibility of South American currencies is much lower, which may increase the relevance of exchange rate risk for these countries. Therefore, although it did not solve intercorrelation problems completely, shift dummies were included to limit the influence of both exchange rate variables to South American countries only.

MOSAIC results suggest that Germans are rather more input orientated than market orientated (see Table 7.6). The market size hypothesis is accepted, but reveals an inelastic relationship and contributes modestly to the regression. Possibly, this coincides with the heavy drop in foreign direct investments in the United States. Per capita income is rejected because of a theoretically incorrect parameter, but this could be due to some intercorrelation with transport costs and exchange rate direction. The labour cost hypothesis on the other hand obtains a significant and highly elastic parameter. Its contribution to explaining the model is intermediate and may coincide with strong growth of foreign investments in some manufacturing industries. The relation with trade is complementary given its significant parameter, and it also shows an intermediate influence. German investments encounter barriers from transport costs and cultural differences. In particular, the transport cost barrier contributes strongly to the explanation of investment flows, as its β-value is highest. Its parameter also implies a highly elastic relationship.

The results for the exchange rate hypotheses show that for foreign direct investments in South American countries unconditional exchange rate volatility is indeed a relevant barrier. However, the parameter's significance is not high and its relative importance is intermediate. The exchange rate direction hypothesis is rejected. A significant positive relationship is found, which is theoretically inappropriate. Possibly, this is due to intercorrelation with the per capita income variable.

The parameters of the period dummies reveal a downward trend of growing importance. This may relate to the strong decline in the shares of North and South America in total German foreign direct investments abroad, particularly those for the United States. However, their β-values suggest their influence to be limited.

With a correlation coefficient above 95 per cent, the explanatory power of the regression is high. However, although of limited relevance, some period dummies obtain significant parameters, which indicates that the explanatory variables are not able to fully cover the observed variation in foreign direct investment shares. The Durbin–Watson test may indicate that the estimation is to some extent distorted by negative autocorrelations in the residuals, but the error terms of individual investment relations do not show large covariances with those of other relations. The high value of the intercept is also an indication for the existence of possible misspecifications in the model. Using other variable definitions in model estimations does not bring about any improvement. Apparently, model estimations are seriously hampered by the limited number of observations in the data set.

Many differences exist between this model and the one for German world investments. Market size is less important for America. Per capita income is not accepted here, but plays a dominant role in the world model. Labour costs are more important for investments in America. The same is true for the barrier from transport costs. Cultural differences show a less strong influence here. Regarding trade, the difference is particularly with the parameter's sign. For world investments the relation is substitutory, whereas for America it is complementary. Finally, the influence from exchange rate movements appears to be different. Exchange rate direction is rejected in both models, whereas exchange rate volatility is more important for (South) America.

The model results indicate input-orientated or upstream simple affiliate integration strategies. This is substantiated by the relevance of labour costs, cultural barriers, trade complementarity and, for South America only, exchange rate volatility. Possibly, this type of strategy prevails if investment flows are dominated by those of manufacturing industries (in South America). The market size variable suggests that some market orientation is included in the motives of German investors. This may relate particularly to the large US market. Perhaps, strategies for North America are downstream orientated rather than upstream. As the model results are not very sustainable, the identification of prevailing corporate strategies remains questionable.

7.4 CONCLUSION

On the whole, foreign direct investments coming from Germany show a steady upward movement between 1982 and 1992. In 1987, investment activity abroad encounters a trough. Yet, until 1990, foreign direct investment activity gains momentum again. By 1991, a stagnation causes another drop in foreign investment activity.

Analysing the geographical distribution of German investments throughout the world leads to the conclusion that most investments from Germany are headed for Western Europe. Another important destination region is North America, where the United States plays a dominant role. The importance of South and Southeast Asia (including Japan) and Latin America is very low. Investments elsewhere are even fewer and can be qualified as marginal. Over the years the importance of Western Europe and North America has changed. In the latter part of the 1980s, the share of

European investments, and particularly that of the European Union, has grown considerably, to the detriment of the share of North America.

The sectoral distribution of German foreign direct investment reveals an emphasis on the group of finance, insurance and business service industries. This group constitutes more than a third of total investments abroad. Manufacturing industries, in particular chemical products and electric and electronic equipment, are important, but have a lower share than the above services grouping and this share is declining. For some manufacturing industries, particularly coal and petroleum products, other transport equipment and other manufacturing, investments abroad show strong growth rates. However, on the whole the share of manufacturing industries is falling to the benefit of service industries.

Table 7.7   Summary of determinants for foreign direct investments from Germany

Determinant	World		Europe		Asia		America	
Market size	✓	++	✓	++	✓	++	✓	+
Per capita income	✓	++	✓	+	✓	++	✗	–
Labour costs	✓	–	✗	–	✗	–	✓	+
ROI differences	n.a.	n.a.	✗	–	n.a.	n.a.	n.a.	n.a.
Transport costs	✓	+	✓	++	O	+	✓	++
Cultural differences	✓	+	✓	+	✗	–	O	–
Trade intensity	✗	–	✗	+	✗	–	✓	+
Exchange rate direction	✗	–	✗	–	✗	–	✗[a]	–
Exchange rate volatility	✗	–	✓	+	✗	+	O[a]	+

Note
a. Influence limited to South American countries only.

Legend
✓ significant   ++ strong influence
O weakly significant   + intermediate influence
✗ not significant or theoretically incorrect parameter   – weak influence

The summary of MOSAIC results for the various regions show large differences (Table 7.7). Determinants of European investments are to some extent surprising. For Asia and America, results are questionable in view of marginal investment flows and data limitations.

Market potential is accepted for all regions. In Western Europe, both market potential hypotheses are significant. Market size contributes substantially to explaining investment flows, whereas the influence of per capita income appears to be lower. In South and Southeast Asia, it is the other way around. Per capita income is the most dominant determinant in the model for this region, but market size also contributes substantially. For North and South America the per capita income hypothesis is rejected. This is considered strange, because in North American markets especially, purchasing power is strong and offers a large sales potential.

Cheap labour costs are an important determinant for German foreign direct investments only in North and South America. This indicates that for this region Germans may have input-orientated motives in mind for undertaking investments there. This may apply to investments in Latin America because low labour costs may be less likely in North America. In Western Europe and South and Southeast Asia, labour costs are not very relevant.

German investors encounter barriers from transport costs and, except for Asia, cultural differences. The transport cost barrier is of major importance, especially for investments in Europe and America. The parameters also suggest a high sensitivity. Cultural differences are important, but less so than transport costs. For Europe, the relevance of both barriers may explain why investments go to neighbouring countries which may have a pro-German orientation.

Strongly diverging results are obtained for the trade hypothesis. Within Western Europe the parameter suggests that trade substitution prevails. For South and Southeast Asia this also seems to be the case, but the hypothesis does not obtain an acceptable parameter. For North and South America a significant complementary relation between trade and foreign direct investment is found. The importance of this determinant varies from intermediate for Europe and America to low for Asia.

For the exchange rate hypotheses the picture varies for the volatility hypothesis. Conditional volatility shows up as a barrier for foreign direct investments within Western Europe. This may imply that German investors favour countries that have pegged their currency to the German mark. However, the parameter value suggests a low elasticity and its importance seems intermediate. For investments in America, unconditional volatility is identified as an influential barrier, but its significance is weak. The barrier applies only to investments in South America. The exchange rate direction hypothesis is not accepted in any of the regions.

The results from MOSAIC estimations for German foreign direct investments throughout the world identified downstream simple affiliate integration and stand-alone strategies as the possible prevailing strategy types (see Table 7.8). Accepting the market potential hypotheses and the barriers from transport costs and cultural differences suggested this. The results for individual world regions seem to be consistent with this observation.

Table 7.8   Summary of overall strategies of corporate structures from Germany

Region	Corporate strategy
Western Europe	Stand alone (regional core networking for German-orientated countries?)
South and Southeast Asia	Stand alone
North and South America	Upstream simple affiliate integration (downstream for North America?)

The stand-alone strategy is identified as the main strategy type of German foreign direct investments in Western Europe. This is supported by the hypotheses on market potential and the relevance of trade substitution. Also, the acceptance of cultural differences, transport costs and volatility of the exchange rate as investment barriers give an indication that this strategy type prevails. In particular, transport costs appear to be a large barrier. The relevance of these barriers could indicate that a difference exists between investments in German-orientated countries and those in other countries in Europe. In view of results from other model estimations, it could be the case that regional core networking strategies exist for the former group of countries.

Asian investments from Germany, although limited in size, seem to be led by stand-alone strategies. Apparently, German investors want to benefit from emerging market potentials in the South and Southeast Asian region, as the market potential hypotheses are strongly supported and dominate the explanatory power of the regression.

In North and South America, German companies seem to pursue an upstream simple affiliate integration strategy. Input orientation, represented by the labour cost hypothesis, obtains a significant parameter and the trade relation with foreign direct investments is complementary. Both variables are of intermediate importance in explaining investments to this region. Other indications for this strategy type are the barriers encountered from cultural differences and exchange rate volatility (in South America only). Market potential seems to be a relevant, but not very important determinant. There is an inclination to believe that this points towards a downstream simple affiliate integration strategy for North America in view of the large North American market.

Applying MOSAIC to German foreign direct investment patterns seems to give sustainable results only for world investments and European investments. For Asia, the model is acceptable, but sensitive to the use of other variable specifications. This may be due to the marginal size of investment flows. Investments in America do not seem to be well explained by the model, because of a limited number of observations and marginal flows to South America. Therefore, support for accepting the hypothesis on the existence of spatial differences creating different locational advantages, seems limited. This shows that data problems can seriously harm the estimation of the model.

NOTES

1. This is due to a large investment from France in that year.
2. OECD (1994f, p. 15) identifies Germany as one of the largest investors in Ireland after the United States. Germany's share in total inflows in Ireland rose from 7 per cent in 1983–87 to 10 per cent in 1988–92.

8. Investments from the Netherlands

8.1 INTRODUCTION

This chapter will deal with the investment patterns of foreign direct investments from the Netherlands and the determinants that can explain them by using MOSAIC estimations. The trends in Dutch investments abroad will be presented in the next section. Afterwards, the results from the model estimates will be discussed.

Model estimations for foreign direct investments from the Netherlands proved to be very difficult. One problem was the limited size of the data set. The available geographical breakdowns of Dutch outward foreign direct investments allowed the inclusion of only a small number of countries. Insufficient labour cost data resulted in losing one of these countries (Switzerland) in the estimations.[1] Analyses for South and Southeast Asia and North and South America appeared to be impossible.[2] A second problem, possibly due to the small data set, was that intercorrelations among explanatory variables existed. In particular, the knowledge variables and the taxation differences variable revealed high correlations with other variables and led to their exclusion from the model estimations.[3] This also seemed appropriate in view of comparability with the models estimated for other home countries. However, this did not eliminate all intercorrelations. A third problem appeared to be the necessary transformation into natural logarithms for estimating the model. The log transformation automatically excluded investment relations with negative (five-year average) flows.[4] The parameter estimations for the remaining investment relations gave very unlikely results, again partly due to intercorrelation problems. A solution to this was raising the dependent variable with a constant.[5]

8.2 INVESTMENT PATTERNS

The trend in Dutch investments abroad is upward from some Dfl. 7 billion in 1982 to Dfl. 24.9 billion in 1992 (see also Figure 8.1). However, there are some substantial deviations from this trend.

Between 1982 and 1988, investments abroad fluctuate. In 1983, a minor decrease can be observed, which is a continuation of the slightly downward movement in investments abroad in the previous year. The years 1984 and 1985 indicate a modest increase, whereas for 1986 another minor reduction can be observed. In the next year, 1987, foreign investments nearly double to more than Dfl. 14 billion, but in 1988 the level of foreign investments goes down considerably again and brings it back to slightly above the 1986 level.

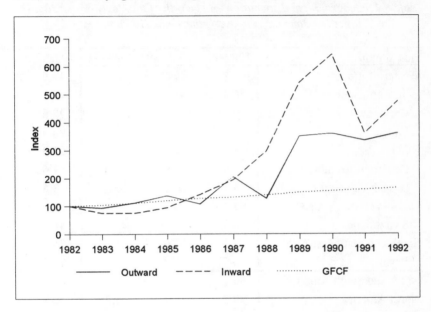

Figure 8.1   Development of foreign direct investment from the Netherlands and gross fixed capital formation (1982 = 100; nominal)

A very strong recovery occurs in 1989, when the level of foreign direct investments from the Netherlands triples to Dfl. 24 billion. According to the Dutch central bank (DNB 1990, pp. 37 and 47), this is probably a reaction to the rather strong increase in Dutch gross domestic product in that year. Also, the economies of other industrialised countries, to which most foreign direct investments are headed, developed favourably. Further, the strong increase in world trade in the previous year may have invoked a lagged investment reaction (DNB 1989, p. 47). The high 1989 level is more or less kept in the subsequent years. This happens despite a declining volume growth in international trade and a reduction in GDP growth.

The developments in foreign direct investments start to deviate from those in domestic investments in the mid-1980s. At the beginning of the 1980s, both outward and inward foreign direct investments show tendencies which are broadly speaking in line with domestic investments. In the latter part of the 1980s, foreign investments grow much stronger than domestic investments. Possibly, the European integration process plays a role here. Inward investments have grown stronger than outward investments, but in 1991 there is a major correction.

Table 8.1   Geographical distribution and growth of total outward foreign direct investments from the Netherlands (1982–92; %)

Host region	1982–86	1985–89	1988–92	1982–92[a]
Western Europe	57.8	49.6	60.6	19.6
European Union (EU12)	56.4	45.5	55.0	18.1
Germany	0.7	5.2	7.0	72.6
France	5.4	5.0	8.1	26.9
Italy	1.5	0.7	1.7	21.0
Belgium/Luxemburg	8.0	9.9	14.9	31.6
United Kingdom	35.1	20.1	15.5	3.5
Other Western Europe	1.3	4.1	5.7	50.7
Switzerland	0.9	2.7	3.3	48.2
South and Southeast Asia	3.3	4.6	4.7	25.5
Japan	0.7	0.5	0.8	21.5
North and South America	36.1	43.0	30.7	15.5
North America	28.8	36.7	26.2	16.8
United States of America	27.9	34.7	23.8	15.6
Latin America	7.3	6.3	4.5	9.4
Other regions	2.8	2.9	3.9	25.4
Central and Eastern Europe	0.0	0.0	1.1	—
Middle East	0.7	0.7	0.3	4.6
Australia and New Zealand	0.9	1.4	1.2	19.2
Africa	1.1	0.6	0.8	13.9
Other	−0.1	0.1	0.5	—
Total	100.0	100.0	100.0	18.6

Note
a. Average nominal growth rate between first and last periods.

Source
DNB.

Table 8.1 shows that two major clusters of host countries can be identified in Dutch foreign direct investments abroad.[6] The first cluster relates to investments made within Western Europe and, in particular, countries of the European Union. The second cluster relates to investments in North America, in particular to the United States.

Table 8.2 Sectoral distribution and growth of total outward foreign direct investments from the Netherlands (1982–92; %)

Industry	1982–86	1985–89	1988–92	1982–92[a]
Agriculture	0.0	0.1	0.0	—
Total manufacturing	60.0	53.7	48.1	10.5
Mining, quarrying, oil and chemistry	47.3	23.6	15.6	–1.9
Metal products and electronics	4.5	13.1	14.4	35.2
Food, beverages and tobacco	4.8	10.4	11.0	27.7
Other manufacturing	3.4	6.7	7.2	36.7
Construction	1.3	0.9	0.6	–2.3
Total commercial services	38.6	45.3	51.3	18.2
Wholesale and retail trade	8.5	10.1	11.9	17.5
Transport, storage and communication	1.3	2.9	3.1	29.6
Banking and insurance	19.2	17.9	17.5	15.3
Other commercial services	9.6	14.4	18.9	20.7
Total	100.0	100.0	100.0	18.6

Note
a. Average nominal growth rate between first and last periods.

Source
DNB.

At first, Dutch foreign direct investments to European countries decline, but during the latter half of the 1980s and at the beginning of the 1990s, shares increase again. Particularly important are investments in the United Kingdom, but this country's share decreases substantially. However, this may be distorted by the existence of two Dutch/British conglomerates (Shell and Unilever). Germany, France and Belgium/Luxemburg, and also Switzerland, are countries which gain substantially in importance. For France, the share is stable at first, but then grows to reach a considerable share by 1988–92. Belgium/Luxemburg shows the same pattern: after a stable share during the pre-1985 years, it grows strongly in subsequent years. Switzerland reveals a relatively small share, but a strong growth rate.

The share of foreign direct investments in the United States increases initially, but in later periods it declines to less than a quarter of the total. This trend was also identified for German investments to this country. Possibly, the European integration process initiated around 1985 may have led to replacing investments in the United States with investments in European Union countries.

Foreign direct investments in other parts of the world show diverging trends. Those in Latin America reveal a decreasing trend, but these investments relate to the Dutch Antilles and Aruba, which are tax havens belonging to the jurisdiction of the Netherlands. Investments in Japan remain below one per cent of the total. For other countries in South and Southeast Asia the trend is upward at first, but stagnant in later periods. As for Germany, foreign direct investments in Central and Eastern Europe seem to have started after the demolition of the Berlin Wall in 1989.

The sectoral distribution of Dutch outward foreign direct investments shows a major emphasis on the mining, quarrying, oil and chemistry industry and on banking and insurance services. The former relates particularly to the large Dutch multinational companies mentioned earlier, which are active in these industries. The latter shows the heavy involvement of Dutch banking and insurance companies in foreign business.

Over the years, a major transition can be noticed. In particular, the large share of investments by multinational companies in the oil and chemistry industries has declined substantially. This is not really due to a decrease of investments abroad by these industries, but rather to an increase in investments abroad by other industries. Most industries in commercial services and the remaining industries in manufacturing show gains in their share of total Dutch foreign direct investments.

8.3 DETERMINANTS

8.3.1 Investments to the World

The data set for foreign direct investment flows from the Netherlands is limited to investments to some European countries plus the United States and Japan. These countries are all strong and well-developed economies, which enable complex international production strategies to be undertaken. Significant parameters for the market potential hypotheses are therefore apparent. In an integrating European market it is likely that Dutch investors seek cheap production locations, integrating their activities within the Netherlands with those abroad into European regional core networks. Therefore, a complementary trade relation and a significant influence of labour costs are expected. Investors may encounter barriers in terms of transport costs. Cultural differences should not be a major barrier, but can be relevant for investments outside Europe, in particular in Japan. Finally, the rather strong Dutch guilder may stimulate Dutch investors to purchase foreign assets, making use of depreciating host currencies towards the guilder. A significant influence of the exchange rate direction hypothesis is therefore likely. Volatility of the exchange rate is expected not to be relevant, at least for Germany, Belgium/Luxemburg and France, as their currencies participate, like the Dutch guilder, in the European Monetary System. For the other countries, the United Kingdom and Italy in Europe and the United States and Japan outside Europe, this may be different, but one may assume that the convertibility of these currencies limits exchange rate risk in the long run.

MOSAIC results (Table 8.3) give some support to the expectations. Dutch investors have indeed a strong market potential orientation in investing abroad.[7] Both the market size and the per capita income hypotheses are accepted. For market size the contribution to the estimation is relatively large, whereas for per capita income the influence is of intermediate importance. However, their elasticities, particularly for market size, reveal a low sensitivity. The labour cost variable also obtains a correct parameter, but its significance is weak and the elasticity is low. This could coincide with the rather strong growth in investments abroad by some manufacturing industries, which may favour cheap labour cost locations. On the other hand, the countries in the data set do not appear to be low labour cost countries. Transport costs are identified as a friction factor which, taking its high β-value into consideration, is highly important. Cultural differences are a barrier of considerable importance and the parameter is highly elastic. The parameter of the trade relation suggests a complementary relationship, but it is insignificant. The exchange rate direction hypothesis is not supported. Exchange rate volatility obtains a significantly positive parameter. This is not in line with the theoretical relationship and suggests an unlikely capital flight motive.

The period dummies may represent the trend in Dutch foreign direct investments abroad. The large leap in 1989 causes the five-year averages to increase over time. This incurred trend may relate to the increasing parameter values over time. However, their β-values suggest a fading influence.

The explanatory power of the model is reasonable. The period-dummy parameters are insignificant or weakly significant, which suggests that the explanatory variables are able to cover the variance adequately. Some concern may follow from the Durbin–Watson test, as it suggests negative autocorrelation in the residuals. In particular, residuals for investments to

Germany, Italy and Japan cause problems. They show rather high covariances among one other. Also, the intercept could raise doubts on the model's results. Further, the model is sensitive to using other variable definitions. Intercorrelations among the market size, per capita income, transport costs and exchange rate volatility variables may cause this. This may be due to the limited number of cases included in the regression. However, other specifications of MOSAIC lead to similar results.

Table 8.3 Dutch investments throughout the world

Information: Periods: 7 (1982–86 to 1988–92) No. of cases: 49 of 49 (100.0%) R^2: 0.832 F: 12.003 R^2 (adjusted): 0.762 DW: 2.321		Countries: 7 Belgium/Luxemburg, France, Germany, Italy, Japan, United Kingdom, United States		
Determinant	Definition[a]	Parameter	T-value	β-value
Market size	1	0.003	4.571	0.722
Per capita income	2b	0.726	1.777	0.233
Labour costs	2c	−0.235	−1.506	−0.127
Transport costs	1	−0.866	−6.908	−0.998
Cultural differences	4	−2.485	−3.883	−0.432
Trade intensity	2c	0.533	1.157	0.188
Exchange rate direction	1	−0.171	−0.934	−0.099
Exchange rate volatility	1	0.849	4.991	0.593
Dummy 1983–87		−0.562	−1.283	−0.152
Dummy 1984–88		−0.904	−1.815	−0.244
Dummy 1985–89		−0.682	−1.273	−0.184
Dummy 1986–90		−0.337	−0.638	−0.091
Dummy 1987–91		−0.026	−0.043	−0.007
Dummy 1988–92		0.243	0.443	0.066
Intercept		5.308	3.147	—

Note
a. For variable definitions, see Appendix IV.

The model results do not really support the existence of complex international production strategies. The strong influence from market size and barriers from transport costs and cultural differences suggest that a stand-alone strategy type seems to prevail. However, although its influence is not large, the complementary trade relation is an indication that downstream simple affiliate integration strategies could exist.

8.3.2 Investments to Western Europe

It was shown that 50 to 60 per cent of Dutch outward foreign direct investment flows are destined to countries in Western Europe. Within this region the countries in the core region of the European Union are the most important host countries.

The expectations regarding determinants of Dutch investments in Europe are, like German investments in this region, largely fed by European integration considerations. The data set analysed here has some similarities with the data set for intra-core investments within the European Union analysed in Chapter 4. Therefore, determinants are expected to support the profile of strategies aiming at regional core networking. Market potential and input orientation should be important determinants for Dutch investors. Cultural barriers may not exist and the relation with trade is likely to be complementary. Possibly, Dutch investors may want to use the strength of the home currency for benefiting from cheap assets in countries with a depreciating currency. Exchange rate volatility seems unlikely here.

The regression results from MOSAIC support most expectations (see Table 8.4). The market potential hypotheses are accepted, but their importance is not very high and their relation with the dependent variable is inelastic. The labour cost hypothesis obtains a positive parameter. This brings the labour quality motive into perspective, but the parameter is insignificant. The transport cost hypothesis is accepted and its β-value identifies it as the most important determinant. Barriers from cultural differences and exchange rate volatility can be considered insignificant. The period-dummy parameters are similar to those for Dutch investments to all countries and thus may reflect the trend in Dutch investments abroad. The results presented here are reasonably consistent with the results obtained for intra-core investments in the European Union (see Chapter 4).

An unexpected result is the significantly negative parameter for the trade variable. With this result the complementary trade hypothesis has to be rejected, which implies that foreign direct investments from the Netherlands have replaced trade from domestic production locations. For European investments from Germany a substitutory relation for trade was found as well, but it was suggested there that substitution could particularly relate to investments in less German-orientated countries. For the Netherlands, a similar suggestion is unlikely. Another explanation may be the strong growth in foreign direct investments made by service industries. The trade-generating effect of service investments abroad may be far less than for manufacturing investments, as intra-firm shipments of products is less apparent in services.[8] However, the variable used suffers from intercorrelation with exchange rate volatility. This may mean that the result presented here is incorrect. Using other variable specifications for either trade or exchange rate volatility did not solve the intercorrelation problem.

Table 8.4 Dutch investments to Western Europe

Information:	Countries: 5		
Periods: 7 (1982–86 to 1988–92)	Belgium/Luxemburg, France,		
No. of cases: 35 of 35 (100.0%)	Germany, Italy, United Kingdom		
R^2: 0.888 F: 10.018			
R^2 (adjusted): 0.799 DW: 2.246			
Determinant	Definition[a]	Parameter	T-value	β-value
---	---	---	---	---
Market size	1	0.003	1.190	0.272
Per capita income	2b	0.861	2.027	0.265
Labour costs	2c	0.121	0.474	0.080
ROI differences	1	0.562	0.902	0.194
Transport costs	1	−1.993	−4.144	−1.344
Cultural differences	4	−1.031	−0.965	−0.158
Trade intensity	2b	−2.074	−2.367	−0.900
Exchange rate direction	1	−0.046	−0.053	−0.007
Exchange rate volatility	2	−0.445	−0.841	−0.294
Dummy 1983–87		−0.615	−1.474	−0.183
Dummy 1984–88		−0.882	−1.921	−0.262
Dummy 1985–89		−0.640	−1.357	−0.190
Dummy 1986–90		−0.480	−0.979	−0.143
Dummy 1987–91		−0.247	−0.490	−0.074
Dummy 1988–92		0.216	0.496	0.064
Intercept		2.993	1.443	—

Note
a. For variable definitions, see Appendix IV.

The model obtains a high correlation coefficient and most period dummies are insignificant. The model is therefore fairly well able to explain the variance in the data set. However, the Durbin–Watson statistic reveals that negative autocorrelations in the residuals could distort the results. This could relate particularly to Dutch foreign direct investments in Germany and Italy, but their covariances with the residuals of other investment relations are low. Other model specifications give no improvement in the regression's quality, but do not qualify the results.

In comparison with the model for world investments – or rather the model for the (core) countries included in the EU model in Chapter 4 plus the United States and Japan – the European model shows more sustainable results. Nevertheless, some parameters can be questioned. In particular, the trade variable parameter raises doubts. It seems that in the world model the large emphasis of the United States and the small flows to Japan cause some distortions in the model estimation.

The corporate strategy which dominates in Dutch investments abroad could be of the regional core networking type, as would be expected in an integrating Europe. This is supported by the acceptance of the market potential hypotheses. Also, the rejection of the cultural differences hypothesis and the exchange rate volatility hypothesis is an indication. However, the substitutory trade parameter argues against this strategy type. In an integrating Europe this implies that economic activities in regional core networks are leaving the Netherlands and are finding better locations elsewhere in Europe without strengthening remaining activities in the network in terms of increased export possibilities.

8.4 CONCLUSION

The overall trend for Dutch investments abroad is upward. However, there are some annual fluctuations. The largest leap is made in 1989, when foreign direct investments abroad nearly triple. Since then, stagnation has set in.

Dutch foreign direct investments concentrate in Western Europe, particularly in the countries of the European Union. Within the Union, the United Kingdom and Belgium/Luxemburg are the most important. Another important destination for Dutch investments abroad is the United States of America. Practically all investments heading for North America are locating in this country.

Looking at the sectoral distribution of foreign direct investment outflows an emphasis is shown for the group of mining, quarrying, oil and chemistry. This is not surprising in view of some large Dutch conglomerates being active in these industries. However, there is a strongly declining trend for this group, which is compensated by strongly growing shares for service industries, in particular wholesale and retail trade, other commercial services, and the remaining manufacturing industries.

Table 8.5   Summary of determinants for foreign direct investments from the
*   Netherlands*

Determinant	World		Europe	
Market size	✓	++	O	+
Per capita income	✓	+	✓	+
Labour costs	O	–	✕	–
ROI differences	n.a.	n.a.	✕	+
Transport costs	✓	++	✓	++
Cultural differences	✓	++	✕	–
Trade intensity	✕	+	✕	++
Exchange rate direction	✕	–	✕	–
Exchange rate volatility	✕	++	✕	+

Legend
✓ significant   ++ strong influence
O weakly significant   +   intermediate influence
✕ not significant or theoretically incorrect parameter   –   weak influence

Dutch investments to the world, or actually to the core region of the European Union plus the United States and Japan, are strongly led by market potential considerations, particularly in terms of market size (see Table 8.5). Cheap labour costs are a determinant, but of low importance. The transport cost barrier is a dominating determinant, which suggests that Dutch investors prefer to invest in the neighbourhood of the home country. However, the large share of US investments implies that this can be compensated by other, more favourable, determinants. Cultural differences seem to bother Dutch investors because they are identified as a significant barrier with a strong influence. The direction of the exchange rate is not relevant and exchange rate volatility is not a barrier to Dutch investors. The significantly positive parameter and the observed strong influence seem to suggest a capital flight motive, which is considered less likely for Dutch investments abroad.

The analysis for West European foreign direct investments from the Netherlands is different from the previous one. Market potential is of intermediate importance. Labour costs do not obtain a significant parameter, but its positive value suggests a labour quality motive instead of a cheap labour motive. Particularly important is the transport cost barrier, whereas other barriers do not seem to be relevant. A major surprise is the significantly negative parameter of the trade variable, which seems to contribute substantially to explaining Dutch investment flows to Europe. The parameter suggests an elastic, substitutory relation between trade and foreign direct investment. However, intercorrelation problems raise doubts about the validity of this parameter.

Table 8.6 Summary of overall strategies of corporate structures from the Netherlands

Region	Corporate strategy
Western Europe	Regional core networking
United States	Stand alone?
Japan	Stand alone?

With some caution, the results could point towards regional core networking strategies of Dutch investors in Western Europe (Table 8.6). Dutch companies are establishing European production networks, because their investments no longer encounter barriers from cultural differences and exchange rate fluctuations and are led by market potentials in other European countries. However, although doubts exist on its validity, the substitutory relation with trade may imply that Dutch corporate structures transfer economic activities in the Netherlands to other parts of Europe where better locational advantages offer a better combination with their ownership advantages. This may not be strange in view of the large share of service industries in investing abroad. Service investments may have a low trade-generating effect.

Strategies of Dutch investors in the United States and Japan can hardly be identified. However, the relative strength of market potential, cultural differences and transport costs in the world model may imply that in these countries, stand-alone strategies could prevail. This may be the case particularly in Japan, where Dutch investments are of a marginal size. If the large share of service industries is taken into consideration again, these strategies may not seem unlikely for the United States either. In the United States, some Dutch companies in banking, insurance and retailing industries have engaged in mergers and acquisitions with similar American companies. These investments may not have triggered intensification of trade relations, as the world model seems to suggest.

MOSAIC's results for Dutch investments abroad seem to support accepting the hypothesis put forward in Chapter 2. Spatial differences in locational advantages exist and allow Dutch investors to combine them with their ownership advantages. However, the results are not very strong. This is caused by the limited size of the data sets.

NOTES

1. This is also the case for the other home countries discussed in previous chapters.
2. Recently, more detailed geographical breakdowns have been published in OECD (1996a).
3. For the small number of host countries included in the data set, in contrast to the analyses made for other home countries in the previous chapters, sufficient knowledge data existed to construct a variable that would not behave as a constant in the model estimations.
4. The natural logarithm of negative figures is not defined.
5. The constant was set equal to one, allowing the dependent variable, the share of an investment relation in total investments, to vary between zero and two.
6. A recent survey among Dutch companies gives a similar picture. See Mensink and Verschoor (1997, p. 317).
7. This is also the conclusion of Mensink and Verschoor (1997, p. 317).
8. Mensink and Verschoor (1997, pp. 316 and 318).

9. Policy Implications

This chapter will discuss the implications of the MOSAIC results for national government policies and international policy-making. First, it will identify a possible policy principle, which could provide a basis for assessing the implications. Second, it will identify the implications for national government policies in countries where complex international production strategies prevail. Then, the same will be done for countries where strategies are less complex. Finally, the implications for international policy-making are dealt with.

9.1 A POLICY PRINCIPLE

For a proper assessment of the policy implications that emanate from the analyses using MOSAIC, it seems appropriate to formulate a general principle for policy-making. This principle allows a view on the policies that home- and host-country governments may pursue *vis-à-vis* internationalisation, corporate networking and foreign direct investment. This view may also apply to international policy-making.

In principle, assuming that market orientation provides the best basis for creating wealth, the allocation of economic activity in geographical space should be based on an optimal combination of market-orientated advantages (in terms of ownership, location and internalisation). These advantages are the result of available endowments in a competitive market environment and can relate to available inputs, market potentials and existing market conditions including any natural barriers. A government is part of this market environment, as it manages and controls its proper functioning. With its policies governments may influence the available endowments without disturbing the market orientation of advantages.

It should be stressed that neither the theoretical framework, nor the tool to test it – MOSAIC – assume advantages to be market orientated. They could very well be based on artificial circumstances created by national or international policies. The theoretical framework allows artificial advantages to be created, for example by creating a trade barrier. The resulting combination of advantages determining an investment location is optimal in view of the theoretical framework, but may be less efficient from a market-orientated perspective. If this is the case, the allocation of economic activities in geographical space is distorted, as it results from an optimal, but inefficient combination of advantages.

Current policy views seem to be consistent with the market orientation assumption.[1] European policies aim at better functioning markets and try to improve the market conditions in backward regions throughout the European Union. National governments appear to introduce more and more market orientation principles in their policies. In development cooperation the improvement of conditions for well-functioning markets and private initiative in developing countries are gaining importance (Michel 1997, pp. 33–5).

National governments have a special interest in the employment situation in their country. An efficient allocation of economic activities in geographical space implies economic activities to be mobile across national borders. This may have consequences for maintaining and improving the employment situation in a country. Therefore, national governments are inclined to pursue policies which stimulate positive effects on employment and curb negative effects. As long as these policies do not disturb a market-orientated allocation of economic activities in geographical space, there seems to be no objection to this. Inevitably, policies have an impact on other countries, which brings policy competition and the need for coordination in international policy-making into perspective.

The above allows the formulation of a general policy principle for both national and international policy-making: policies should be directed towards a market-orientated allocation of economic activities in geographical space. This implies that policies can try to strengthen advantages, but should avoid distorting the market-orientated allocation. This can be done by stimulating domestic companies to invest in creating new ownership advantages, by maintaining a competitive market environment with good quality location conditions and by eliminating (natural and political) barriers to foreign trade, foreign direct investment and other types of internationalisation. Policies to create artificial advantages and barriers to economic interaction should not be pursued.

9.2 NATIONAL GOVERNMENT POLICIES AND COMPLEX INTERNATIONAL PRODUCTION STRATEGIES

Complex international production strategies appear to be possible on foreign direct investment relations, where companies may not encounter (natural and political) barriers, or in which barriers have become of little importance.

Policy Implications

179

One may assume that the resulting allocation of economic activity may be close to a fully market-orientated geographical allocation. Government policies may be such that they do not distort this allocation and thus seem to comply with the above policy principle of strengthening advantages.

This study may give support to the importance of economic integration policies for the strengthening of advantages. For foreign direct investments within the core region of the European Union, the results may suggest that economic integration has reached a level in which foreign direct investments within this region have started to behave like domestic investments. This means that mainly market-orientated endowments determine the advantages and artificial advantages may have become minimal. Further, indications were found that corporate networks in the core region are extending their linkages to periphery countries in the Union. This means that locational advantages in periphery countries become available to core investors, possibly due to current integration processes. Also, the results seem to give evidence that further economic integration, such as establishing an Economic and Monetary Union and improving infrastructure and education and training particularly in the periphery, is important for supporting these network extensions and strengthening existing corporate networks.

However, the results for foreign direct investments from the Netherlands to other countries in the core region of the European Union seem to indicate that economic activities may leave the country. This could mean that activities find better combinations of advantages in those other countries. As a result, a small country in a larger geographical unit could lose employment. For the national government of such a country, this is a challenging situation: it may have to combat political pressures to engage in policies violating the policy principle. This principle requires that the government persists in efforts to strengthen advantages further in non-distortive ways in order to improve the competitiveness of existing activities and to create opportunities for new activities.

The results for American foreign direct investments in Europe and Japanese investments in Europe and Asia show that complex international production strategies can exist when there are more important barriers to economic interaction. This means that corporate networks can develop at lower levels of economic integration and lower levels of host-country development. An explanation could be that in these investment relations, corporate networks have found ways to circumvent barriers by creating appropriate (ownership) advantages. Further, it may be the case that policies are consistent with international treaties regarding the liberalisation of trade and capital (GATT/WTO).

The above results allow the derivation of a policy lesson for national governments. National governments should continue to engage in strengthening market-orientated advantages. This can be done by stimulating knowledge creation and application by companies and developing attractive good-quality location conditions for economic activities. Further, it seems appropriate to engage in economic integration with other countries into larger geographical units.

An interesting application of the above policy lesson is the plea for a quality strategy for social economic policy-making in the medium term by the Social–Economic Council (SER 1996, pp. 143–202) of the Netherlands. SER proposes to pursue policies that aim at improving knowledge and innovation in companies, enhancing education of (future) employees and enriching the living environment. Also, according to SER, policies should be directed towards creating a better physical infrastructure, competitive conditions on product markets and properly functioning capital markets. Further, policies should eliminate rigidities on labour markets, but sustain a moderate development of labour costs in comparison to other countries. In the view of SER, these policies should be pursued within the framework of a sound budgetary policy, in which the use of fiscal incentives is strengthened. With this policy mix, SER envisages an improvement in employment from the establishment of new economic activities and from better competitive positions of existing activities.

A possible danger of policies aimed at improving ownership advantages in a country is that companies may decide to apply these advantages abroad. It may be the case that companies find better combinations of their (new) ownership advantages with locational advantages elsewhere. This implies that the direct employment effect from such policies does not materialise in the home country, but at foreign locations. The only positive employment effect for the home country may then come in an indirect way: the international network to which the (domestic) company belongs may strengthen its competitive position, incurring higher output for both domestic and foreign companies in the network. The question can be raised whether the use of national budgets in such cases is still appropriate. It seems more obvious to use international funds. For example, in the field of technology policy in European countries stimulating technology creation and diffusion in large European corporate structures, it seems more effective for national governments to participate in European technology programmes, rather than to pursue such policies on their own.[2]

The cheap labour cost hypothesis obtained different results in the various estimations of MOSAIC. Intra-EU foreign direct investments and American investments in Europe do not seem to be made in view of a low level of labour costs. Instead, these investments show a positive relation with labour costs, which may suggest that investors favour locations with comparatively expensive labour. Possibly, the quality of the labour force is relevant here.[3]

However, for Japanese investments in Asia, cheap labour was a relevant determinant. Possibly, this has something to do with the type of activities that is transferred. Knowledge-intensive activities may require expensive high-quality labour, whereas knowledge-extensive activities may prefer cheap labour. Also, the state of development of Asian host countries *vis-à-vis* Japan may be an explanation.

The above results imply a careful consideration of cheap labour cost policies when complex international production strategies prevail. If policies aim at creating a favourable environment for knowledge-intensive activities, it may be better to pay more attention to developing labour quality, rather than to lowering labour costs. For other types of activity maintaining a low level of labour costs may be more appropriate.

9.3 NATIONAL GOVERNMENT POLICIES AND LESS COMPLEX STRATEGIES

Less complex strategies appear on investment relations, where there are quite a number of considerable barriers. If these barriers are purely natural, the allocation of economic activities is fully market orientated and can therefore be considered efficient. However, many political barriers may have been created and maintained by national governments for many – and sometimes very legitimate – reasons. This may imply that the resulting allocation of economic activities in geographical space is not in line with a fully market-orientated allocation. In such cases, compliance with the policy principle formulated earlier is low.

Strategies of a less complex nature are generally aimed at using specific local endowments. In simple affiliate integration strategies, corporate structures want to use specific inputs for activities abroad or establish sales outlets for products made elsewhere. The affiliate belongs to the corporate's international network, but does not seem to be fully integrated. In stand-alone strategies, the corporate structure has transplanted or even copied a set of activities into a country for which barriers prohibit other modes of internationalisation. Linkages with the corporate network are weak.

This study may indicate that the allocation of foreign direct investments encounters substantial natural and political barriers. This is based on the identification of less complex international production strategies on many foreign direct investment relations. Investments in South and Southeast Asia from the United States, Germany and the Netherlands seem to be made in view of stand-alone strategies. For North and South America, stand-alone and simple affiliate integration strategies seem to prevail. Hence, the investments may be the result of a combination of advantages that may not be fully market orientated.

The policy lesson which may be derived from the above is that national government policies should try to integrate domestic economic activities into international corporate networks. For this it seems appropriate to aim at developing the potential for existing corporate strategies to move towards complex international production strategies. Again, a market-orientated strengthening of advantages is the obvious road to achieve this. However, priority should be given to the elimination of existing political barriers. And if natural barriers may impede a transition to complex strategies, policies should try to diminish their impact. This may require a long road of policies strengthening advantages.[4]

In this respect, the policy actions to be taken in African countries formulated by the United Nations (1995b, Chapter VI) give a rather complete overview. The United Nations recommends that governments formulate sustainable long-term policy objectives and develop instruments to achieve this. Developing a nation's infrastructure in terms of transportation and telecommunication is considered highly important and may be a first move towards diminishing a strong natural barrier. Also, according to the United Nations, a sufficient legal system and educational facilities should be developed in order to offer foreign activities an appropriate legal environment and labour with suitable skills. Further, the United Nations expresses the need for adequate exchange provisions with no transfer of funds restrictions. Ideally, in its view local currencies should be convertible. In addition, less complex regulations for investment authorization and for production operations are favoured. Finally, the United Nations gives suggestions for improving investment incentive schemes and for marketing a country's locational advantages in the international environment.

Locating foreign direct investments in a country is not a sufficient condition for integrating national economies into international corporate networks. If indigenous activities are not able to create linkages with the foreign affiliate's activity, this affiliate may remain in an isolated position. Many developing countries have been successful in attracting foreign direct investments, particularly in activities for which specific locational advantages were available.[5] Cheap labour, natural resources and interesting market potentials are among these advantages. However, the role of domestic activities as input providers or sales outlets for the foreign affiliate has generally remained limited due to insufficient capabilities of domestic companies. It also seems appropriate to direct policies to improving the capabilities, or ownership advantages, of indigenous firms.[6]

The results of the EU model in this study for intra-EU foreign direct investments by corporate structures from the Union's core region in the

Union's periphery countries indicate that favourable taxation policies may have an influence. This means that taxation policies may be a way to locate economic activities from abroad in a (periphery) country. Because on core-to-periphery investment relations strategies seem to develop towards regional core networking, this may also suggest that favourable taxation policies can be an effective policy instrument for developing corporate strategies. However, the results also show that the importance of favourable taxation is stronger for core-to-periphery investments than for intra-core investment relations where strategies have already achieved the complex international production type. This may mean that when complex international production strategies have become possible, governments should refrain from using favourable taxation.

9.4 INTERNATIONAL POLICY-MAKING

The growing internationalisation raises the question, what is a 'national' company? Multinational companies manage large international corporate networks. These companies can now barely be identified with the nation from which they developed. They do not have a national orientation any more, but their perspective and scope of business has grown into an international or even global one. The activities in their networks have become geographically mobile.

As a result, the position of national governments *vis-à-vis* (multinational) corporate structures has changed (Kline 1995). The geographical scope of national governments is limited to their national economies, whereas the scope of multinationals is international. Corporate structures have become more powerful in evaluating alternative locations in various countries for their activities, or in the words of Doz (1986, p. 226): 'national governments can no longer regulate, but have to negotiate'.

The higher geographical mobility of economic activities may have created policy competition among national governments.[7] They are forced more than ever to maintain the quality of location conditions for existing activities in comparison to those elsewhere and to create more attractive conditions for the settlement of new activities.[8] For this, governments may use many policies.[9] As long as policies comply with the above policy principle, there seems to be no objection to such policy competition. However, violation of the policy principle can occur easily, if political pressures require this. Therefore, it seems appropriate to come to some kind of international arrangement on the way national governments should deal with foreign direct investment.

Multilateral regulation in the field of foreign direct investment is still insufficient despite a myriad of bilateral, plurilateral and multilateral agreements, codes of conduct and conventions.[10] Various countries active in investing abroad, especially OECD countries, have engaged in bilateral agreements with other (non-OECD) countries. These Investment Protection Agreements stipulate basic rules for the treatment of foreign direct investments complying with principles agreed in international fora. There is a possibility that existing (bilateral) international investment agreements have paved the way for the current mosaic of foreign direct investment patterns, but may have blocked investments to other geographical destinations because of differences in rules for different destinations. Hence, this may have distorted the efficient allocation of foreign direct investments in geographical space and may have diverted investments away from developing countries and economies in transition. Current WTO rules, agreed upon in the Uruguay Round Final Act concluded in Marrakesh and in earlier rounds, have already provided the means to curb distortive effects and to settle disputes.[11]

In view of the above, an all-encompassing international agreement which is consistent with the policy principle formulated earlier, is relevant. It is considered beneficial if a general treaty on investments could be arranged within the World Trade Organisation (Huner and Schuurman 1995, p. 1062). According to the United Nations (1996, p. 166), such a treaty should be comprehensive and multilateral and should create a stable, predictable and transparent enabling framework. The scope of the treaty should include the globe as a whole, as business is globalising. It should also encompass trade, since trade and foreign direct investment, as was already suggested in the theoretical framework in this study, are closely intertwined. However, concluding such a treaty is likely to be a long-term issue. It is therefore appropriate to continue with current arrangements and to conclude new agreements in the short term. In this respect, the current negotiations within the OECD to conclude the Multilateral Agreement on Investment seem beneficial.

A point to note in international agreements is the current trend in bloc formation: many countries in geographical regions decide to engage in some kind of integration of their economies. In most cases, these are regional free trade agreements, such as the North American Free Trade Area (NAFTA), the Association of South East Asian Nations (ASEAN), the Asia–Pacific Economic Cooperation (APEC) and the Common Market of South America (the Mercado Común del Sur; MERCOSUR), possibly with some initiatives to come to some integration in other fields (free movement of production factors and policy coordination).[12] These treaties also contain rules on foreign direct investment (WTO 1996, Chapter IV). In other cases, such as the European Union, integration ambitions are much higher and treaties include stricter rules in the field of, among others, investing abroad. This growing bloc formation may result in a dichotomy between countries belonging to integrating economic areas and those which do not. This may cause new barriers for internationalisation, not only in trade, but also in foreign direct investment.

For American and Japanese investments in Europe, this study found indications that the Internal Market programme within the European Union did not cause major barriers. There was little evidence of a Fortress Europe. This may suggest that bloc formation does not necessarily trigger distortive effects on the geographical allocation of economic activities.

However, economic integration may still have a diverting effect on the geographical allocation of foreign direct investments. The economic importance of integrating areas may change, as the results for intra-core investments in the European Union suggest. The results may indicate that the core region in the European Union has become 'one country' for foreign investors established there. MOSAIC results for Japan could imply that a similar view exists among Japanese investors in Europe. These investors may favour investing in the integrating area rather than investing elsewhere. It should be noted that this is consistent with the policy principle, as integration creates new market-orientated advantages.

NOTES

1. Safarian (1991) shows that in the past government policies *vis-à-vis* multinational enterprises were substantially less market orientated.
2. A similar recommendation was based on an analysis of international licensing by multinational enterprises. See Morsink (1992, p. 176).
3. Other research shows that labour availability and labour relations are location factors of stable importance, but that labour quality and skills are a critical factor of increasing importance in location decisions, especially in knowledge-intensive activities. See NEI (1993, p. 108).
4. Campa and Guillén (1996, p. 227) conclude that government policies of political and economic stabilisation, liberalisation and market opening, including accession into the European Union, pursued from the 1960s until now have transformed Spain into a prospering economy and an important participant in foreign direct investments.
5. Lall (1996, p. 440) calls such policies 'passive open door policies'.
6. For example, Shanghai has been very successful in attracting foreign direct investments to its Pudong area, but still encounters problems with the involvement of indigenous activities in the operations of these investments. A strengthening of ownership advantages seems a good way to improve this. See Zou, Morsink and Liu (1996).
7. With a 'multiple principle (many governments) – single agent (one multinational)' model Haaparanta (1996, p. 152) finds that the allocation of foreign direct investment may be affected by subsidy competition.
8. Langille (1996, p. 237) calls this 'regulatory arbitrage'.
9. A historical overview of policies by national governments to regulate inward and outward foreign direct investment is given in Safarian (1993).

10. For an overview of the various regulations in the field of foreign direct investment, see WTO (1996, Chapter IV) and Trebilcock and Howse (1995, Chapter 11).
11. The WTO report (1996, Chapter V) mentions the General Agreement on Trade in Services, the Agreement on Trade-Related aspects of Intellectual Property rights (TRIPs), the Agreement on Trade-Related Investment Measures (TRIMs), the Agreement on Subsidies and Countervailing Measures (ASCM) and the Plurilateral Agreement on Government Procurement.
12. For an overview of existing regional trade arrangements, see Harmsen and Leidy (1994, Appendix I).

10. Evaluation

At the end of this book it seems appropriate to evaluate the aims set and the sustainability of the results obtained. In this study the emphasis lies with the geographical dimension: the question why investments go to one country and not to others. The time dimension, the question why investments to a certain country develop in the way they do, gets less attention. This approach diverts from other analyses of foreign direct investment patterns. It is interesting to consider whether this diverting methodology could give a more consistent view on spatial differences in investment determinants and allow a better understanding of the mosaic of geographical patterns in foreign direct investment.

Regarding the aims of this study, it appears that they have been reached. For various spatial foreign direct investment clusters a set of determinants was derived using MOSAIC, the gravity-type MOdel for Spatial Analysis of Investment Conditions. Further, the study was able to identify some overall corporate strategies prevailing in the various spatial investment clusters from the sets of determinants. Also, it was possible to derive some implications for national and international policy-making.

To some extent the results of the estimations using MOSAIC seem to be consistent with the research of others. For most spatial investment clusters, results did not contradict those of other investigations. However, it should be noted that many of those investigations considered the development of investments on specific foreign direct investment relations (the time dimension) and not the spatial differences in determinants of alternative locations.[1] The use of gravity-type models for the analysis of foreign direct investment patterns has not been very common. This seems logical in view of a considerable number of limitations in using such a model for this purpose.

A first limitation is that model estimations appear to be good when sufficient data are available. For foreign direct investment clusters where data availability was limited, such as for investments from Germany and the Netherlands and for investments destined for countries in North and South America, the model results were doubtful. These are also investment relations, where less advanced corporate strategies were identified. This raises the question whether a good performance of the model estimation automatically coincides with complex international production strategies.

Another limitation is that for some determinants, varying variable definitions have been used. This was necessary to meet with intercorrelation problems, but makes the comparability of determinants for different investment clusters difficult. It may also raise suspicion about an inclination in the analyses to use different definitions just in order to get a proper model fit.

Further, the question can be raised whether MOSAIC contains all relevant determinants. In the analyses of intra-EU foreign direct investments only one ownership advantage was included: the level of technological development as a push factor. In the analyses of investments from the four individual home countries, this advantage had to be left out due to insufficient variation. Alternative variables, such as capital intensity and skilled-labour intensity, may also give a good indication of ownership advantages. Regarding pull factors, other determinants such as the availability of energy and the quality of the environment could be important, next to market potential and labour costs. Also, additional stimulus and friction factors could be included, such as the costs of information transfer. Another question is whether all determinants in MOSAIC have been properly proxied with the variables used. For example, the proxy for transportation costs, straight-line physical distance, is rather coarse and the variables for taxation and cultural differences are measured for a specific time period only. Other variables may give a better representation of these determinants and thus a more appropriate analysis with the model.

In addition to the above question one may wonder if the theoretical framework developed here provides a good basis for MOSAIC. It should be noted that the framework is based on theories developed from a manufacturing perspective. In the analyses, it was shown that most foreign direct investments relate to foreign direct investments in service industries. The implicit assumption that the framework also holds for service activities needs further appraisal.

A problem which needs considerable attention is the way in which geographical clusters are identified. In this study, clusters were derived from geographical distributions. However, due to insufficient data availability a geographical cluster for one home country may contain a set of countries which is different from the same cluster for another home country. As a result, the set of determinants for the same cluster of host countries may already differ from one home country to another for this particular reason.

Another limitation of the results presented here is that they relate to macro-economic foreign direct investment flows. This makes the analyses of a rather general nature and sensitive to their underlying compositions. It is obvious that the set of determinants for mining investments differs considerably from the set for investments in banking. If in one investment cluster mining investments have a large share in the total and if banking dominates in another cluster, the identified investment determinants from the macro-economic flows must be substantially different. However, a consistent use of gravity-type modelling for foreign direct investments at the industry level is still impossible due to insufficient data collection.

Finally, data quality is a limitation for interpreting the results. As is shown in Appendix I, inconsistencies in foreign direct investment data are large despite international agreements on how to register foreign direct investment transactions. Simple calibration techniques, such as in Appendix III, can be used to derive consistent data sets, but they may introduce new distortions.

Despite these limitations, it seems that MOSAIC or other (improved) gravity-type models can be a useful tool for analysing spatial differences in determinants for different clusters of foreign direct investment. In this respect, it would be interesting to develop data sets for foreign direct investment flows within the new European Union of 15 member countries or among the countries belonging to the European Economic Area. Possibly, one may include the transition countries in Central and Eastern Europe in such a data set. Further, the development of a data set for intra-Asia investments may be appropriate, as foreign direct investment by Asian nations other than Japan are increasing rapidly.[2] Such a data set may extend to Australia and New Zealand, as the importance of these countries is rising. In addition, it would be interesting to apply the model on investments at a lower level of geographical aggregation, such as among regions within countries. For example, analysing investment patterns among the states of the United States or those among NUTS regions in the European Union could give insights in the determinants of interregional investments.[3] However, the use of gravity-type models for analysing these investment patterns requires good solutions for the problems of using this tool and proper ways to cope with its limitations. It seems advisable to use this tool in conjunction with other tools of analysis.

Gravity-type models may also be used for other modes of internationalisation. Some such use has already been made in analysing trade patterns. For other modes, such as joint ventures and international strategic alliances, this tool may also be appropriate if sufficient data are available. Comparing the sets of determinants in the different modes may give further insights into the reasons for mode switching in internationalisation and the existence of complementarity among modes in corporate networks.[4]

NOTES

1. Wang and Swain (1995, p. 361) recently used a model with a strong resemblance with MOSAIC in a time-series analysis of foreign direct investments in Hungary and China during 1978–92. However, their analysis was heavily criticised by Mátyás and Körösi (1996).
2. The work of Chen (1993) could provide an interesting basis.
3. NUTS regions are regions geographically demarcated according to the Nomenclature of Territorial Units for Statistics.
4. Recently, Pfaffermayr (1996) has analysed foreign direct investment and trade patterns using a comparable model.

11. Summary

This book considers the phenomenon of internationalisation by analysing the mosaic of macro-economic foreign direct investment patterns in geographical space. It tries to identify the determinants explaining this mosaic using a model specifically developed for this purpose. As different spatial investment clusters are analysed with the model, the study tries to identify differences in the set of determinants for the various spatial clusters. The results of the analyses should be consistent with the results of other studies. This also allows a view on the ability of the model to explain foreign direct investment flows appropriately. From the sets of determinants for the various spatial investment clusters, the study makes an effort to derive the prevailing corporate strategy in macro-economic investment patterns. Different strategies for different geographical regions are identified. The results allow different implications for national and international policy-making to be assessed.

11.1 THEORETICAL FRAMEWORK

Dunning has developed the OLI paradigm in the theory of international production. In this paradigm, a company engages in internationalisation when it can combine its ownership advantages with locational advantages abroad. Ownership advantages emanate from particular endowments owned by the company. Locational advantages relate to the availability of specific endowments at a certain location. If there are internalisation advantages, the combination results in a foreign direct investment. Internalisation is based on strategy considerations. In modern corporate structures combinations of various modes of internationalisation are made, which make these modes complementary rather than substitutory.

Many factors influence the occurrence of combinations of ownership and locational advantages and the internalisation question. New knowledge provides a company with new ownership advantages, which can also be exploited in foreign locations. Processes of economic integration erase (political) barriers and bring new locational advantages into perspective. Within regions, synergies arise when production and consumption concentrate. These synergies add to the ownership advantages of companies located in the region and may create new locational advantages for foreign companies. As a result, new possibilities for combining ownership and locational advantages may appear, and new internalisation advantages for these combinations may lead to more foreign direct investments.

The above developments have created possibilities for establishing networks of interlinked economic activities. Each economic activity can locate in such a way that an optimal combination of ownership and locational advantages exists. In this way, the economic activity contributes to the competitive position of a complete international production system. The strength of one economic activity improves the strength of other economic activities, or, networking creates ownership advantages for economic activities and contributes to locational advantages. Further, it may change internalisation advantages.

The way in which advantages are used depends on a corporate's strategy. Three types of corporate strategy are identified. Stand-alone strategies prevail if many barriers to economic interaction exist, but the market is attractive enough to locate subsidiaries there. However, the subsidiary is unlikely to be part of the corporate structure's international network of activities. It will reap the benefits of a profitable local market by manufacturing and selling products locally. Simple affiliate integration strategies prevail when companies want to use specific local endowments. These can relate to input production (upstream) or to local sales potentials (downstream). The affiliate contributes to the structure's network of activities by providing cheap inputs or a profitable sales outlet, but is not fully integrated into the network because of existing barriers. When the affiliate no longer encounters barriers in its interactions with other activities in the corporate structure, one may speak of complex international production strategies. In the latter type of strategies networking is most developed.

11.2   METHODOLOGY

The above theoretical framework needs to be tested. Therefore, the hypothesis is put forward that different countries offer different opportunities for internalising optimal combinations of ownership and locational advantages in foreign direct investment. To test this hypothesis, MOSAIC is developed: the MOdel for Spatial Analysis of Investment Conditions. This model is of the gravity type and contains a set of potential determinants for explaining the geographical distribution of foreign direct investment flows:

1. push factors:
   - knowledge transfer: companies want to use their knowledge, or in Dunning's terminology ownership advantages, in foreign locations;
2. pull factors:
   - market potential: the volume of potential customers in a market (market size) and the purchasing power of potential customers in a market (per capita income);
   - labour costs: the availability of cheap inputs, in particular labour, to foreign investors;
3. stimulus and friction factors:
   - return on investment differences: based on the traditional portfolio selection theory, investments are made when higher profits can be realised abroad;
   - taxation differences: the role of taxation policies, proxied by the after-tax return on investment;
   - transport costs: the geographical distance between home and host country as a proxy for transaction costs between parent company and a foreign subsidiary;
   - cultural differences: barriers from language and differences in customs and personal relations;
   - trade intensity: the relation between trade and investments indicating a complementary or substitutory relationship and, if relevant, trade barriers;
   - exchange rates: the barrier or stimulus caused by the direction in which changes in the mutual exchange rate move (exchange rate direction) and the risk caused by the fluctuations in the mutual exchange rate (exchange rate volatility).

MOSAIC is transformed into a 'generalized linear regression model' in which cross-section data for investment relations are pooled over different time periods. In order to diminish large annual fluctuations in the dependent variable, the cross-section data are converted into five-year moving averages. Pooling is necessary in order to circumvent problems regarding the degrees of freedom in cross-section analyses for individual time periods. Dummies for the time periods are added for reducing covariance problems in the residuals.

Estimation of MOSAIC is done for various (pooled) data sets. These data sets consist of the geographical distribution of investment flows and the explanatory variables representing the investment determinants. Data problems regarding explanatory variables of some host countries, particularly in Asia and Latin America, require a flexible approach in estimating the model. The results of the estimations are compared with those of other studies. This comparison allows a conclusion to be drawn on the robustness of the model for identifying determinants for geographical investment patterns.

In order to derive prevailing corporate strategies, the results of the model estimations are compared with the profiles of three corporate strategy types. In these profiles the relevance of the above investment determinants is indicated. In stand-alone strategies market orientation and barriers from cultural differences and exchange rates are strong and investment replaces trade. In simple affiliate integration strategies the trade intensity indicates a complementary relationship, but barriers in terms of cultural differences and exchange rates continue to prevail. Investors seek either an interesting market potential (downstream) or a specific locationally available input (upstream). In complex international production strategies barriers no longer influence investment patterns considerably and the investments are made in view of a combination of market potentials and available inputs. If such strategies relate to a specific geographical region one may speak of regional core networking strategies. If the model estimation results are consistent with any of the three strategy profiles, one may conclude that the corresponding corporate strategy type prevails. As the three strategy types differ in terms of the extent of networking, this may also indicate the level of integration of economic activities in a geographical region in international corporate networks.

Identification of policy implications is made by an assessment of the results of the analyses in this study and their consequences for government policies in home and host countries and for policy initiatives by international institutions. The results on investment determinants and the prevailing strategies that emanate from these results may provide footholds for policies to integrate economic activities within countries into international networks of activity. These footholds differ for the various strategy types.

11.3   GEOGRAPHICAL DISTRIBUTIONS OF FOREIGN DIRECT INVESTMENT FLOWS

The geographical distributions of foreign direct investment flows that are analysed using MOSAIC relate to foreign direct investment patterns within the European Union and to outward world foreign direct investments from four individual home countries. For the geographical distribution of investments throughout the European Union a distinction is made between core and periphery countries. Core countries are countries with high levels of outward and inward intra-EU foreign direct investments, whereas periphery countries have, in comparison to core countries, low levels. The four home countries that are considered, are: the United States, Japan, Germany and the Netherlands.

Table 11.1   *Geographical distribution and growth of interregional and intra-regional foreign direct investments within the EU (1980–92; %)*

Investment relation	1980–84	1984–88	1988–92	1980–92[a]
Core to core	77.2	80.0	71.3	30.2
Core to periphery	19.8	15.8	22.2	33.3
Periphery to core	2.7	3.6	5.0	42.2
Periphery to periphery	0.4	0.6	1.5	55.7

Note
a.   Average annual nominal growth rate.

Source
Appendix III.

   Within the European Union foreign direct investments concentrate in the core region (see Table 11.1). However, investors from the core show an increasing interest in investments in the periphery of the Union. Investments from periphery countries grow most strongly, but their size remains marginal. Germany, France, the Netherlands and the United Kingdom are most active in investing abroad. When looking at inward investment flows, Belgium/Luxemburg and France are important, but over the years they lose their position to the United Kingdom, Germany and Spain.
   Investments from the United States cluster mainly in Western Europe and North and South America (see Table 11.2). In Europe, the United Kingdom is the most important host country, whereas in America, investments go to Canada, Mexico and Brazil. Canada and Mexico may be important in view of the establishment of the NAFTA agreement. South and Southeast Asia is of minor importance to US investors.
   The most important host region for Japanese investments is North and South America. Within this region, the United States is by far the most important host country: more than half of Japanese world investments go to this country. The share of Latin-American countries has declined substantially over the years. Western Europe ranks second. The share of this region in the total has grown over the years to about a fifth. This could coincide with the creation of the Internal Market and Japanese investors' fear of a 'Fortress Europe'. South and Southeast Asia appears to be less important in relative terms as its share in the total is lower than Europe's and remains stable over the years. The growing share of the group of other

regions coincides with growing investment activity in Australia and New Zealand.

Table 11.2   Geographical distribution and growth of world foreign direct investments from four home countries (1982–92; %)

Investment relation	1982–86	1985–89	1988–92	1982–92[a]
From the USA to:				
Western Europe	58.3	50.1	47.2	16.3
South and Southeast Asia	15.2	6.9	10.6	13.3
North and South America	20.5	41.2	37.3	33.2
Other regions	6.0	2.0	5.0	16.7
From Japan to:				
Western Europe	15.1	19.5	21.9	34.3
South and Southeast Asia	14.2	12.3	13.4	25.2
North and South America	63.0	61.1	55.9	23.9
Other regions	7.6	7.1	9.0	29.6
From Germany to:				
Western Europe	42.9	48.0	69.7	25.4
South and Southeast Asia	3.1	2.7	3.0	14.9
North and South America	50.9	46.9	23.5	1.6
Other regions	3.2	2.6	3.8	19.5
From the Netherlands to:				
Western Europe	50.1	39.1	55.5	20.0
South and Southeast Asia	3.4	4.0	4.4	22.8
North and South America	35.9	42.9	29.8	14.0
Other regions	5.1	8.9	2.7	6.4

Note
a. Average annual nominal growth rate.

Source
OECD.

German investors show an increasing interest for countries in Western Europe. This coincides with the Internal Market programme. Another important destination is, as for Japanese investors, the United States. However, the share of investments to this country in total German investments abroad has declined substantially, particularly in the latter half of the 1980s. Investments in South and Southeast Asia are of marginal size, but growing. The same is true for the group of other regions, which is particularly due to increasing investments in Central and Eastern Europe at the beginning of the 1990s. Possibly, these trends indicate that German investors have been replacing their investments in North and South America with those in Western (and Eastern) Europe in order to reap the benefits of (future) European integration.

Dutch corporate structures invest particularly in the United Kingdom, Belgium/Luxemburg and the United States. For the latter country, a considerable decline in the share can be noticed. Investments in Germany are also important, but as for the United States its share decreases substantially over the years. Investments in Asia are, like German investments in this region, marginal, but growing.

11.4 MOSAIC AND INTRA-EU FOREIGN DIRECT INVESTMENTS

Table 11.3 summarizes the overall strategy profiles that are identified for the four main investment relations: intra-core, core-to-periphery, periphery-to-core and intra-periphery investments.

Table 11.3   Summary of corporate strategies within the European Union

To → ↓ From	Core countries	Periphery countries
Core countries	Regional core networking	Downstream simple affiliate integration moving to regional core networking
Periphery countries	Portfolio ?	Portfolio ?

Intra-core investments are not modelled very well using MOSAIC. The estimations suggest that market size, per capita income and cultural differences are not relevant. There is an inclination to believe that this is the result of economic integration processes such as the Internal Market programme. Spatial differences within the core region may have become minor, rendering these determinants less suitable. Instead, investors may consider the corresponding variables for the core region as a whole more appropriate and not the spatial differences among core countries. For labour costs a significantly positive parameter is found. This may suggest that investors prefer locations with more expensive, high-quality labour rather than locations where cheap labour is available. This could coincide with the large share of investments in service industries. Regarding exchange rate movements, the estimation results suggest that the influence of exchange rate risk has disappeared, possibly as a result of exchange rate policies such as the European Monetary System. In view of the above, there is an inclination to accept that regional core networking strategies prevail within the core region of the Union. The results may even indicate that intra-core foreign direct investments have started to behave like domestic investments.

MOSAIC's results for core-to-periphery investments suggest that there is a strong relation with market size. Investors still encounter barriers from cultural differences and transport costs. The barrier from exchange rate volatility is relevant for the beginning of the 1980s, but in later years it seems to have disappeared. This may explain the growth in the share of core-to-periphery investments in the EU total since the mid-1980s. A possible stimulus factor may come from beneficial taxation policies in periphery countries regarding inward foreign direct investment. Further, for labour costs again a significantly positive parameter is found, implying that labour quality is a relevant determinant. All in all, these results seem to suggest that in view of the strong emphasis on market size, downstream simple affiliate integration strategies prevail. However, the elimination of exchange rate risk as a relevant determinant may indicate a transition towards regional core networking in which core investors extend their networks from the core region to the periphery.

For investments made by companies from periphery countries, the results from the MOSAIC estimations are indeterminate. The limited size of investment flows and the incidental nature of investments on some of the investment relations hamper model estimation considerably. If the obtained results can be interpreted at all, it may be the case that portfolio-orientated strategies prevail. An indication for such strategies is that there seems to be a consistently positive relation between investments and exchange rate volatility. Possibly, this means that periphery investors want to hedge the value of their investment capital. Favourable taxation may be another (portfolio-orientated) reason for them to invest in other periphery countries. However, it should be stressed that the results obtained for periphery investments should be interpreted very carefully.

In general, the results of the MOSAIC estimations support acceptance of the hypothesis that different countries give different opportunities for internalising optimal combinations of ownership and locational advantages in foreign direct investment. This is particularly the case for investors from the core region of the European Union. They constitute the bulk of intra-EU investments. For those from periphery countries, the model is less able to support the hypothesis.

11.5 MOSAIC AND OUTWARD FOREIGN DIRECT INVESTMENTS FROM FOUR HOME COUNTRIES

MOSAIC estimations for investment relations to the geographical clusters of host countries identified earlier gave different views on the prevailing strategies. Table 11.4 summarises the conclusions drawn.

Table 11.4   Summary of overall strategies of corporate structures from four home countries in some world regions

To → ↓ From	Western Europe	South and Southeast Asia	North and South America
United States	Regional core networking	Stand alone	Stand alone (regional core networking for NAFTA countries?)
Japan	Regional core networking	Regional core networking	Simple affiliate integration (trade substituting regional core networking in North America?; stand alone in South America?)
Germany	Stand alone (regional core networking for German-orientated countries?)	Stand alone	Upstream simple affiliate integration (downstream for North America?)
Netherlands	Regional core networking	Stand alone?	Stand alone?

Investments from the United States are motivated by various determinants. Market potential is an important determinant, particularly in terms of market size. For Europe, barriers from exchange rate movements and cultural differences seem to be absent and the relation with trade is complementary. This supports the regional core networking strategy for US–European investments. A significant positive parameter for labour costs may indicate that American investors are inclined to search for investment locations with good-quality, and thus more expensive, labour. For investments in Asia, a substitutory relation with trade is found, which implies substitution of home-country production. Barriers arise from cultural differences and exchange rate volatility on investment relations to Asia and America. These are indications for the stand-alone strategy type for these regions. Regarding investments in NAFTA countries (Canada and Mexico) it could be the case that regional core networking strategies exist, as the barriers from cultural differences and exchange rate volatility apply particularly to South American countries.

For Japanese investments both the market potential hypotheses and the labour cost hypothesis are accepted for all investment regions. This suggests that Japanese investors have both market orientations and input orientations. However, for Europe the labour cost parameter is insignificant. Transport costs seem to stimulate investments abroad, as a consistently positive parameter is found for all investment relations. This leads to rejecting the transport costs hypothesis, but it could imply that Japanese investors favour the foreign direct investment mode above other modes of inter-nationalisation. For investments in Europe, the regional core networking strategy is particularly supported by the complementary trade relation and the irrelevance of exchange rate movements. The existence of cultural differences is considered a counter indication. The regional core networking strategies in Asia are supported by the relevance of market potential and labour costs. Further, the complementary trade relation is an indication. There seems to be an influence from barriers from cultural differences and exchange rate volatility, but it is outnumbered by influences from trade intensity and market potential. Investments in North and South America may coincide with simple affiliate integration strategies, as exchange rate volatility is a significant and important barrier. A substitutory trade relation may coincide with trade barriers from voluntary export restraints and local content requirements for the United States, as most investments are destined for this country. There is an inclination to believe that Japanese investors transplant their corporate structures (including input providers) to the US market in order to circumvent these barriers. The resulting American core network is controlled from headquarters in Japan. In South America stand-alone strategies may be more appropriate in view of the relevance of cheap labour costs and the exchange rate volatility barrier.

The stand-alone strategies of investments by German corporate structures in Europe are supported by the significantly negative parameter found for the trade intensity hypothesis and acceptance of the market potential hypotheses and those on exchange rate volatility and cultural differences. The latter could mean that German investors favour investments in German-orientated countries. Possibly, German corporate structures develop regional core networks with this group of countries. In North and South America the identification of upstream simple affiliate integration strategies is based on the indication that cheap labour is a determinant of intermediate influence and on the complementary relation with trade. However, as market size is also identified as a relevant determinant and cheap labour is less likely in North America, simple affiliate integration strategies may be of the downstream type in the latter region. In Asia, accepting the market orientation hypotheses in view of the very limited size of investments in this region supports the identification of the stand-alone strategy type.

Dutch corporate bodies may develop West European core networks in view of the absence of cultural barriers and of exchange rate volatility barriers. However, it has to be taken into account that most investments are made in Europe's core region for which such barriers may not exist any more. For other investment relations these barriers may still prevail. A concern may be that a substitutory relation with trade is found, which implies that investments abroad coincide with diminishing trade to and from the Netherlands. Possibly, investments may relate to industries, where trade activities are less obvious. In this respect, a connection may exist with the large share of investments abroad by service industries. For the United States and Japan, Dutch investors may follow a stand-alone strategy in view of the importance of market orientation in the MOSAIC results for Dutch world investments. However, the prevailing strategy type for these particular investment relations could not be identified using MOSAIC.

As for intra-EU investments, the results for world investment flows support the hypothesis that different countries offer different opportunities for foreign direct investment. Various locational advantages may explain the occurrence of foreign investments. Locational advantages vary from one region to another. Corporate structures are led by different strategies to combine these advantages with their ownership advantages.

11.6 POLICY IMPLICATIONS

The policy implications of this study are assessed by putting forward a general policy principle. This principle is that the allocation of economic activity in geographical space should be based on market-orientated advantages in a competitive market environment. As long as government policies do not interfere with the market orientation, they may contribute to the endowments that determine sets of advantages.

When complex international production strategies prevail, it seems likely that government policies are generally in line with the policy principle. Barriers may still exist, but they do not appear to disturb a market-orientated allocation of economic activities in geographical space. Policies should engage in a further strengthening of advantages by stimulating knowledge creation and application with indigenous companies (ownership advantages), offering good location conditions for existing and new economic activities (locational advantages), integrating the domestic market into larger geographical entities and diminishing existing (natural) barriers. Policies aiming at cheap labour costs and favourable taxation appear to be less effective.

When less complex strategies prevail, government policies may have caused an allocation of economic activities in geographical space, which may not be fully market orientated. This is the case when political barriers influence the set of advantages on which the allocation is based. In order to enable more advanced corporate strategies, it seems appropriate for national governments to eliminate political barriers in the long run. As long as they are temporary and are abolished when international networking is achieved, it may be legitimate to use these political barriers in the transition to more complex corporate strategies (such as favourable taxation). When complex international production strategies have become possible, governments should engage in policies to strengthen advantages further as described above.

It could be the case that less complex strategies prevail and the allocation of economic activities is fully market orientated. This occurs when only natural barriers exist and prevent strategies from developing into complex international production. In this case, government policies should not only engage in strengthening market-orientated advantages further, but also in diminishing the impact of natural barriers.

For international policy-making the above policy principle also applies. In this respect, three elements are important. The first element relates to political pressures. Political pressures may force national governments to engage in policies that may not comply with the policy principle. This may cause onerous policy competition among governments. The second element, an international agreement on foreign direct investments, may create a good framework for curbing onerous policy competition. This agreement should replace the current practice of bilateral, plurilateral and multilateral regulations, which in itself may cause political barriers. The third element, which should be taken into account in drafting an international agreement, is bloc formation. Currently, in many geographical regions regional free trade agreements are concluded with all kinds of regulations on dealing with foreign direct investment. Although integration of countries in larger geographical units is necessary, there could be a basis for creating new political barriers between countries signatory to such agreements and those which are not and between countries belonging to different trade blocs.

11.7   EVALUATION

It seems that the study was able to achieve the aims set at the beginning. It appeared to be possible to identify investment determinants for different investment clusters using MOSAIC, the model specifically developed for this purpose. It also turned out to be possible to derive some general corporate strategies from these determinants and to formulate some policy implications.

However, many limitations and data problems must be taken into account when interpreting the results obtained using MOSAIC. As far as studies were found that analyse similar investment patterns, the results obtained here generally seem to be consistent with the results of those studies. This suggests that gravity-type models such as MOSAIC can be an interesting tool of analysis used in conjunction with other tools provided that its limitations are taken into account and solutions can be found for its problems.

Appendix I. Difficulties with Foreign Direct Investment Data

Considerable difficulties exist in measuring foreign direct investment flows. The definition specified by the IMF states that foreign direct investment refers to 'investment that is made to acquire a lasting interest in an enterprise operating in an economy other than that of the investor, the investor's purpose being to have an effective voice in the management of the enterprise'.[1] This definition is unclear in various ways:

- it does not specify what to do with reinvested profits (undistributed earnings). Although the IMF manual elsewhere stipulates inclusion in foreign direct investment figures, some countries do not do this;
- it does not specify what is considered an 'effective voice'. Countries therefore use varying criteria: Germany uses 25 per cent of stock ownership as a threshold; the United States uses 10 per cent;[2]
- it does not specify how to classify investments by type of industry. Countries use various classifications based on their own practices. This could lead to serious differences in the case of inter-industry investments, that is, a company operating in one type of industry taking over another company active in another. Some countries classify this foreign direct investment in the industry in which the parent company is active; other countries in the industry where the company that is taken over operates;
- it does not specify when an investment is a foreign direct investment. Some countries consider an investment to be foreign only when it is approved or authorized by the relevant authorities.

There are also a number of practical problems when measuring foreign direct investment. One involves the question of what foreign direct investment actually is. Is it only the financial transfer of funds which is measured on the balance of payments or is it the total capital needed for the foreign establishment irrespective of the fund's origin? According to Gilman (1981) there are three ways to finance foreign direct investment: home-currency sources, foreign-currency borrowing, and foreign-generated cash flows of foreign affiliates.[3] Only the transfer of home-currency sources is registered directly on the balance of payments. A second problem is the moment of registration in statistics. A declaring country may register a specific foreign direct investment transaction in one year, whereas the receiving country may register it in the next year. Another practical problem is the 'nationality' of an investment. A multinational company can no longer be identified with a particular nation just because its headquarters is located there. Hence, is an investment made by a German subsidiary of a Dutch multinational in another country, an investment originating from Germany or from the Netherlands?

The OECD through its Committee on International Investment and Multinational Enterprises has made an effort to deal with some of the major problems by expanding on the IMF definition.[4] The Committee has developed the following Detailed Benchmark Definition of Foreign Direct Investment: 'a foreign direct investment enterprise is one in which a single foreign investor either controls 10 per cent or more of the ordinary shares or voting power of an incorporated enterprise or the equivalent of an unincorporated enterprise, or controls less than 10 per cent (or none) of the ordinary shares or voting power of the enterprise but has an effective voice in the management of the enterprise'.

Some deviations on the OECD definition exist. The definition stipulates that an investment is considered to be a foreign direct investment when a firm holds 10 per cent or more of the voting stock. However, if it can be shown that the firm exerts control holding less than 10 per cent of total voting stock, the investment is also classified as foreign direct investment. Similarly, in the case of a firm holding more than 10 per cent without exerting control, the investment is considered to be a portfolio investment.[5]

The OECD also recommends the inclusion of all intra-firm debt and equity flows and the parent's share in the affiliates' retained earnings in balance of payments statistics. To consider the latter as a capital flow is somewhat paradoxical: it is recorded as capital earnings 'paid' by the affiliate to the parent on the current account and immediately 'transferred' from the parent to the affiliate as invested capital on the capital account.

Nieuwkerk and Sparling (1985, Appendix B) give arguments both in favour of and against inclusion of retained earnings in the balance of payments. Arguments in favour basically relate to the ability to establish the actual level of foreign involvement and the return on investment. Arguments against inclusion relate to the relevance of retained earnings for a national economy. These earnings in fact add to national savings and national income.

In view of the above, it is no surprise that statistics on foreign direct investments show large asymmetries. Comparability among countries, let alone industries, is low. This implies that the results of analyses using these statistics need to be interpreted very carefully. However, if it can be assumed that inconsistencies in data collection are 'consistently' made, then the analyses may still be able to identify major trends and relationships.

NOTES

1.   EUROSTAT (1992) refers in its methodological annexe to the *Balance of Payments Manual*, 4th Edition, International Monetary Fund, 1977, Chapter 18, paragraph 408.
2.   Reference to the American threshold value is made in Scholl (various issues).
3.   See also Crone and Overbeek (1981), who mention domestic funds (the actual transfer of money by the investor), funds borrowed on local or international capital markets, and reinvested profits and depreciations.
4.   For the complete OECD definition, see EUROSTAT (1992), Methodological annexe.
5.   Hymer (1976) has stressed the importance of the difference between the extent of control and the legal ownership. A majority ownership can go together with a minimum of interference in management from the parent company; on the other hand a non-equity agreement could go together with severe restrictions on the firm's operations.

Appendix II. History of Gravity Modelling

Gravity modelling has its origin in physical science. In 1687, Sir Isaac Newton formulated the law of universal gravitation: two bodies in the universe attract each other in proportion to the product of their masses and inversely with the square of their distance (Haggett 1979, p.437). In the 18th century, according to Fernández (1991), Charles Coulomb presented a similar law of gravitation: the force between two electrical charges is proportional to the product of the charges and inversely proportional to the square of the distance between them.

Carrothers (1956) presents an overview on the developments in using the gravity model for non-physical phenomena. He claims that in social sciences the idea of gravitation has probably first been used by Carey (1858–59) in his book *Principles of Social Science*. Carey considered human interaction to be based on the fundamental law of gravitation, as the greater the number (of people) collected in a given space, the greater is the attractive force exerted. Gravitation is the direct ratio of the mass and the inverse one of distance. In 1885, according to Carrothers, the British demographer Ravenstein used gravitational concepts for the explanation of flows of migrants between cities. These flows appeared to be directly related to the size of the cities involved and inversely proportional to the distance separating them. Other applications followed in the 1920s when Young tried to explain migration and when Reilly formulated his law of retail gravitation, in which a city attracted retail trade from individuals located in its surrounding territory. In the early 1930s, a sociological application was made by Bossard who found an inverse relationship between concluded marriages and the distance between the former residences of the involved partners.

For an initial specification of the model, Carrothers mentions Stewart and Zipf. In the early 1940s, they formulated the gravity concept into a basic 'energy of interaction' equation:

$$E_{ij} = k \cdot \frac{P_i \cdot P_j}{D_{ij}}. \tag{AII.1}$$

where:

E_{ij} = energy of interaction between centres i and j;
P = population of centres i and j;
D_{ij} = distance of interaction between centres i and j;
k = a constant of proportionality, equivalent to the gravitational constant of physics.

Carrothers signals modifications to the basic equation in later years. Various authors suggested that the impact of distance is not uniform, as it depends on time and costs of traversing the physical distance (effective or economic distance), and thus introduced functions of distance into the denominator. For example, an exponent α was added to the distance variable (D_{ij}^{α}). Other authors suggested modifications to the population factor in order to take into account gender, income, education and so on. This led to introducing population functions into the numerator, in which weighing factors and exponents became popular. Some authors even replaced the population variable with other variables. Carrothers mentions Isard and Freutel, who introduced the income potential measured by national or regional income, and Harris who included a measure of market potential.

In the early 1960s, gravitation models were developed for analysing international trade flows. Tinbergen and Pöyhönen were among the first to present such models. Although their models are very similar, they developed them completely independently.[1] Tinbergen's model is as follows (Tinbergen 1962, pp. 262–6):

$$E_{ij} = \alpha_0 \cdot Y_i^{\alpha_1} \cdot Y_j^{\alpha_2} \cdot D_{ij}^{\alpha_3}. \tag{AII.2}$$

where:

E = exports;
Y = gross national product;
D = distance;
i = home country;
j = host country.

Tinbergen presented a simple model in which the volume of trade between any two countries is determined by gross national product (GNP) in the home country, GNP in the host country and the geographic distance between their main economic centres. GNP of the home country represented its economic size as a supplier and could thus be interpreted as a proxy for production costs. GNP of the host country represented the size of its market demand. This made this variable a proxy for market potential. Geographic distance was a proxy for transportation costs or broader, transaction costs. Pöyhönen used similar variables.[2]

More specific determinants have been included by Linnemann (1966, pp. 34–6), who built on the model of Tinbergen. For the home country he identified factors indicating its total potential supply to the world market, such as national product, population size and per capita income. These factors could be seen as determinants of production costs. For the host country these factors indicated its total potential demand on the world market. Hence, these were determinants of a country's market potential. Finally, he attempted to find factors representing the 'resistance' to a trade flow from potential supplier to potential buyer. Such factors were impediments because of transport costs, transport time, psychological distance and cultural differences. Such factors might represent transaction costs. The following model was presented:

$$X_{ij} = \delta_0 \cdot Y_i^{\delta_1} \cdot N_i^{-\delta_2} \cdot Y_j^{\delta_3} \cdot N_j^{-\delta_4} \cdot D_{ij}^{-\delta_5} \cdot P_{ij}^{\delta_6}.$$
(AII.3)

where:

X = trade volume;
Y = national income;
N = population size;
D = distance;
P = trade preference;
i = home country;
j = host country.

Although Tinbergen, Pöyhönen and Linnemann developed the specification of the gravity model, their theoretical substantiation was not strong. Apparently, Carey's perception that human interaction is based on the fundamental law of gravitation from physical science, continued to be a sufficient basis for application in social sciences and legitimated (social) indicators to replace the physical variables in this law (Carrothers 1956, p. 94).

Anderson (1979) provided a more fundamental theoretical explanation when he developed a gravity-type model for the occurrence of commodity flows. His theoretical explanation is based on the properties of expenditure systems: a set of N countries among which tradables are supplied by manufacturers and demanded by consumers. Equilibrium in all expenditure systems implies that trade between two countries is determined by the shares of tradable goods in total income, the host country's population and a transit cost factor representing any barriers to trade and transport. This transit cost factor increases with distance.

Bergstrand (1985) extends on Anderson's idea of expenditure systems by developing a general equilibrium model for world trade. This model describes a world of N countries (markets). In each country a homogeneous good X is manufactured and consumed. Consumers purchase the good from outlets in both the domestic and foreign markets. Manufacturers provide the good to these outlets, again in both the domestic and foreign markets. For consumption, Bergstrand derives demand equations from N constant elasticity of substitution utility functions constrained by the same number of income expenditure equations. Income is determined by the volume of the good bought, its unit price, transport costs, any relevant trade barriers (tariffs or taxes) and exchange rates. For production, Bergstrand derives supply equations from N constant elasticity of transformation production functions. Production is determined by profit maximisation, which results from domestic and foreign sales of good X and its production costs. With some assumptions the equilibrium for the N markets results in Bergstrand's 'generalized' gravity equation: a function in which X_{ij} is determined by income in home and host country (Y), transport costs (C), tariff rates (T) and the exchange rate (E):[3]

$$X_{ij} = f\left(Y_i, Y_j, C_{ij}, T_{ij}, E_{ij}\right) / P_{ij}. \qquad\qquad i,j = 1, 2, ..., N \ \ (\text{AII.4})$$

Later, Bergstrand (1989) develops his model further by presenting a general equilibrium model with three adaptations. First, he introduces two differentiated-product industries, which results in separate demand and supply equations for the two products. Second, he allows two production factors (labour and capital) incorporating differences in relative factor endowments and thus different technologies in the constant elasticity of transformation function. Third, he includes non-homothetic tastes in consumption behaviour with a 'nested' constant elasticity of substitution (Cobb–Douglas–CES–Stone–Geary) utility function, which includes per capita income (y). The resulting gravity equation is not fundamentally different from the earlier model:

$$X_{ij} = f\left[Y_i^K, \left(\frac{K_i^*}{L_i^*}\right), Y_j, y_j, C_{ij}, T_{ij}, E_{ij}\right] / P_{ij}. \qquad i, j = 1, 2, ..., N \quad \text{(AII.5)}$$

where:

X = trade flow of good X;
Y^K = national output in terms of units of capital;
K^* = capital stock;
L^* = labour stock;
Y = income;
y = per capita income;
C = transport cost factor (cif/fob factor);
T = tariff rate;
E = exchange rate;
P = price of good X;
i = home country;
j = host country.

Equation (AII.5) shows that the volume of trade in good X between a pair of countries i and j depends on a considerably large set of determinants. The income variables for the host country can be seen as determinants of market potential. National output in home country i and the capital–labour ratio in home country i may represent determinants of production costs. Determinants of transaction costs can be considered the costs of transportation, tariffs and the exchange rate between the two countries.

Many economists have used the gravity model. For the analysis of trade flows the model was used not only by Tinbergen, Pöyhönen and Linnemann, but also by Pulliainen, van Bergeijk and Ménil and Maurel. Pulliainen (1963) tested the model of Pöyhönen on trade flows among 62 countries over the 1948–60 period. Van Bergeijk (1990) used the model for determining the relevance of political factors to international trade flows. Ménil and Maurel (1994), using a gravity model, investigated the breaking up of the customs union of the Austro-Hungarian empire in 1919. The model was also applied to other types of human interaction. Vanderkamp (1977) studied migration behaviour using a gravity model. Heijke and Klaassen (1979) analysed regional labour migration within four European countries using a gravity-type model. Molle and van Mourik (1988) applied the model on international labour movements within Western Europe. In addition, many other applications can be found in studying other geographical interaction processes, such as commuting, tourism and commodity shipping.

NOTES

1. The editor of Weltwirtschaftliches Archiv in which Pöyhönen's article was published, added a note indicating that Tinbergen and Pöyhönen elaborated the same theory 'simultaneously but independently at two different research centres'. Pöyhönen had already submitted his article in November 1961, whereas Tinbergen published his book in 1962. See Pöyhönen (1963a, p. 93).
2. Replacing some of Pöyhönen's variables with those of Tinbergen gives Tinbergen's gravity equation. See Pöyhönen (1963a, p. 95). Pöyhönen (1963b, pp. 72–4) himself confirms the resemblance in a later article.
3. Bergstrand (1985, pp. 479–80) does not mention the exchange rate any more, but in his empirical investigation the exchange rate is included. Apparently, the exchange rate variable (E) was accidentally omitted.

Appendix III. Data Sets on Intra-EU Foreign Direct Investments

The creation of comprehensive and consistent data sets on intra-EU foreign direct investments is extremely difficult and many problems are encountered. In 1983, Pelkmans (1983) produced a draft for an origin-destination matrix of foreign direct investment flows for the years 1966 and 1970 among the six member states of the then European Community plus the United Kingdom.

In later years, EUROSTAT and the OECD have drafted several overviews with statistical information on foreign direct investment.[1] Among others, geographical breakdowns have been presented on the origins of a country's inward foreign direct investment flows and on the destinations of a country's outward flows. This information has been used to calibrate data sets on intra-EU foreign direct investments.

Despite the efforts of the OECD and EUROSTAT to harmonise the collection and processing of data on foreign direct investments, they have not been able to create fully consistent data. Differences in definitions and measurement in the various countries, as described in Appendix I, account for this. A particular problem is how to deal with reinvested profits. For the European Union, data generally relate to foreign direct investment flows excluding reinvested profits.[2]

In order to create reasonably consistent data sets, a simple calibration methodology is followed.[3] This method consists of four steps:

1. creation of an origin-destination matrix based on information on net outward foreign direct investment flows as collected by the home country;
2. creation of an origin-destination matrix based on information on net inward foreign direct investment flows as collected by the host country;
3. assessment of information quality in both matrices;
4. calibration of a new origin-destination matrix.

In the four steps the following is done. First, the information for a specific year on net outward foreign direct investment flows is put into an origin-destination matrix for all EU countries.[4] Second, the same is done for net inward foreign direct investment flows in the same year. The result is two sets of origin-destination matrices on intra-EU foreign direct investments in a particular year. Third, an assessment is made of the information quality by comparing the two data sets. This comparison reveals asymmetries for particular flows, caused by measurement problems. It also indicates for which cells in the matrices information is available from either the first or the second data set. Finally, a new origin-destination matrix for the year considered is calibrated. In case both initial data sets provide information for one cell in the new matrix, the information is averaged by adding both sets of information and dividing the result by two unless the quality of any of the two values in these sets is considered insufficient. If there is only one source, or if one of the two sources' quality is too low, the best information is transferred to the new matrix.

It must be admitted that the methodology does not eliminate all measurement problems. It can even be argued that it effectively ignores them. However, for the purpose of this study, identifying determinants for the mosaic of geographical patterns in intra-EU foreign direct investment flows, this methodology seems acceptable.

In order to circumvent many statistical problems and to moderate large fluctuations in annual data, five-year totals are calculated. This results in the following data sets (see Tables AIII.1–9).

NOTES

1. EUROSTAT initiated the overviews with EUROSTAT (1989), EUROSTAT (1991) and EUROSTAT (1992). The work was continued in a joint effort by OECD and EUROSTAT and resulted in OECD (1993c), OECD (1994a), OECD (1995d) and OECD (1996a).
2. The inclusion of reinvested profits is likely to have a major impact: speculative estimates show that outward investment flows can be 28 to 51 per cent higher; inward investment flows can be 17 to 53 per cent higher. See EUROSTAT (1992, Section 2.4).
3. The methodology resembles the one followed by Pelkmans. See Pelkmans (1983, p. 45, notes to Table I).
4. This relates to the membership situation of the European Union before 1 January 1995 (EU12). Belgium and Luxemburg are considered as one country.

Table AIII.1 Intra-EU foreign direct investments, 1980–84 (ECU million; current prices)

↓ From \ To →	Germany	France	Italy	Netherlands	Belgium/ Luxemburg	United Kingdom	Denmark	Ireland	Spain	Portugal	Greece	EU12
Germany	—	1343	891	547	2171	560	117	73	800	74	93	6669
France	610	—	681	376	562	499	-6	50	816	139	44	3772
Italy	207	477	—	221	673	191	-19	1	85	3	12	1851
Netherlands	-146	997	217	—	1197	832	39	269	338	16	33	3791
Belgium/ Luxemburg	534	536	59	400	—	15	4	14	130	9	6	1708
United Kingdom	880	1206	490	-1359	513	—	78	307	508	126	41	2789
Denmark	29	79	6	39	15	135	—	4	11	6	1	324
Ireland	-23	22	21	3	-1	58	0	—	3	12	0	94
Spain	-2	43	19	-8	21	44	-9	3	—	55	0	167
Portugal	2	29	0	0	1	8	-2	0	0	—	0	38
Greece	13	9	2	0	0	2	0	0	1	0	—	27
EU12	2104	4740	2387	219	5153	2344	201	719	2692	442	229	21230

215

Table AIII.2 Intra-EU foreign direct investments, 1981–85 (ECU million; current prices)

To → ↓ From	Germany	France	Italy	Netherlands	Belgium/ Luxemburg	United Kingdom	Denmark	Ireland	Spain	Portugal	Greece	EU12
Germany	—	1382	1080	696	2150	691	90	84	967	67	88	7296
France	612	—	619	412	534	811	–3	50	805	168	105	4112
Italy	258	518	—	572	612	350	–14	1	144	5	14	2460
Netherlands	244	989	387	—	1112	1284	38	277	392	18	68	4808
Belgium/ Luxemburg	445	585	75	201	—	204	8	12	95	18	6	1649
United Kingdom	774	1305	885	–186	695	—	69	444	622	286	28	4922
Denmark	47	78	7	38	19	145	—	4	38	5	0	380
Ireland	–59	29	22	–5	–3	36	0	—	22	13	0	55
Spain	0	47	21	–2	19	68	–12	3	—	71	0	215
Portugal	0	27	0	0	5	6	–2	0	2	—	0	38
Greece	11	7	2	0	0	–1	0	0	1	0	—	20
EU12	2332	4967	3099	1726	5141	3593	174	874	3088	653	309	25955

216

Table AIII.3 Intra-EU foreign direct investments, 1982–86 (ECU million; current prices)

To → ↓ From	Germany	France	Italy	Netherlands	Belgium/ Luxemburg	United Kingdom	Denmark	Ireland	Spain	Portugal	Greece	EU12
Germany	—	1462	1130	1409	2111	920	111	101	1473	82	141	8941
France	723	—	717	574	522	1231	2	47	756	145	94	4810
Italy	389	745	—	662	850	580	-11	4	213	14	28	3475
Netherlands	622	1033	518	—	911	2694	81	224	561	22	73	6741
Belgium/ Luxemburg	389	647	20	450	—	557	6	18	120	25	7	2240
United Kingdom	836	1506	1071	1003	679	—	14	443	750	310	46	6657
Denmark	90	101	6	33	18	226	—	5	43	4	0	525
Ireland	-67	28	23	-4	18	60	0	—	24	13	0	96
Spain	11	81	26	12	36	80	-14	3	—	101	0	336
Portugal	0	23	0	-1	6	1	-2	0	2	—	0	29
Greece	8	10	2	0	0	0	0	0	1	0	—	20
EU12	3001	5635	3512	4138	5152	6351	188	846	3942	716	389	33870

Table AIII.4 Intra-EU foreign direct investments, 1983–87 (ECU million; current prices)

To → ↓ From	Germany	France	Italy	Netherlands	Belgium/ Luxemburg	United Kingdom	Denmark	Ireland	Spain	Portugal	Greece	EU12
Germany	—	1788	1262	1644	2086	1160	105	103	1541	109	137	9936
France	603	—	997	1065	1183	2475	-4	85	993	157	122	7675
Italy	382	1049	—	717	844	566	-2	13	623	15	26	4232
Netherlands	906	967	794	—	516	4606	-31	217	954	26	75	9030
Belgium/ Luxemburg	321	875	83	672	—	1317	2	16	218	20	11	3534
United Kingdom	981	1821	1318	2158	835	—	-18	568	996	393	58	9109
Denmark	126	112	8	38	39	305	—	7	111	6	2	753
Ireland	-70	32	21	2	18	110	0	—	26	13	0	152
Spain	100	111	37	67	51	92	-16	3	—	141	0	585
Portugal	-1	-3	0	-3	3	3	-2	0	5	—	0	4
Greece	1	11	1	0	-2	0	-1	0	0	0	—	10
EU12	3349	6761	4521	6362	5573	10633	34	1011	5467	879	430	45020

218

Table AIII.5 Intra-EU foreign direct investments, 1984–88 (ECU million; current prices)

To → ↓ From	Germany	France	Italy	Netherlands	Belgium/Luxemburg	United Kingdom	Denmark	Ireland	Spain	Portugal	Greece	EU12
Germany	—	1992	1601	1792	2352	1567	114	102	1913	161	152	11745
France	908	—	1689	1437	3093	3962	4	213	1297	186	136	12926
Italy	436	1642	—	1016	830	662	5	18	640	19	27	5295
Netherlands	1018	1376	929	—	757	6004	21	208	1660	60	69	12102
Belgium/Luxemburg	105	1422	263	1116	—	1517	11	40	305	42	22	4842
United Kingdom	1472	3769	1742	4695	934	—	5	598	1646	523	66	15450
Denmark	218	112	11	46	65	469	—	8	136	11	2	1079
Ireland	-75	39	27	176	27	319	1	—	29	7	0	550
Spain	129	208	56	106	218	182	-19	3	—	209	1	1092
Portugal	-1	12	0	-3	6	2	-1	0	22	—	1	38
Greece	0	9	0	0	4	-8	-1	0	0	0	—	6
EU12	4210	10581	6318	10381	8287	14677	138	1190	7648	1218	476	65124

219

Table AIII.6 Intra-EU foreign direct investments, 1985–89 (ECU million; current prices)

to → ↓ from	Germany	France	Italy	Netherlands	Belgium/ Luxemburg	United Kingdom	Denmark	Ireland	Spain	Portugal	Greece	EU12
Germany	—	2692	1594	2110	2354	3291	126	397	2480	234	172	15450
France	2018	—	2797	2335	4865	5998	366	332	2434	374	179	21697
Italy	652	1763	—	1186	948	761	16	19	797	30	35	6206
Netherlands	1433	2455	1202	—	1876	9432	63	220	2417	111	119	19329
Belgium/ Luxemburg	1092	1682	-683	1943	—	2289	14	137	410	92	38	7013
United Kingdom	2289	5849	2446	7240	1350	—	48	752	2493	799	103	23369
Denmark	335	303	16	410	64	765	—	9	157	20	10	2089
Ireland	-40	27	15	269	44	647	2	—	32	4	0	1000
Spain	180	265	148	241	314	345	-16	8	—	484	1	1971
Portugal	0	13	0	-1	5	15	-1	0	47	—	1	79
Greece	-3	6	-1	0	-2	-12	-4	0	1	0	—	-16
EU12	7957	15055	7535	15732	11817	23530	613	1875	11267	2147	658	98186

Table AIII.7 Intra-EU foreign direct investments, 1986–90 (ECU million; current prices)

To → ↓ From	Germany	France	Italy	Netherlands	Belgium/ Luxemburg	United Kingdom	Denmark	Ireland	Spain	Portugal	Greece	EU12
Germany	—	3374	1838	3112	4069	5657	180	1348	3218	350	187	23333
France	3092	—	4184	4323	6177	8803	387	364	5159	630	197	33316
Italy	1013	2294	—	942	2380	720	9	29	1160	47	41	8635
Netherlands	1776	3070	973	—	3748	10622	132	242	4008	175	133	24879
Belgium/ Luxemburg	2956	2118	−907	2664	—	2374	9	402	650	182	74	10522
United Kingdom	2083	6576	2474	8238	921	—	145	638	3385	866	155	25480
Denmark	349	491	28	462	44	955	—	51	160	28	11	2579
Ireland	4	49	57	392	71	958	2	—	26	4	0	1562
Spain	322	367	176	364	453	679	−8	11	—	756	10	3127
Portugal	1	20	5	−1	1	33	−1	0	78	—	1	138
Greece	9	8	1	0	−5	−15	−4	0	1	0	—	−5
EU12	11605	18367	8829	20496	17859	30786	850	3084	17845	3038	809	133566

Table AIII.8 Intra-EU foreign direct investments, 1987–91 (ECU million; current prices)

From ↓ \ To →	Germany	France	Italy	Netherlands	Belgium/ Luxemburg	United Kingdom	Denmark	Ireland	Spain	Portugal	Greece	EU12
Germany	—	5065	1993	3144	5809	6243	218	3036	3415	397	192	29512
France	3956	—	4759	4754	7703	10058	488	486	7447	838	210	40698
Italy	1033	2382	—	1097	1848	822	6	23	1380	68	73	8732
Netherlands	2358	3740	828	—	5016	11727	121	220	6592	299	194	31095
Belgium/ Luxemburg	5747	2238	-663	2872	—	2498	131	451	996	234	104	14609
United Kingdom	1862	6735	2196	7750	1336	—	241	827	4682	1024	167	26821
Denmark	450	513	87	502	27	1018	—	311	251	96	12	3267
Ireland	6	71	7	462	97	1125	2	—	42	42	0	1855
Spain	328	525	575	781	622	900	-3	17	—	1108	10	4864
Portugal	2	51	12	1	30	42	-1	0	268	—	2	408
Greece	8	4	-25	0	3	-19	-4	0	1	0	—	-33
EU12	15750	21324	9770	21363	22491	34414	1199	5370	25077	4106	964	161828

Table AIII.9 Intra-EU foreign direct investments, 1988–92 (ECU million; current prices)

From ↓ \ To →	Germany	France	Italy	Netherlands	Belgium/ Luxemburg	United Kingdom	Denmark	Ireland	Spain	Portugal	Greece	EU12
Germany	—	5839	2043	3646	8500	7616	506	3207	3962	511	201	36031
France	5193	—	5404	5930	9547	9820	499	506	8675	1025	216	46816
Italy	1041	3718	—	1627	1979	781	22	29	1364	185	245	10991
Netherlands	2508	5042	782	—	6195	11093	311	329	8573	390	255	35478
Belgium/ Luxemburg	8059	3932	-271	3773	—	1317	168	675	1629	218	131	19632
United Kingdom	2163	7071	2084	7470	1085	—	296	1280	4899	1337	284	27968
Denmark	482	575	85	557	65	1228	—	348	260	121	13	3733
Ireland	-12	95	1	573	187	1005	24	—	40	69	2	1984
Spain	272	704	637	1121	638	1033	2	102	—	1346	11	5865
Portugal	0	90	18	3	54	74	-1	0	571	—	1	810
Greece	2	5	-25	0	19	-19	-4	0	2	0	—	-19
EU12	19708	27069	10756	24698	28269	33948	1825	6477	29976	5202	1361	189288

Appendix IV. Definitions of Variables Used in the Regressions

A. Knowledge transfer

1. Gross Domestic Expenditure on R&D in the home country as a percentage of Gross Domestic Product
    Source: OECD, Main Science and Technology Indicators

2. Business Enterprise Expenditure on R&D in the home country as a percentage of Domestic Product of Industry
    Source: OECD, Main Science and Technology Indicators

B. Market size

1. Population in the host country (million)
    Sources: EUROSTAT
             OECD
             World Bank, World Tables

C. Per capita income

1a. GDP per capita in the host country (ECU 1000)
1b. GDP per capita in the host country (% change previous year)
     Source: EUROSTAT

2a. GDP per capita in the host country in the currency of the home country (USA: US$1000; JPN: yen million; BRD: DM 1000; NL: DFL 1000)
2b. GDP per capita in the host country in the currency of the home country (% change previous year)
     Source: World Bank, World Tables

D. Labour costs

1a. Compensation of employees per wage and salary earner in the host country (ECU 1000; 1985 prices and exchange rates)

1b. Compensation of employees per wage and salary earner in the host country (index; home country = 100)

1c. Compensation of employees per wage and salary earner in the host country (% change to previous year)
Source: EUROSTAT, ESA National Accounts

2a. Real earnings per employee in the host country (index; 1987 = 100)

2b. Real earnings per employee in the host country (index; home country = 100)

2c. Real earnings per employee in the host country (% change to previous year)
Source: World Bank, World Tables

E.   Return on investment differences

1. Difference in Government Bond Yield in percentages, corrected with the GDP deflator, between host and home country
Source: IMF, International Financial Statistics

F.   Taxation differences

1. Difference in the tax indicator between the host and home country (tax indicator = the required return on investment before taxation to achieve a 5 per cent after tax return on investment)
Source: Devereux and Pearson (1989)

G.   Transport costs

1. Distance between the capitals or economic centres between home and host country (in 1000 kilometres)
Source: measured from maps

H.   Cultural differences

1. Difference in the Power Difference Index, the extent of hierarchical inequality between a boss and his or her subordinates (index; home country = 100)
Source: Hofstede (1984)

2. Difference in the Uncertainty Avoidance Index, the extent of tolerance towards future uncertainties (index; home country = 100)
Source: Hofstede (1984)

3.   Difference in the Individualism Index, the extent of dominance of individuals versus that of the collectivity (index; home country = 100)
       Source: Hofstede (1984)

4.   Difference in the Masculinity Index, the extent of a nation's population to endorse goals usually more popular among men than among women (index; home country = 100)
       Source: Hofstede (1984)

I.   Trade intensity

1.   Trade intensity between home and host country calculated as a quote from the share of the bilateral trade in total home country's exports to the EU12 plus the share of this trade flow in the host country's imports from EU12 (lagged 1 year)
       Source: EUROSTAT

2a.   Trade intensity between home and host country calculated as a quote from the share of the bilateral trade in total home country's world exports plus the share of this trade flow in the host country's world imports (lagged 1 year)

2b.   Trade between home and host country as a share of total home country's exports (lagged 1 year)

2c.   Trade between home and host country (percentage change to previous year; lagged 1 year)
       Source: United Nations, International Trade Statistics

J.   Exchange rate direction

1.   Average relative deviation of monthly real bilateral exchange rates
       Sources: EUROSTAT
                IMF, International Financial Statistics

2.   The sum of deviations of monthly real bilateral exchange rates divided by the average of monthly real bilateral exchange rates
       Sources: EUROSTAT
                IMF, International Financial Statistics

K. Exchange rate volatility

1. The quotient of the difference between the maximum and the minimum value in monthly real bilateral exchange rates and the average of monthly real bilateral exchange rates
    Sources: EUROSTAT
    IMF, International Financial Statistics

2. The standard deviation of monthly real bilateral exchange rates divided by the average of monthly real bilateral exchange rates
    Sources: EUROSTAT
    IMF, International Financial Statistics

3. The standard deviation of the deviations of the actual monthly real bilateral exchange rate from its twelve-month moving average
    Sources: EUROSTAT
    IMF, International Financial Statistics

4. The standard deviation of the month-to-month percentage change of the real bilateral exchange rate
    Sources: EUROSTAT
    IMF, International Financial Statistics

5. The standard deviation of the percentage change in the monthly real bilateral exchange rate versus its value in the same month in the previous year
    Sources: EUROSTAT
    IMF, International Financial Statistics

Bibliography

Abrams, R.K. (1980), 'International Trade Flows under Flexible Exchange Rates', *Economic Review*, Federal Reserve Bank of Kansas City, March, pp. 3–10.

Acocella, N. (1992), 'Trade and Direct Investment within the EC: The Impact of Strategic Considerations', in Cantwell, J. (ed.), *Multinational Investment in Modern Europe, Strategic Interaction in the Integrated Community*, Aldershot: Edward Elgar, pp. 192–213.

Agarwal, J.P. (1980), 'Determinants of Foreign Direct Investment: A Survey', *Weltwirtschaftliches Archiv*, Vol. 116, pp. 739–73.

Aliber, R.Z. (1970), 'A Theory of Direct Foreign Investment', in Kindleberger, C.P. (ed.), *The International Corporation*, Cambridge MA: MIT Press, pp. 17–34.

Aliber, R.Z. (1971), 'The Multinational Enterprise in a Multiple Currency World', in Dunning, J.H. (ed.), *The Multinational Enterprise*, London: Allen & Unwin, pp. 49–60.

Amin, A. and M. Dietrich (eds) (1991), *Towards a New Europe*, Aldershot: Edward Elgar.

Anderson, J.E. (1979), 'A Theoretical Foundation for the Gravity Equation', *American Economic Review*, Vol. 69, pp. 106–16.

Andriessen, J.E. and R.F. van Esch (1993), *Globalisering: Een Zekere Trend*, (Globalisation: A Certain Trend), Discussion Paper No. 9301, Ministry of Economic Affairs, The Hague.

Arge, R. d' (1969), 'Note on Customs Unions and Direct Foreign Investment', *Economic Journal*, Vol. 79, pp. 324–33.

Aristotelous, K. and S. Fountas (1996), 'An Empirical Analysis of Inward Foreign Direct Investment Flows in the EU with Emphasis on the Market Enlargement Hypothesis', *Journal of Common Market Studies*, Vol. 34, No. 4, pp. 571–83.

Artisien, P., M. Rojec and M. Svetlicic (eds) (1993), *Foreign Investment in Central and Eastern Europe*, New York: St. Martin's Press.

Audretsch, D.B., L.I.E. Sleuwaegen and H. Yamawaki (1989a), 'The Dynamics of Export Competition', in Audretsch, D.B., L.I.E. Sleuwaegen and H. Yamawaki (eds), *The Convergence of International and Domestic Markets*, Amsterdam: North-Holland, pp. 211–45.

Audretsch, D.B., L.I.E. Sleuwaegen and H. Yamawaki (eds) (1989b), *The Convergence of International and Domestic Markets*, Amsterdam: North-Holland.

Axelsson, B. and G. Easton (eds) (1992), *Industrial Networks, A New View of Reality*, London: Routledge.

Bagchi-Sen, S. (1995), 'FDI in US Producer Services: A Temporal Analysis of Foreign Direct Investment in the Finance, Insurance and Real Estate Sectors', *Regional Studies*, Vol. 29, No. 2, pp. 159–70.

Bajo-Rubio, O. and S. Sosvilla-Rivero (1994), 'An Econometric Analysis of Foreign Direct Investment in Spain, 1964–89', *Southern Economic Journal*, Vol. 61, No. 1, pp. 104–20.

Balassa, B. (1961), *The Theory of Economic Integration*, London: Allen & Unwin.

Balassa, B. (ed.) (1975), *European Economic Integration*, Amsterdam: North-Holland.

Balassa, B. (1976), 'Types of Economic Integration', in Machlup, F. (ed.), *Economic Integration Worldwide, Regional, Sectoral*, London: Macmillan.

Balassa, B. and L. Bauwens (1988), 'The Determinants of Intra-European Trade in Manufactured Goods', *European Economic Review*, Vol. 32, pp. 1421–37.

Balasubramanyam, V.N. (1985), 'Foreign Direct Investment and the International Transfer of Technology', in Greenaway, D. (ed.), *Current Issues in International Trade, Theory and Policy*, London: Macmillan.

Balasubramanyam, V.N. and D. Greenaway (1992), 'Economic Integration and Foreign Direct Investment: Japanese Investment in the EC', *Journal of Common Market Studies*, Vol. 30, No. 2, pp. 175–93.

Balasubramanyam, V.N. and D. Greenaway (1994), 'East Asian Foreign Direct Investment in the EC', in Balasubramanyam, V.N. and D. Sapsford (eds), *The Economics of International Investment*, Aldershot: Edward Elgar, pp. 103–28.

Balasubramanyam, V.N. and M.A. Salisu (1991), 'Export Promotion, Import Substitution and Direct Foreign Investment in Less Developed Countries', in Koekkoek, A. and L.B.M. Mennes (eds), *International Trade and Global Development, Essays in Honour of Jagdish Bhagwati*, London: Routledge, pp. 191–207.

Balasubramanyam, V.N. and D. Sapsford (eds) (1994), *The Economics of International Investment*, Aldershot: Edward Elgar.

Baldwin, R.E. (1979), 'Determinants of Trade and Foreign Investment: Further Evidence', *Review of Economics and Statistics*, Vol. 61, pp. 40–8.

Baldwin, R.E. (1994), 'The Effects of Trade and Foreign Direct Investment on Employment and Relative Wages', *OECD Economic Studies*, No. 23, pp. 7–54.

Baldwin, R., P. Haaparanta and J. Kiander (eds) (1995), *Expanding Membership of the European Union*, Cambridge: Cambridge University Press.

Ball, G.W. (ed.) (1975), *Global Companies, The Political Economy of World Business*, London: Prentice-Hall.

Balvers, R. and L. Szerb (1996), 'Location in the Hotelling Duopoly Model with Demand Uncertainty', *European Economic Review*, Vol. 40, pp. 1453–61.

Batra, R.N. and R. Ramachandran (1980), 'Multinational Firms and the Theory of International Trade and Investment', *American Economic Review*, Vol. 70, No. 3, pp. 278–90.

Beije, P., J. Groenewegen and O. Nuys (eds) (1993), *Networking in Dutch Industries*, Leuven/Apeldoorn: Garant.

Belderbos, R.A. (1988), *De Internationalisering van de Nederlandse Economie: Een Studie naar Omvang en Determinanten van Directe Buitenlandse Investeringen*, (The Internationalisation of the Dutch Economy: A Study into the Size and the Determinants of Direct Foreign Investments), SEO Research Memorandum, No. 8801, Stichting voor Economisch Onderzoek, Amsterdam.

Belderbos, R.A. (1991), 'Tariff Jumping DFI and Welfare under Cournot Duopoly', mimeo, Tinbergen Institute, Rotterdam.

Belderbos, R.A. (1992), 'Large Multinational Enterprises Based in a Small Economy: Effects on Domestic Investment', *Weltwirtschaftliches Archiv*, Vol. 128, pp. 543–57.

Belderbos, R.A. (1994), *Strategic Trade Policy and Multinational Enterprises, Essays on Trade and Investment by Japanese Electronics Firms*, Tinbergen Institute Research Series, No. 68, Amsterdam.

Belderbos, R.A. and L.I.E. Sleuwaegen (1996a), 'Japanese Firms and the Decision to Invest Abroad: Business Groups, Regional Core Networks and Corporate Development', *Review of Economics and Statistics*, pp. 1–31.

Belderbos, R.A. and L.I.E. Sleuwaegen (1996b), 'Tariff Jumping Direct Foreign Investment: Japanese Electronic Firms in Europe', *International Journal of Industrial Organisation*.

Bergeijk, P.A.G. van (1990), 'Handel en Diplomatie', (Trade and Diplomacy), Dissertation, State University Groningen.

Bergeijk, P.A.G. van (1992), 'Diplomatic Barriers to Trade', *De Economist*, Vol. 140, No. 1, pp. 45–64.

Bergsman, J. and X. Shen (1995), 'Foreign Direct Investment in Developing Countries: Progress and Problems', *Finance and Development*, December, pp. 6–8.

Bergstrand, J.H. (1985), 'The Gravity Equation in International Trade: Some Microeconomic Foundations and Empirical Evidence', *Review of Economics and Statistics*, Vol. 67, pp. 474–81.

Bergstrand, J.H. (1989), 'The Generalized Gravity Equation, Monopolistic Competition, and the Factor-proportions Theory in International Trade', *Review of Economics and Statistics*, Vol. 71, pp. 143–53.

Bhagwati, J.N. (1987), 'VERs, Quid Pro Quo FDIs and VIEs: Political Economy Theoretic Analysis', *International Economic Journal*, Vol. 1, pp. 1–14.

Bhagwati, J.N., E. Dinopoulos and K. Wong (1992), 'Quid Pro Quo Foreign Investment', *American Economic Review*, Vol. 82, No. 2, pp. 186–190.

Bhagwati, J.N. and R.E. Hudec (eds) (1996), *Fair Trade and Harmonization, Prerequisites for Free Trade?*, Cambridge, MA: MIT Press.

Bikker, J.A. (1992), 'Internal and External Trade Liberalization in the EEC: An Econometric Analysis of International Trade Flows', *Economie Appliquée*, Vol. XLV, No. 3, pp. 91–119.

Bishop M. and J. Kay (ed.) (1993), *European Mergers and Merger Policy*, Oxford: Oxford University Press.

Bliss, C. and J. Braga de Macedo (eds) (1990), *Unity with Diversity in the European Economy: The Community's Southern Frontier*, Cambridge: Cambridge University Press.

Blom, M.J. (1995), 'Regionale Dispariteiten en Werkgelegenheidsstructuur in het Europese Integratieproces', (Regional Disparities and the Employment Structure in the European Integration Process), doctoraalscriptie Erasmus Universiteit Rotterdam.

Blomström, M. (1989), *Foreign Investment and Spillovers*, London: Routledge.

Blomström, M., A. Kokko and M. Zejan (1994), 'Host Country Competition, Labor Skills, and Technology Transfer by Multinationals', *Weltwirtschaftliches Archiv*, Vol. 130, pp. 521–33.

Blomström, M., R.E. Lipsey, K. Kulchycky (1988), 'U.S. and Swedish Direct Investment and Exports', in Baldwin, R.E. (ed.), *Trade Policy Issues and Empirical Analysis*, Chicago.

Boadway, R. and A. Shah (1992), *How Tax Incentives Affect Decisions to Invest in Developing Countries*, Policy Research Working Papers WPS 1011, Country Economics Dept, World Bank, Washington, DC.

Bondt, R. de and L.I.E. Sleuwaegen (1988), *Innovatie en Multinationals*, (Innovation and Multinationals), Leuven: Universitaire Pers.

Bondt, R. de, L.I.E. Sleuwaegen and R. Veugelers (1988), 'Innovative Strategic Groups in Multinational Industries', *European Economic Review*, Vol. 32, pp. 905–25.

Borensztein, E., J. De Gregorio and J.-W. Lee (1995), *How Does Foreign Direct Investment Affect Economic Growth?*, NBER, Working Paper No. 5057, Cambridge, MA.

Bovenberg, A.L., K. Andersson, K. Aramaki and S.K. Chand (1990), 'Tax Incentives and International Capital Flows: The Case of the United States and Japan', in Razin, A. and J. Slemrod (eds), *Taxation in the Global Economy*, Chicago: University of Chicago Press and NBER, pp. 283–328.

Boyd, G. (1995), *Competitive and Cooperative Macromanagement, The Challenges of Structural Interdependence*, Aldershot: Edward Elgar.

Boyer, R. and D. Drache (eds) (1996), *States Against Markets, The Limits of Globalization*, London: Routledge.

Bramezza, I. (1994), *Measuring the Competitive Position and the Performance of Regions*, Tinbergen Institute Research Bulletin, Vol. 6, No. 2, pp. 47–61.

Branson, W.H. (1979), *Macroeconomic Theory and Policy*, 2nd edition, New York: Harper & Row.

Broll, U. and I. Zilcha (1991), *International Production, Investments and Borrowing with Exchange Rate Risk and Futures Markets*, Sonderforschungsbereich 178 'Internationalisierung der Wirtschaft', Diskussionsbeiträge Serie II, Nr. 148, Universität Konstanz.

Broll, U. and I. Zilcha (1992), 'Exchange Rate Uncertainty, Futures Markets and the Multinational Firm', *European Economic Review*, Vol. 36, pp. 815–26.

Broll, U. and J.E. Wahl (1992), 'International Investments and Exchange Rate Risk', *European Journal of Political Economy*, Vol. 8, pp. 31–40.

Buck (1995), *Buitenlandse Investeringen in West-Europa, Marktanalyse*, (Foreign Investments in Western Europe, Market Analysis), Nijmegen: Buck Consultants International BV.

Buckley, P.J. and P. Artisien (1987), *North–South Direct Investment in the European Communities*, London: Macmillan.

Buckley, P.J. and M.C. Casson (1976), *The Future of the Multinational Enterprise*, London: Macmillan.

Buckley, P.J. and M.C. Casson (1981), 'The Optimal Timing of a Foreign Direct Investment', *Economic Journal*, Vol. 91, pp. 75–87.

Buckley, P.J. and M.C. Casson (1992), *Multinational Enterprises in the World Economy, Essays in Honour of John Dunning*, Aldershot: Edward Elgar.

Buckley, P.J. and R.D. Pearce (1981), 'Market Servicing by Multinational Manufacturing Firms: Exporting versus Foreign Production', *Managerial and Decision Economics*, Vol. 2, No. 4, pp. 229–46.

Buigues, P. and A. Jacquemin (1989), 'Strategies of Firms and Structural Environments in the Large Internal Market', *Journal of Common Market Studies*, Vol. XXVIII, No. 1, pp. 53–67.

Bulcke, D. van den and Ph. de Lombaerde (1992), 'The Belgian Metalworking Industries and the Large European Internal Market: The Role of Multinational Investment', in Cantwell, J. (ed.), *Multinational Investment in Modern Europe, Strategic Interaction in the Integrated Community*, Aldershot: Edward Elgar, pp. 107–49.

Bürgenmeier, B. and J.L. Mucchielli (eds) (1991), *Multinationals and Europe 1992, Strategies for the Future*, London: Routledge.

Calderón, A., M. Mortimore and W. Peres (1996), 'Mexico, Foreign Investment as a Source of International Competitiveness', in Dunning, J.H. and R. Narula (eds), *Foreign Direct Investment and Governments, Catalysts for Economic Restructuring*, London: Routledge, pp. 240–79.

Calderón-Rossell, J.R. (1985), 'Towards the Theory of Foreign Direct Investment', *Oxford Economic Papers*, Vol. 37, pp. 282–91.

Calvet, A.L. (1980), *Markets and Hierarchies: Toward a Theory of International Business*, Boston: MIT Press.

Calvet, A.L. (1981), 'A Synthesis of Foreign Direct Investment Theories and Theories of the Multinational Firm', *Journal of International Business Studies*, Spring/Summer, pp. 43–59.

Campa, J.M. and M.F. Guillén (1996), 'Spain, A Boom from Economic Integration', in Dunning, J.H. and R. Narula (eds), *Foreign Direct Investment and Governments, Catalysts for Economic Restructuring*, London: Routledge, pp. 207–39.

Cantwell, J. (1989), *Technological Innovation and Multinational Corporations*, Oxford: Basil Blackwell.

Cantwell, J. (ed.) (1992), *Multinational Investment in Modern Europe, Strategic Interaction in the Integrated Community*, Aldershot: Edward Elgar.

Capel, J.J. (1991), 'The Choice of Market-servicing Mode under Uncertainty, A Real Option Approach', Research Memorandum No. 9101, Department of Economics, University of Amsterdam.

Capel, J.J. (1993), *Exchange Rates and Strategic Decisions of Firms*, Tinbergen Institute Research Series, No. 47, Amsterdam.

Carrothers, G.A.P. (1956), 'An Historical Review of the Gravity and Potential Concepts of Human Interaction', *Journal of the American Institute of Planners*, pp. 94–102.

Carson, M. (1982), 'The Theory of Foreign Direct Investment', in Black, J. and J.H. Dunning (eds), *International Capital Movements*, London: Macmillan, pp. 22–58.

Casal, C. (1989), 'Die Problematik mittelfristiger Wechselkursschwankungen für international tätige Unternehmen', (The Problem of medium-term Exchange rate

Movements for Internationally Active Companies), Dissertation Hochschule St. Gallen (CH), Verlag Rüegger, Grüsch.

Casson, M. (1987), *The Firm and the Market, Studies on Multinational Enterprise and the Scope of the Firm*, Oxford: Basil Blackwell.

Caves, R.E. (1971), 'International Corporations: The Industrial Economics of Foreign Investment', *Economica*, Vol. 38, pp. 1–27.

Caves, R.E. (1982), *Multinational Enterprise and Economic Analysis*, Cambridge: Cambridge University Press.

Caves, R.E. (1988), *Exchange-Rate Movements and Foreign Direct Investment in the United States*, Harvard Institute of Economic Research, Discussion Paper Series, No. 1383.

Caves, R.E. (1993), 'Japanese Investment in the United States: Lessons for the Economic Analysis of Foreign Investment', *The World Economy*, Vol. 16, pp. 279–300.

Chan Kim, W. and P. Hwang (1992), 'Global Strategy and Multinationals' Entry Mode Choice', *Journal of International Business Studies*, 1st Quarter, pp. 29–53.

Chen, E.K.Y. (1992), 'Changing Pattern of Financial Flows in the Asia-Pacific Region and Policy Responses', *Asian Development Review*, Vol. 10, No. 2, pp. 46–85.

Chen, E.K.Y. (1993), 'Foreign Direct Investment in East Asia', *Asian Development Review*, Vol. 11, No. 1, pp. 24–59.

Chesnais, F. (1995), 'Some Relationships Between Foreign Direct Investment, Technology, Trade and Competitiveness', in Hagedoorn, J. (ed.), *Technical Change and the World Economy, Convergence and Divergence in Technology Strategies*, Aldershot: Edward Elgar, pp. 6–33.

Clegg, J. (1996), 'The Determinants of Intra-European Foreign Direct Investment Flows: Market Integration and Policy Issues', paper presented at the conference 'Globalisation et Regionalisation dans le Commerce et les Investissements Internationaux', Université Paris-I Pantheon-Sorbonne.

Commission of the European Communities (CEC) (1985), *Completing the Internal Market*, Cockfield White Paper, Brussels/Luxemburg.

Commission of the European Communities (CEC) (1990), *One Market, One Money, An Evaluation of the Potential Benefits and Costs of Forming an Economic and Monetary Union*, European Economy No. 44, Luxemburg.

Commission of the European Communities (CEC) (1991), *The Economics of EMU, Background Studies for European Economy No. 44 'One Market, One Money'*, European Economy special edition No. 1, Luxemburg.

Commission of the European Communities (CEC) (1993), *The European Community as a World Trade Partner, The Second Trade Report*, European Economy, No. 52, Luxemburg.

Commission of the European Communities (CEC) (1995), *A Level Playing Field for Direct Investment World-wide*, Communication to the Council, the European Parliament and the Economic and Social Committee, Europe Documents, No. 1926.

Crone, F. and H. Overbeek (1981), *Nederlands Kapitaal over de Grenzen, Verplaatsing van Produktie en Gevolgen voor de Nationale Ekonomie*, (Dutch

Capital across the Border, Relocation of Production and the Consequences for the National Economy), Amsterdam: SUA.

Culem, C.G. (1988), 'The Locational Determinants of Direct Investments Among Industrialized Countries', *European Economic Review*, Vol. 32, pp. 885–904.

Cushman, D.O. (1985), 'Real Exchange Rate Risk, Expectations, and the Level of Direct Investment', *Review of Economics and Statistics*, Vol. 67, pp. 297–308.

Cushman, D.O. (1988), 'Exchange-rate Uncertainty and Foreign Direct Investment in the United States', *Weltwirtschaftliches Archiv*, Vol. 124, pp. 322–36.

De Nederlandsche Bank (DNB) (1989), *Jaarverslag 1988*, (Annual Report 1988), Amsterdam: DNB.

De Nederlandsche Bank (DNB) (1990), *Jaarverslag 1989*, (Annual Report 1989), Amsterdam: DNB.

Deardorff, A.V. and R.M. Stern (eds) (1994), *Analytical and Negotiating Issues in the Global Trading System*, Ann Arbor, MI: University of Michigan Press.

Dei, F. (1985), 'Voluntary Export Restraints and Foreign Direct Investment', *Journal of International Economics*, Vol. 19, pp. 305–12.

Demsetz, H. (1986), 'The Market for Corporate Control, Corporate Control, Insider Trading, and Rates of Return', *American Economic Review*, Vol. 76, No. 2, pp. 313–16.

Dent, C.M. (1997), *The European Economy, The Global Context*, London: Routledge.

Devereux, M.P. and H. Freeman (1995), 'The Impact of Tax on Foreign Direct Investment: Empirical Evidence and the Implications for Tax Integration Schemes', *International Tax and Public Finance*, Vol. 2, pp. 85–106.

Devereux, M. and M. Pearson (1989), *Corporate Tax Harmonisation and Economic Efficiency*, Institute for Fiscal Studies, IFS Report Series No. 35, London.

Dicken, P. (1986), *Global Shift, Industrial Change in a Turbulent World*, London: Harper & Row.

Dicken, P. (1988), 'The Changing Geography of Japanese Foreign Direct Investment in Manufacturing Industry: A Global Perspective', *Environment and Planning*, Vol. 20, pp. 633–53.

Dicken, P. and M. Quévit (eds) (1994), 'Transnational Corporations and European Regional Restructuring', *Netherlands Geographical Studies*, Vol. 181, Utrecht.

Dijk, J.W.A. van and L.G. Soete (eds) (1992), *Technologie in een Economie met Open Grenzen*, (Technology in an Economy with Open Borders), Beleidsstudies Technologie Economie, Alphen aan den Rijn: Samson.

Dinopoulos, E. and K.-y. Wong (1991), 'Quid Pro Quo Foreign Investment and Policy Intervention', in Koekkoek, A. and L.B.M. Mennes (eds), *International Trade and Global Development, Essays in Honour of Jagdish Bhagwati*, London: Routledge, pp. 162–90.

Dobosiewicz, Z. (1992), *Foreign Investment in Eastern Europe*, London: Routledge.

Doz, Y.L. (1986), 'Government Policies and Global Industries', in Porter, M.E. (ed.), *Competition in Global Industries*, Harvard.

Doz, Y.L. (1987), 'International Industries: Fragmentation versus Globalization', in Guile, B.R. and H. Brooks (eds), *Technology and Global Industry, Companies and Nations in the World Economy*, Washington, DC: National Academy Press.

Drake, T.A. and R.E. Caves (1992), 'Changing Determinants of Japanese Foreign Investment in the United States', *Journal of the Japanese and International Economies*, Vol. 6, pp. 228–46.

DRI (1995), 'Typical Forms of Transnational Investments by EU Firms Outside the EU', in European Commission, *Panorama of EU-industry 95/96*, Luxemburg, pp. 41–53.

Dunning, J.H. (1971) (ed.), *The Multinational Enterprise*, London: Allen & Unwin.

Dunning, J.H. (1973), 'The Determinants of International Production', *Oxford Economic Papers*, Vol. 25, pp. 289–336.

Dunning, J.H. (ed.) (1974), *Economic Analysis and the Multinational Enterprise*, London: Allen & Unwin.

Dunning, J.H. (1979), 'Explaining Changing Patterns of International Production: In Defence of the Eclectic Theory', *Oxford Bulletin of Economics and Statistics*, Vol. 41, No. 4, pp. 269–95.

Dunning, J.H. (1981), 'Explaining the International Direct Investment Position of Countries: Towards a Dynamic or Developmental Approach', *Weltwirtschaftliches Archiv*, Vol. 117, pp. 30–64.

Dunning, J.H. (ed.) (1985), *Multinational Enterprises, Economic Structure and International Competitiveness*, Chichester: John Wiley & Sons/IRM.

Dunning, J.H. (1986), *Japanese Participation in British Industry*, London: Routledge.

Dunning, J.H. (1988a), *Explaining International Production*, London: Unwin Hyman.

Dunning, J.H. (1988b), 'The Eclectic Paradigm of International Production: a Restatement and some Possible Extensions', *Journal of International Business Studies*, Vol. 19, No. 1, pp. 1–31 (also published in Dunning 1988a).

Dunning, J.H. (1991), *Dunning on Porter: Reshaping the Diamond of Competitive Advantage*, paper to the Annual Meeting of the Academy of International Business, Toronto, October 1990, published as Working Paper WP6–91, Institute of International Economics and Management, Copenhagen.

Dunning, J.H. (1992), 'Multinational Investment in the EC: Some Policy Implications', in Cantwell, J. (ed.), *Multinational Investment in Modern Europe, Strategic Interaction in the Integrated Community*, Aldershot: Edward Elgar, pp. 349–81.

Dunning, J.H. (1993), *The Globalisation of Business, The Challenge of the 1990s*, London: Routledge.

Dunning, J.H. (1997a), 'The European Internal Market Programme and Inbound Foreign Direct Investment, Part I', *Journal of Common Market Studies*, Vol. 35, No. 1, pp. 1–30.

Dunning, J.H. (1997b), 'The European Internal Market Programme and Inbound Foreign Direct Investment, Part II', *Journal of Common Market Studies*, Vol. 35, No. 2, pp. 189–223.

Dunning, J.H. and J. Cantwell (1987), *IRM Directory of Statistics of International Investment and Production*, Institute for Research and Information on Multinationals, London: Macmillan.

Dunning, J.H. and J.A. Cantwell (1991), 'Japanese Direct Investment in Europe', in Bürgenmeier, B. and J.L. Mucchielli (eds), *Multinationals and Europe 1992, Strategies for the Future*, London: Routledge, pp. 155–84.

Dunning, J.H. and M. McQueen (1981), 'The Eclectic Theory of International Production: A Case of the International Hotel Industry', *Managerial and Decision Economics*, Vol. 2, No. 4, pp. 197–210.

Dunning, J.H. and R. Narula (eds) (1996), *Foreign Direct Investment and Governments, Catalysts for Economic Restructuring*, London: Routledge.

Durán Herrera, J.J. (1992), 'Cross-direct Investment and Technological Capability of Spanish Domestic Firms', in Cantwell, J. (ed.), *Multinational Investment in Modern Europe, Strategic Interaction in the Integrated Community*, Aldershot: Edward Elgar, pp. 214–55.

Economic Institute for Small and Medium-sized Enterprises (EIM) (1993), *Ontwikkeling van Buitenlandse Vestigingen, Een Internationale Vergelijking*, (The Development of Foreign Subsidiaries, An International Comparison), Zoetermeer: EIM.

El-Agraa, A. (1985), 'International Economic Integration', in Greenaway, D. (ed.), *Current Issues in International Trade, Theory and Policy*, London: Macmillan.

Erdilek, A. (ed.) (1985), *Multinationals as Mutual Invaders: Intra-industry Foreign Investment*, London and Sydney: Croom Helm.

Ernst, A. and H.G. Hilpert (1990), *Japans Direktinvestitionen in Europa – Europas Direktinvestitionen in Japan, Bestandsaufnahme und wirtschaftspolitische Empfehlungen*, (Japan's Direct Investments in Europe – Europe's Direct Investments in Japan), IFO Studien zur Japanforschung No. 4, IFO-Institut für Wirtschaftsforschung, München.

Etemad, H. (1995), 'International Production Networks and Alliances', in Boyd, G., *Competitive and Cooperative Macromanagement, The Challenges of Structural Interdependence*, Aldershot: Edward Elgar, pp. 153–85.

Ethier, W.J. (1986), 'The Multinational Firm', *Quarterly Journal of Economics*, Vol. 101, November, pp. 805–33.

Ethier, W.J. (1988), *Modern International Economics*, 2nd Edition, New York: Norton.

EUROSTAT (1989), 'Direct Investment, European Community/USA/Japan', Luxemburg (not published).

EUROSTAT (1991), *European Community Direct Investment, 1984–1988*, Luxemburg.

EUROSTAT (1992), *European Community Direct Investment, 1984–1989*, Luxemburg.

EUROSTAT (1994), *European Community Direct Investment, 1984–1991*, Luxemburg.

EUROSTAT (1995a), *European Union Direct Investment, 1984–92*, Luxemburg.

EUROSTAT (1995b), *European Union Direct Investment, 1984–93*, Luxemburg.

FAST e.V. (1993), 'Inward and Outward Foreign Direct Investment in Western Europe', in Commission of the European Communities, *Panorama of EC Industry 93*, Luxemburg, pp. 55–64.

Feenstra, R.C. (ed.) (1989), *Trade Policies for International Competitiveness*, Chicago: University of Chicago Press.

Feenstra, R.C. and G.H. Hanson (1995), *Foreign Investment, Outsourcing and Relative Wages*, NBER, Working Paper No. 5121, Cambridge, MA.

Fenedex (1994), *Global Sourcing, Een Onderzoek naar de Verplaatsing van Bedrijfsactiviteiten door Nederlandse Bedrijven*, (Global Sourcing, An Investigation into the Relocation of Company Activities by Dutch Enterprises), Amsterdam: Fenedex.

Fernández, P. (1991), *Modelling the Balance of Services for Link Project*, Centro Lawrence R. Klein, Facultad de Ciencias Económicas y Empresariales, Universidad Autónoma de Madrid, Documento 91/9.

Finger, J.M. (ed.) (1993), *Antidumping, How It Works and Who Gets Hurt*, Ann Arbor, MI: University of Michigan Press.

Fokkema, T. and P. Nijkamp (1994), 'The Changing Role of Governments: The End of Planning History?', *International Journal of Transport Economics*, Vol. XXI, No. 2, pp. 127–45.

Folmer, H. and J. Oosterhaven (eds) (1979), *Spatial Inequalities and Regional Development*, The Hague: Nijhoff.

Fry, M.J. (1993), *Foreign Direct Investment in a Macroeconomic Framework: Finance, Efficiency, Incentives and Distortions*, World Bank, Policy Research Working Paper Series, WPS 1141.

Fukasaku, K., D. Wall and M. Wu (1994), *China's Long March to An Open Economy*, OECD Development Centre, Paris: OECD.

Gales, B.P.A. and K.E. Sluyterman (1993), 'Outward Bound. The Rise of Dutch Multinationals', in Jones, G. and H.G. Schröter (eds), *The Rise of Multinationals in Continental Europe*, Aldershot: Edward Elgar.

Garnaut, R. (1996), 'The Asia-Pacific: Role Model and Engine of Growth', in OECD, *Globalisation and Linkages to 2020, Challenges and Opportunities for OECD Countries*, OECD Proceedings, Paris: OECD, pp. 19–31.

Geraci, V.J. and W. Prewo (1977), 'Bilateral Trade Flows and Transport Costs', *Review of Economics and Statistics*, Vol. 59, pp. 67–74.

Gevel, A.J.W. van de (1983), 'Integratie van Theorieën van Internationale Handel en Directe Investeringen', (Integration of International Trade Theories and Direct Investment Theories), *Maandschrift Economie*, Vol. 47, pp. 342–58.

Giddy, I.H. (1981), 'The Cost of Capital in the International Firm', *Managerial and Decision Economics*, Vol. 2, No. 4, pp. 263–71.

Gilman, M.G. (1981), *The Financing of Foreign Direct Investment: A Study of the Determinants of Capital Flows in Multinational Enterprises*, London: Pinter.

Gold, D., P. Economou and T. Tolentino (1991), *Trade Blocs and Investment Blocs: The Triad in Foreign Direct Investment and International Trade*, New York: UNCTC.

Graham, E.M. (1992), 'Direct Investment between the United States and the European Community Post-1986 and Pre-1992', in Cantwell, J. (ed.), *Multinational Investment in Modern Europe, Strategic Interaction in the Integrated Community*, Aldershot: Edward Elgar, pp. 46–70.

Graham, E.M. and P.R. Krugman (1989), *Foreign Direct Investment in the United States*, Washington, DC: Institute for International Economics.

Greenaway, D. (1991), 'Trade Related Investment Measures: Political Economy Aspects and Issues for GATT', *The World Economy*, pp. 367–85.

Greenaway, D. (1993), 'Trade and Foreign Direct Investment', in Commission of the European Communities, *The European Community as a World Trade Partner, The Second Trade Report*, European Economy, No. 52, Luxemburg.

Greenhut, J.G. and M.L. Greenhut (1975), 'Spatial Price Discrimination, Competition and Locational Effects', *Economica*, Vol. 42, November, pp. 401–19.

Greenhut, M.L. and G. Norman (1986), 'Spatial Pricing with a General Cost Function: The Effects of Taxes on Imports', *International Economic Review*, Vol. 27, No. 3, pp. 761–76.

Greenhut, M.L., G. Norman and C.-S. Hung (1987), *The Economics of Imperfect Competition, A Spatial Approach*, Cambridge: Cambridge University Press.

Grewlich, K.W. (1978), *Direct Investment in the OECD Countries*, Alphen aan den Rijn: Sijthoff & Noordhoff.

Groenewegen, J. (1991), 'Japan en de Regio', (Japan and the Region), *Economisch Statistische Berichten*, pp. 620–23.

Grossman, G.M. and E. Helpman (1991), 'Trade, Knowledge Spillovers and Growth', *European Economic Review*, Vol. 35, pp. 517–26.

Grubaugh, S.G. (1987), 'Determinants of Direct Foreign Investment', *Review of Economics and Statistics*, pp. 149–52.

Guile, B.R. and H. Brooks (eds), *Technology and Global Industry, Companies and Nations in the World Economy*, Washington, DC: National Academy Press.

Haack, G. (1986), 'Internationale Investeringen en de Nederlandse Economie', (International Investments and the Dutch Economy), *Tijdschrift voor Politieke Economie*, Vol. 9, No. 4, pp. 63–78.

Haaparanta, P. (1996), 'Competition for Foreign Direct Investments', *Journal of Public Economics*, Vol. 63, pp. 141–53.

Hacche, G. (1983), *The Determinants of Exchange Rate Movements*, Working Paper, OECD Economics and Statistics Department, Paris.

Hagedoorn, J. (ed.) (1995), *Technical Change and the World Economy, Convergence and Divergence in Technology Strategies*, Aldershot: Edward Elgar.

Haggett, P. (1979), *Geography, A Modern Synthesis*, 3rd edition, New York: Harper & Row.

Håkanson, L. (1979), 'Towards a Theory of Location and Corporate Growth', in Hamilton, F.E.I. and G.J.R. Linge (eds), *Industrial Systems*, Vol. I, Chichester: John Wiley & Sons, pp. 115–38.

Hallwood, C.P. (1994), 'A Reconsideration of the Theory of the Multinational Corporation', *Keio Economic Studies*, Vol. 31, No. 2, pp. 1–10.

Hamilton, F.E.I. and G.J.R. Linge (eds) (1979), *Industrial Systems*, Vol. I, Chichester: John Wiley & Sons.

Harmsen, R. and M. Leidy (1994), 'Regional Trading Arrangements', in IMF, *International Trade Policies, The Uruguay Round and Beyond*, Vol. II, Background Papers, Washington DC, pp. 88–133.

Head, K., J. Ries and D. Swenson (1993), 'Agglomeration Benefits and Location Choice: Evidence from Japanese Manufacturing Investments in the United States', paper, Vancouver, Davis.

Heijke, J.A.M. and L.H. Klaassen (1979), 'Human Reactions to Spatial Diversity: Mobility in Regional Labour Markets', in Folmer, H. and J. Oosterhaven (eds), *Spatial Inequalities and Regional Development*, The Hague: Nijhoff.

Heilbron, J. and N. Wilterdink (eds) (1995), *Mondialisering, De Wording van de Wereldsamenleving*, (Globalisation, The Creation of a World Society), Groningen: Wolters-Noordhof.

Heitger, B. and J. Stehn (1990), 'Japanese Direct Investments in the EC – Response to the Internal Market 1993?', *Journal of Common Market Studies*, Vol. 29, No. 1, pp. 1–15.

Hekman, C.R. (1981), 'Foreign Exchange Risk: Relevance and Management', *Managerial and Decision Economics*, Vol. 2, No. 4, pp. 256–62.

Helpman, E. and P.R. Krugman (1985), *Market Structure and Foreign Trade, Increasing Returns, Imperfect Competition, and the International Economy*, Hemel Hempstead: Harvester Wheatsheaf.

Hertz, S. (1992), 'Towards More Integrated Industrial Systems', in Axelsson, B. and G. Easton (eds), *Industrial Networks, A New View of Reality*, London: Routledge, pp. 105–28.

Hill, C.W.L., P. Hwang, W. Chan Kim (1990), 'An Eclectic Theory of the Choice of International Entry Mode', *Strategic Management Journal*, Vol. 11, pp. 117–28.

Hindle, T. (1993), 'Cross-border Mergers and Acquisitions in the EC', in Commission of the European Communities, *Panorama of EC Industry 93*, Luxemburg, pp. 49–54.

Hirsch, S. (1976), 'An International Trade and Investment Theory of the Firm', *Oxford Economic Papers*, Vol. 28, pp. 258–70.

Hirschey, M. (1986), 'Mergers, Buyouts and Fakeouts', *American Economic Review*, Vol. 76, No. 2, pp. 317–22.

Hoesel, R. van (1993), *Third World Multinationals: Retrospect and New Issues*, Discussion Paper Series, No. 90, Centre for Development Planning, Erasmus University, Rotterdam.

Hoesel, R. van (1994), 'Taiwanese en Zuidkoreaanse Multinationals in Europa', (Taiwanese and South Korean Multinationals in Europe), *Economisch Statistische Berichten*, pp. 86–8.

Hofstede, G. (1984), *Culture's Consequences, International Differences in Work-related Values*, Abridged edition, Cross-cultural Research and Methodology Series, Vol. 5, Sage.

Hofstede, G. (1991a), *Cultures and Organizations, Software of the Mind, Intercultural Cooperation and Its Importance for Survival*, New York: McGraw-Hill.

Hofstede, G. (1991b), *Allemaal Andersdenkenden, Omgaan met Cultuurverschillen*, Amsterdam (translation of Hofstede 1991a).

Horst, T. (1972), 'Firm and Industry Determinants of the Decision to Invest Abroad: An Empirical Study', *Review of Economics and Statistics*, pp. 258–66.

Horstmann, I.J. and J.R. Markusen (1989), 'Firm-specific Assets and the Gains from Direct Foreign Investment', *Economica*, Vol. 56, pp. 41–8.

Hufbauer, G.C. (1975), 'The Multinational Corporation and Direct Investment', in Kenen, P. (ed.), *International Trade and Finance, Frontiers for Research*, Cambridge: Cambridge University Press, pp. 253–319.

Hufbauer, G.C. (ed.) (1990), *Europe 1992: An American Perspective*, Washington, DC: The Brookings Institution.

Huijser, A.P. (1984), 'Het Kapitaalverkeer van de Private Sector; Een Gedesaggregeerd Model voor de Periode 1970–1980', (Capital Flows in the Private Sector, A Desaggregated Model for the 1970–1980 Period), *Maandschrift Economie*, Vol. 48, pp. 175–92.

Huner, J.P. and P. Schuurman (1995), 'Toename Buitenlandse Investeringen', (Growth of Foreign Investments), *Economisch Statistische Berichten*, pp. 1062–3.

Hymer, S.H. (1976), *The International Operations of National Firms: A Study of Direct Foreign Investment*, Cambridge, MA: MIT Press.

Isard, W. (1956), *Location and Space-economy, A General Theory Relating to Industrial Location, Market Areas, Land Use, Trade and Urban Structure*, Cambridge, MA: MIT Press.

Jacobs, D. (1994), *Concurrentie, Samenwerking en Innovatie, Een Overzicht van de Problematiek*, (Competition, Cooperation and Innovation, An Overview), Publicatiereeks Economische Structuur, The Hague: Ministry of Economic Affairs.

Jacquemin, A. and D. Wright (1993), 'Corporate Strategies and European Challenges Post-1992', *Journal of Common Market Studies*, Vol. 31, No. 4, pp. 525–37.

Jagersma, P.K. (1993a), 'Multinationale Concernstructuren', (Multinational Corporate Structures), *Economisch Statistische Berichten*, pp. 104–9.

Jagersma, P.K. (1993b), 'Vestigingsmotieven van Buitenlandse Multinationals', (Location Motives of Foreign Multinationals), *Economisch Statistische Berichten*, pp. 774–7.

Jagersma, P.K. (1993c), 'Internationale Acquisities van Nederlandse Multinationals', (International Acquisitions of Dutch Multinationals), *Economisch Statistische Berichten*, pp. 914–9.

Jagersma, P.K. (1994a), 'Multinationalisatie van het Uitgeefwezen', (Internationalisation in the Publishing Industry), *Economisch Statistische Berichten*, pp. 241–5.

Jagersma, P.K. (1994b), 'De Multinationalisering van het Verzekeringswezen', (Internationalisation in the Insurance Services Industry), *Economisch Statistische Berichten*, pp. 661–4.

Jagersma, P.K. and J. Bell (1992), 'Internationale Joint Ventures; Een Empirische Analyse', (International Joint Ventures; An Empirical Analysis), *Economisch Statistische Berichten*, pp. 1064–8.

Jannink, J. (1993), 'Naar een Multinationaal MKB', (Towards Multinational Small and Medium-sized Enterprises), *Economisch Statistische Berichten*, pp. 62–4.

Jansson, H. (1994), *Transnational Corporations in Southeast Asia, An Institutional Approach to Industrial Organisation*, Aldershot: Edward Elgar.

Johnson, H.G. (1970), 'The Efficiency and Welfare Implications of the International Corporation', in Kindleberger, C.P., *The International Corporation*, Cambridge, MA: MIT Press.

Jones, G. and H.G. Schröter (eds) (1993), *The Rise of Multinationals in Continental Europe*, Aldershot: Edward Elgar.

Juhl, P. (1985), 'The Federal Republic of Germany', in Dunning, J.H. (ed.), *Multinational Enterprises, Economic Structure and International Competitiveness*, Chichester: John Wiley & Sons/IRM, pp. 127–54.

Julius, D. (1991), *Foreign Direct Investment: The Neglected Twin of Trade*, Group of Thirty, Occasional Papers No. 33, Washington, DC.

Jun, J. (1990), 'U.S. Tax Policy and Direct Investment Abroad', in Razin, A. and J. Slemrod (eds), *Taxation in the Global Economy*, Chicago: University of Chicago Press and NBER, pp. 55–78.

Kemp, M.C. (1964), *The Pure Theory of International Trade*, Englewood Cliffs, NJ: Prentice-Hall.

Kindleberger, C.P. (1969), *American Business Abroad, Six Lectures on Direct Investment*, New Haven and London: Yale University Press.

Klaassen, L.H. and P. Drewe (1973), *Migration Policy in Europe, A Comparative Study*, Netherlands Economic Institute, Farnborough, UK and Lexington, USA: Saxon House and Lexington Books.

Klaassen, L.H. and W.T.M. Molle (eds) (1983), *Industrial Mobility and Migration in the European Community*, Netherlands Economic Institute, Aldershot: Gower Publishing.

Klein, M.W. and E. Rosengren (1992), 'Foreign Direct Investment Outflow from the United States: An Empirical Assessment', in Klein, M.W. and P.J.J. Welfens (eds), *Multinationals in the New Europe and Global Trade*, Berlin and Heidelberg: Springer-Verlag.

Klein, M.W. and P.J.J. Welfens (eds) (1992), *Multinationals in the New Europe and Global Trade*, Berlin and Heidelberg: Springer-Verlag.

Kleinknecht, A. and J. ter Wengel (1996), 'Feiten over Globalisering', (Facts on Globalisation), *Economisch Statistische Berichten*, pp. 831–3.

Kline, J.M. (1995), 'Transnational Enterprises and National Political Economies', in Boyd, G., *Competitive and Cooperative Macromanagement, The Challenges of Structural Interdependence*, Aldershot: Edward Elgar, pp. 1–19.

Klodt, H. (1988), 'International Trade, Direct Investment, and Regulations in Services', *World Competition Law and Economics Review*, Vol. 12, No. 2, pp. 49–67.

Kmenta, J. (1971), *Elements of Econometrics*, New York: Macmillan.

Koekkoek, A. and L.B.M. Mennes (eds) (1991), *International Trade and Global Development, Essays in Honour of Jagdish Bhagwati*, London: Routledge.

Koizumi, T. and K.J. Kopecky (1977), 'Economic Growth, Capital Movements and the International Transfer of Technical Knowledge', *Journal of International Economics*, Vol. 7, pp. 45–65.

Kojima, K. (1973), 'A Macroeconomic Approach to Foreign Direct Investment', *Hitotsubashi Journal of Economics*, Vol. 14, pp. 1–21.

Kojima, K. (1975), 'International Trade and Foreign Investment: Substitutes or Complements', *Hitotsubashi Journal of Economics*, Vol. 16, pp. 1–12.

Kojima, K. (1978), *Direct Foreign Investment, A Japanese Model of Multinational Business Operations*, London: Croom Helm.

Korten, D.C. (1995), *When Corporations Rule the World*, London: Earthscan Publications.

Kox, H. and L. van Velzen (1985), *Kapitaalexport vanuit Nederland*, (Exporting Capital from the Netherlands), Amsterdam: Somo.

Krägenau, H. (1975), *Internationale Direktinvestitionen 1950–1973, Vergleichende Untersuchungen und Statistische Materialien*, (International Direct Investments 1950–1973, Comparative Research and Statistical Materials), Hamburg: Verlag Weltarchiv.

Krägenau, H. (1982), *Internationale Direktinvestitionen*, (International Direct Investments), Ergänzungsband 1982, Hamburg: Verlag Weltarchiv.

Krugman, P. (1991a), *Geography and Trade*, Leuven; Cambridge, MA: Leuven University Press ; MIT Press.

Krugman, P. (ed.) (1991b), *Trade with Japan, Has the Door Opened Wider?*, Chicago: University of Chicago Press.

Krugman, P.R and M. Obstfeld (1988), *International Economics, Theory and Policy*, Glenview, IL: Scott.

Krugman, P.R. and A.J. Venables (1990), 'Integration and the Competitiveness of Peripheral Industry', in Bliss, C. and J. Braga de Macedo (eds), *Unity with Diversity in the European Economy: the Community's Southern Frontier*, Cambridge: Cambridge University Press.

Krugman, P.R. and A.J. Venables (1995), *The Seamless World: A Spatial Model of International Specialization*, CEPR Discussion Paper No. 1230, London.

Kume, G. (1993), 'Recent Trends and Prospects for Japanese Direct Investment in Asia', in OECD, *Foreign Direct Investment Relations between the OECD and the Dynamic Asian Economies*, The Bangkok Workshop, Informal Dialogue with the DAEs, Paris, pp. 55–60.

Lall, S. (1993), 'Foreign Direct Investment in South Asia', *Asian Development Review*, Vol. 11, No. 1, pp. 103–19.

Lall, S. (1996), 'The Investment Development Path, Some Conclusions', in Dunning, J.H. and R. Narula (eds), *Foreign Direct Investment and Governments, Catalysts for Economic Restructuring*, London: Routledge, pp. 423–41.

Langhammer, R.J. (1995), 'Regional Integration in East Asia. From Market-driven Regionalisation to Institutionalised Regionalism?', *Weltwirtschaftliches Archiv*, Vol. 131, pp. 167–201.

Langille, B.A. (1996), 'General Reflections on the Relationship of Trade and Labour (Or: Fair Trade is Free Trade's Destiny)', in Bhagwati, J.N. and R.E. Hudec (eds), *Fair Trade and Harmonization, Prerequisites for Free Trade?*, Vol. 2, Legal Analysis, Cambridge, MA: MIT Press, pp. 231–66.

Lemmen, J.J.G. and S.C.W. Eijffinger (1996), 'The Fundamental Determinants of Financial Integration in the European Union', *Weltwirtschaftliches Archiv*, Vol. 132, pp. 432–56.

Lensink, R. (1993), *External Finance and Development*, Groningen: Wolters-Noordhoff.

Lensink, R. and M. Antuma (1991), 'Directe Investeringen in Ontwikkelingslanden', (Direct Investments in Developing Countries), *Economisch Statistische Berichten*, pp. 1128–35.

Liemt, G. van (ed.) (1992), *Industry on the Move, Causes and Consequences of International Relocation in the Manufacturing Industry*, Geneva: ILO.

Lin, A. (1995), 'Trade Effects of Foreign Direct Investment: Evidence for Taiwan with Four ASEAN Countries', *Weltwirtschaftliches Archiv*, pp. 737–47.

Lindert, P.H. (1986), *International Economics*, 8th edition, Homewood, IL: Irwin.

Linnemann, H. (1966), *An Econometric Study of International Trade Flows*, Amsterdam: North-Holland.

Lipsey, R.E. (1994), *Outward Direct Investment and the U.S. Economy*, NBER Working Paper Series, No. 4691, Cambridge, MA.

Lipsey, R.E. and I.B. Kravis (1985), 'The Competitive Position of US Manufacturing Firms', *Banca Nazionale del Lavoro Quarterly Review*, No. 153, pp. 127–54.

Lizondo, J.S. (1991), *Foreign Direct Investment, in IMF, Determinants and Systemic Consequences of International Capital Flows*, Occasional Papers No. 77, Washington, DC.

Lloyd, P.E. and P. Dicken (1977), *Location in Space, A Theoretical Approach to Economic Geography*, 2nd edition, London: Harper & Row.

Lösch, A. (1954), *The Economics of Location*, translated from the 2nd revised edition by W.H. Woglom with the assistance of W.F. Stolper, New Haven, CT: Yale University Press.

Lubbers, R.F.M. (1995), 'Globalisering, Naar een Nieuwe Kijk op Political Economy', (Globalisation, Towards a New Vision on Political Economy), Inaugural lecture Catholic University Brabant, Tilburg.

Lunn, J. (1980), 'Determinants of US Direct Investment in the EEC, Further Evidence', *European Economic Review*, Vol. 13, pp. 93–101.

Lunn, J. (1983), 'Determinants of US Direct Investment in the EEC, Revisited Again', *European Economic Review*, Vol. 21, pp. 391–3.

MacDonald, G. (1989), *The Nordic Countries and Multinational Enterprises: Employment Effects and Foreign Direct Investment*, Working Paper No. 57, Multinational Enterprises Programme, Geneva: ILO.

Machlup, F. (ed.) (1976), *Economic Integration Worldwide, Regional, Sectoral*, London: Macmillan.

Markusen, J. (1983), 'Factor Movements and Commodity Trade as Complements', *Journal of International Economics*, Vol. 14, pp. 341–56.

Martijn, J.K. (1993), *Exchange-rate Variability and Trade, Essays on the Impact of Exchange-rate Variability on Trade Policy and Trade Flows*, Tinbergen Institute Research Series No. 42, Amsterdam.

Martin, P. and C.A. Rogers (1995), 'Trade Effects of Regional Aid', in Baldwin, R., P. Haaparanta and J. Kiander (eds), *Expanding Membership of the European Union*, Cambridge: Cambridge University Press, pp. 166–88.

Mátyás, L. and G. Körösi (1996), 'The Determinants of Foreign Direct Investment in Transforming Economies: A Comment', *Weltwirtschaftliches Archiv*, Vol. 132, pp. 390–93.

McCulloch, R. (1993), 'Foreign Direct Investment in the United States', *Finance and Development*, March, pp. 13-15.

McKinsey (1988), *The Attractiveness of the Netherlands for Foreign Investors, An Opinion Survey of Foreign Companies*, Amsterdam: McKinsey & Company.

Melo, J. de and D.G. Tarr (1995), *VERs Under Imperfect Competition and Foreign Direct Investment: A Case Study of the US–Japan Auto VER*, CEPR Discussion Paper Series, No. 1173, London.

Ménil, G. de and M. Maurel (1994), 'Breaking Up a Customs Union: The Case of the Austro–Hungarian Empire in 1919', *Weltwirtschaftliches Archiv*, Vol. 130, pp. 553–75.

Mensink, N.W. and W.F.C. Verschoor (1997), 'Globalisering van de Nederlandse Industrie', (Globalisation of the Dutch Manufacturing Industry), *Economisch Statistische Berichten*, pp. 316–18.

Messerlin, P.A. (1995), 'The Impact of Trade and Capital Movements on Labour: Evidence on the French Case', *OECD Economic Studies*, No. 24, pp. 89–124.

Michel, J.H. (1997), 'A New Approach to Development', *The OECD Observer*, No. 204.

Micossi, S. and S. Rossi (1986), 'Restrictions on International Capital Flows: The Case of Italy', paper prepared for the symposium on 'European Factor Mobility: Trends and Consequences', Canterbury.

Miller, R.R. (1993), 'Determinants of US Manufacturing Investment Abroad', *Finance and Development*, March, pp. 16–18.

Milner, C. and E. Pentecost (1994), 'The Determinants of the Composition of US Foreign Direct Investment in UK Manufacturing', in Balasubramanyam, V.N. and D. Sapsford (eds), *The Economics of International Investment*, Aldershot: Edward Elgar, pp. 85–102.

Ministry of Economic Affairs (1990), *Economie met Open Grenzen*, (An Economy with Open Borders), The Hague: Ministry of Economic Affairs.

Molle, W.T.M. (1990), *The Economics of European Integration, Theory, Practice, Policy*, Aldershot: Dartmouth.

Molle, W.T.M. (1994), *The Economics of European Integration, Theory, Practice, Policy*, 2nd edition, Aldershot: Dartmouth.

Molle, W.T.M. (1995), 'De Economie van de Europese Integratie, Overzicht van een Groeiend Vakgebied', (The Economics of European Integration, Overview of a Growing Profession), *Internationale Spectator*, pp. 142–49.

Molle, W.T.M. and R.L.A. Morsink (1991), 'Intra-European Direct Investment', in Bürgenmeier, B. and J.L. Mucchielli (eds), *Multinationals and Europe 1992, Strategies for the Future*, London: Routledge, pp. 81–101.

Molle, W.T.M. and A. van Mourik (1988), 'International Movement of Labour under Conditions of Economic Integration; The Case of Western Europe', *Journal of Common Market Studies*, Vol. 26, No. 3, pp. 317–42.

Moore, M.O. (1993), 'Determinants of German Manufacturing Direct Investment: 1980–1988', *Weltwirtschaftliches Archiv*, Vol. 129, pp. 120–37.

Morawetz, R. (1991), *Recent Foreign Direct Investment in Eastern Europe: Towards a Possible Role for the Tripartite Declaration of Principles Concerning Multinational Enterprises and Social Policy*, Working Paper No. 71, Multinational Enterprises Programme, Geneva: ILO.

Morsink, R.L.A. (1991), 'Direct Investments within the European Community, Main Trends and the Factors Behind', paper presented at the EuroInvest Conference on 'Investment Prospects in Europe for 1992 and Medium-term Trends', Paris.

Morsink, R.L.A. (1992), 'Internationale Overdracht van Technologische Kennis', (International Technology Transfer), in Dijk, J.W.A. van and L.G. Soete (eds), *Technologie in een economie met open grenzen*, Beleidsstudies Technologie Economie, Alphen aan den Rijn: Samson, pp. 165–77.

Morsink, R.L.A. and W.T.M. Molle (1991a), 'Direct Investments and Monetary Integration', in European Economy, *The Economics of EMU, Background Studies for European Economy No. 44 'One Market, One Money'*, special edition No. 1, Luxemburg, pp. 36–55.

Morsink, R.L.A. and W.T.M. Molle (1991b), 'Direct Investment and European Integration', paper presented at the seminar on 'Foreign Direct Investment in Europe' at the Université Catholique de Louvain, Louvain-la-Neuve.

Mortensen, J. (1992), 'The Allocation of Savings in a Liberalised European Capital Market', in Steinherr, A. (ed.), *The new European Market Place*, London: Longman.

Motta, M. (1992), 'Multinational Firms and the Tariff-jumping Argument, A Game Theoretic Analysis with some Unconventional Conclusions', *European Economic Review*, Vol. 36, pp. 1557–71.

Mucchielli, J.L. (1985), *Les Firmes Multinationales: Mutations et Nouvelles Perspectives*, (Multinationals: Developments and New Perspectives), Centre d'Etudes et de Recherches Internationales et Communautaires Université Aix-Marseille III Faculté de Droit et de Science Politique, Economica, Paris.

Munday, M. (1990), *Japanese Manufacturing Investment in Wales*, Cardiff: University of Wales Press.

Mundell, R.A. (1957), 'International Trade and Factor Mobility', *American Economic Review*, pp. 321–35.

Nakamoto, S. (1992), 'Japanese Direct Investment in the U.S., Character and Perspective', *Osaka City University Economic Review*, Vol. 27, No. 1, pp. 15–32.

Narula, R. (1996), *Multinational Investment and Economic Structure, Globalisation and Competitiveness*, London: Routledge.

Netherlands Economic Institute (NEI) (1993), *New Location Factors for Mobile Investment in Europe*, in cooperation with Ernst & Young, Commission of the European Communities, DG for Regional Policies, Regional Development Studies, No. 6, Luxemburg.

Neven, D.J. and L.-H. Röller (1991), 'European Integration and Trade Flows', *European Economic Review*, Vol. 35, pp. 1295–309.

Nicolaides, P. (1991), 'Investment Policies in an Integrated World Economy', *The World Economy*, Vol. 14, No. 2, pp. 121–37.

Nicolaides, P. and S. Thomsen (1991a), 'Can Protectionism Explain Direct Investment?', *Journal of Common Market Studies*, Vol. 29, No. 6, pp. 635–43.

Nicolaides, P. and S. Thomsen (1991b), 'The Impact of 1992 on Direct Investment in Europe', *European Business Journal*, Vol. 3, No. 2, pp. 8–16.

Nieuwkerk, M. van (1986), 'De Internationalisering van de Nederlandse Economie', (The Internationalisation of the Dutch Economy), *Economisch Statistische Berichten*, pp. 1088–93.

Nieuwkerk, M. van and R.P. Sparling (1985), *De Internationale Investeringspositie van Nederland*, (The International Investment Position of the Netherlands), Monetaire Monographieën No. 4, De Nederlandsche Bank, Deventer: Kluwer.

Nieuwkerk, M. van, P. Speelman (1980), 'Dutch Investments Abroad and Foreign Investments in the Netherlands', *Kwartaalbericht De Nederlandsche Bank*, No. 3.

Nooteboom, B. (1996), 'Innoveren, Globaliseren', (Innovate, Internationalise), *Economisch Statistische Berichten*, pp. 828–30.

OECD (1989a), *Investment Incentives and Disincentives: Effects on International Direct Investment*, Paris.

OECD (1989b), *International Direct Investment and the New Economic Environment, The Tokyo Round Table, International Investment and Multinational Enterprises*, Paris.

OECD (1990), 'Towards New Forms of Corporate Organisation', Draft Chapter 5 of Draft Background Report, Technology Economy Programme, Paris.

OECD (1992), *International Direct Investment, Policies and Trends in the 1980s*, Paris.

OECD (1993a), *Promoting Foreign Direct Investment in Developing Countries*, Paris.

OECD (1993b), *Foreign Direct Investment Relations between the OECD and the Dynamic Asian Economies*, The Bangkok Workshop, Informal Dialogue with the DAEs, Paris.

OECD (1993c), *International Direct Investment Statistics Yearbook*, Paris.

OECD (1993d), *OECD Reviews on Foreign Direct Investment, Sweden*, Paris.

OECD (1993e), *OECD Reviews on Foreign Direct Investment, New Zealand*, Paris.

OECD (1993f), *Foreign Direct Investment in Selected Central and Eastern European Countries and New Independent States, Policies and Trends in Fourteen Economies in Transition*, OECD Working Papers, No. 11, Paris.

OECD (1994a), *International Direct Investment Statistics Yearbook*, Paris.

OECD (1994b), *Trade and Investment: Transplants*, Paris.

OECD (1994c), *Assessing Investment Opportunities in Economies in Transition*, Centre for Cooperation with the Economies in Transition, Paris.

OECD (1994d), *Taxation and Investment Flows: An Exchange of Experiences Between the OECD and the Dynamic Asian Economies*, Paris.

OECD (1994e), *The Performance of Foreign Affiliates in OECD Countries*, Paris.

OECD (1994f), *OECD Reviews of Foreign Direct Investment, Ireland*, Paris.

OECD (1994g), *OECD Reviews on Foreign Direct Investment, Portugal*, Paris.

OECD (1994h), *OECD Reviews of Foreign Direct Investment, Greece*, Paris.

OECD (1994i), *OECD Reviews of Foreign Direct Investment, Italy*, Paris.

OECD (1994j), *Industrial Policy in OECD Countries*, Annual Review 1994, Paris.

OECD (1995a), *The OECD STAN Database for Industrial Analysis 1974–1993*, Paris.

OECD (1995b), *Taxation and Foreign Direct Investment, The Experience of the Economies in Transition*, Centre for Cooperation with the Economies in Transition, Paris.

OECD (1995c), *Foreign Direct Investment, OECD Countries and Dynamic Economies of Asia and Latin America*, Paris.

OECD (1995d), *International Direct Investment Statistics Yearbook*, Paris.

OECD (1995e), *OECD Reviews of Foreign Direct Investment, Denmark*, Paris.

OECD (1995f), *OECD Reviews of Foreign Direct Investment, Finland*, Paris.

OECD (1995g), *OECD Reviews of Foreign Direct Investment, Norway*, Paris.

OECD (1995h), *OECD Reviews of Foreign Direct Investment, United States*, Paris.

OECD (1996a), *International Direct Investment Statistics Yearbook*, Paris.

OECD (1996b), *Investment Guide for Uzbekistan*, Paris.

OECD (1996c), *Globalisation of Industry, Overview and Sector Reports*, Paris.

OECD (1996d), *Globalisation and Linkages to 2020, Challenges and Opportunities for OECD Countries*, OECD Proceedings, Paris.

OECD (1997), *Investment Policies in Latin America and Multilateral Rules on Investment*, OECD Proceedings, Paris.

Oerlemans, L., J. Dagevos and F. Boekema (1993), 'Networking; Risk-reduction in a Turbulent Environment', in Beije, P., J. Groenewegen and O. Nuys (eds), *Networking in Dutch Industries*, Leuven/Apeldoorn: Garant, pp. 165–89.

Olsson, G. (1965), *Distance and Human Interaction, A Review and Bibliography*, Philadelphia, PN: Regional Science Research Institute.

Onoda, K., H. Kohama and S. Urata (1991), 'Industrial Restructuring by Japanese Firms and Government Policies', in Nakakita, T. and S. Urata (eds), *Industrial Adjustment in Japan and its Impact on Developing Countries*.

Ozawa, T. (1985), 'Japan', in Dunning, J.H. (ed.), *Multinational Enterprises, Economic Structure and International Competitiveness*, Chichester: John Wiley & Sons/IRM, pp. 155–85.

Ozawa, T. (1991), 'Japanese Multinationals and 1992', in Bürgenmeier, B. and J.L. Mucchielli (eds), *Multinationals and Europe 1992, Strategies for the Future*, London: Routledge, pp. 135–54.

Paliwoda, S.J. (1981), 'Multinational Corporations: Trade and Investment Across the East–West Divide', *Managerial and Decision Economics*, Vol. 2, No. 4, pp. 247–55.

Panglaykim, J. (1983), *Japanese Direct Investment in ASEAN: The Indonesian Experience*, Singapore: Maruzen Asia.

Panic, M. and C. Schioppa (1986), 'Europe's Long Term Capital Flows since 1971', paper presented at an International Symposium on 'European Factor Mobility', University of Cambridge.

Park, Y.C. and W.-A. Park (1991), 'Changing Japanese Trade Patterns and the East Asian NICs', in Krugman, P. (ed.), *Trade with Japan, Has the Door Opened Wider?*, Chicago: University of Chicago Press.

Pearce, R.D. (1993), *The Growth and Evolution of Multinational Enterprise, Patterns of Geographical and Industrial Diversification*, Aldershot: Edward Elgar.

Pelkmans, J. (1983), 'European Direct Investments in the European Community', *Journal of European Integration*, Vol. VII, No. 1, pp. 41–69.

Perée, E. and A. Steinherr (1989), 'Exchange Rate Uncertainty and Foreign Trade', *European Economic Review*, Vol. 33, pp. 1241–64.

Perrucci, A. (1991), 'The Internationalisation Process of OECD Countries: A Sectoral Analysis', Unpublished paper, ENEA, Research Department, Rome.

Petrochilos, G.A. (1989), *Foreign Direct Investment and the Development Process, The Case of Greece*, Aldershot: Avebury.

Pfaffermayr, M. (1996), 'Foreign Outward Direct Investment and Exports in Austrian Manufacturing: Substitutes or Complements?', *Weltwirtschaftliches Archiv*, Vol. 132, pp. 501–22.

Piggott, J. and M. Cook (eds) (1993), *International Business Economics: A European Perspective*, London: Longman.

Porter, M.E. (1990), *The Competitive Advantage of Nations*, London: Macmillan.

Pöyhönen, P. (1963a), 'A Tentative Model for the Volume of Trade Between Countries', *Weltwirtschaftliches Archiv*, Vol. 90, pp. 93–100.

Pöyhönen, P. (1963b), 'Toward a General Theory of International Trade', *Economiska Samfundets Tidskrift*, Vol. 16, pp. 69–77.

Prahalad, C.K. and Y.L. Doz (1987), *The Multinational Mission, Balancing Local Demands and Global Vision*, New York: Free Press.

Prewo, W. (1978), 'Determinants of the Trade Pattern among OECD Countries from 1958 to 1974', *Jahrbücher für Nationalekonomie und Statistik*, Vol. 193, August, pp. 341–58.

Pronk, C. (1992), 'De Economische Relatie tussen Nederland en Oost-Europa', (The Economic Relationship between the Netherlands and Eastern Europe), *Economisch Statistische Berichten*, pp. 735–7.

Pugel, T.A. (1981), 'The Determinants of Foreign Direct Investment: An Analysis of US Manufacturing Industries', *Managerial and Decision Economics*, Vol. 2, No. 4, pp. 220–28.

Pugel, T.A. (1985), 'The United States', in Dunning, J.H. (ed.), *Multinational Enterprises, Economic Structure and International Competitiveness*, Chichester: John Wiley & Sons/IRM, pp. 57–90.

Pulliainen, K. (1963), 'A World Trade Study: An Econometric Model of the Pattern of the Commodity Flows in International Trade in 1948–1960', *Ekonomiska Samfundets Tidskrift*, Vol. 16, pp. 78–91.

Purvis, D.D. (1972), 'Technology, Trade and Factor Mobility', *Economic Journal*, pp. 991–9.

Ramstetter, E.D. (ed.) (1991), *Direct Foreign Investment in Asia's Developing Economies and Structural Change in the Asia-Pacific Region*, Boulder, CO: Westview Press.

Ramstetter, E.D. (1993), 'Prospects for Foreign Firms in Developing Economies of the Asian and Pacific Region', *Asian Development Review*, Vol. 11, No. 1, pp. 151–85.

Ray, E.J. (1989), 'The Determinants of Foreign Direct Investment in the United States, 1979–85', in Feenstra, R.C. (ed.), *Trade Policies for International Competitiveness*, Chicago: University of Chicago Press, pp. 53–83.

Razin, A. and J. Slemrod (eds) (1990), *Taxation in the Global Economy*, Chicago: University of Chicago Press and NBER, pp. 79–122.

Rich, D.C. and G.J.R. Linge (eds) (1991), *The State and the Spatial Management of Industrial Change*, London: Routledge.

Richardson, J.D. (1971), 'On "Going Abroad": The Firm's Initial Foreign Investment Decision', *Quarterly Review of Economics and Business*, Vol. 11, pp. 7–22.

Rietbergen, T. van, J. Bosman and M. de Smidt (1991), 'Internationalisering van de Dienstensector', (The Internationalisation of the Service Industry), *Economisch Statistische Berichten*, pp. 624–8.

Rietbergen, T. van and H. van Hastenberg (1993), 'Nederlandse Investeringen in Centraal-Europa', (Dutch Investments in Central Europe), *Economisch Statistische Berichten*, pp. 387–9.

Robson, P. (1987), *The Economics of International Integration*, 3rd edition, London: Allen & Unwin.

Robson, P. and I. Wooton (1993), 'The Transnational Enterprise and Regional Economic Integration', *Journal of Common Market Studies*, Vol. 31, No. 1, pp. 71–90.

Roman, D.D. and J.F. Puett, Jr. (1983), *International Business and Technological Innovation*, New York: North-Holland.

Root, F.R. (1987), *Entry Strategies for International Markets*, revised edition of *Foreign Market Entry Strategies* of 1982, Lexington, MA: Lexington Books.

Ruffin, R.J. (1993), 'The Role of Foreign Investment in the Economic Growth of the Asian and Pacific Region', *Asian Development Review*, Vol. 11, No. 1, pp. 1–23.

Rugman, A.M. (1980), 'Internalization as a General Theory of Foreign Direct Investment: A Re-appraisal of the Literature', *Weltwirtschaftliches Archiv*, Vol. 116, pp. 365–79.

Rugman, A.M. (1981a), 'A Test of Internalization Theory', *Managerial and Decision Economics*, Vol. 2, No. 4, pp. 211–19.

Rugman, A.M. (1981b), *Inside the Multinationals: The Economics of Internal Markets*, London: Croom Helm.

Rugman, A.M. (1985), 'Internalization is still a General Theory of Foreign Direct Investment', *Weltwirtschaftliches Archiv*, Vol. 121, pp. 570–75.

Rugman, A.M., A. Verbeke and J.R. D'Cruz (1995), 'Internalization and De-internalization: Will Business Networks Replace Multinationals?', in Boyd, G., *Competitive and Cooperative Macromanagement, The Challenges of Structural Interdependence*, Aldershot: Edward Elgar, pp. 107–28.

Ruigrok, W. and R. van Tulder (1995), 'Misverstand: Globalisering', (A Misunderstanding: Globalisation), *Economisch Statistische Berichten*, pp. 1140–43.

Safarian, A.E. (1991), 'Firm and Government Strategies', in Bürgenmeier, B. and J.L. Mucchielli (eds), *Multinationals and Europe 1992, Strategies for the Future*, London: Routledge, pp. 187–203.

Safarian, A.E. (1993), *Multinational Enterprise and Public Policy, A Study of the Industrial Countries*, Aldershot: Edward Elgar.

Sander, H., K.S. Kim, S.F. Foster and M.S.S. El-Namaki (eds) (1996), *Economic and Corporate Restructuring: Experiences and Challenges of the Decade*, Leiderdorp: LANSA.

Sanna-Randaccio, F. (1993), 'The Non Equivalence of Tariff and Non-tariff Barriers: the case of Foreign Direct Investments', paper presented at the EIBA Annual Meeting, Lisbon.

Sapir, A. (1996), 'The Effects of Europe's Internal Market Program on Production and Trade: A First Assessment', *Weltwirtschaftliches Archiv*, Vol. 132, pp. 457–75.

Sapir, A., K. Sekkat and A.A. Weber (1994), *The Impact of Exchange Rate Fluctuations on European Union Trade*, CEPR, Discussion Paper Series, No. 1041, London.

Sauvant, K.P. and Z. Zimny (1987), 'Foreign Direct Investment in Services: The Neglected Dimension in International Service Negotiations', *World Competition Law and Economics Review*, No. 31, pp. 27–55.

Savary, J. (1992), 'Cross-investments between France and Italy and the New European Strategies of Industrial Groups', in Cantwell, J. (ed.), *Multinational Investment in Modern Europe, Strategic Interaction in the Integrated Community*, Aldershot: Edward Elgar, pp. 150–91.

Scaperlanda, A. and R.S. Balough (1983), 'Determinants of US Direct Investment in the EEC, Revisited', *European Economic Review*, Vol. 21, pp. 381–90.

Scaperlanda, A.E. and L.J. Mauer (1969), 'The Determinants of US Direct Investment in the EEC', *American Economic Review*, Vol. 59, pp. 558–68.

Schmitz, A. (1970), 'The Impact of Trade Blocs on Foreign Direct Investment', *Economic Journal*, Vol. 80, pp. 724–31.

Schmitz, A. and J. Bieri (1972), 'EEC Tariffs and US Direct Investment', *European Economic Review*, Vol. 3, pp. 259–70.

Schmitz, A. and P. Helmberger (1970), 'Factor Mobility and International Trade: the Case of Complementarity', *American Economic Review*, Vol. 60, pp. 761–67.

Scholl, R.B. (1987), 'The International Investment Position of the United States in 1986', *Survey of Current Business*, June, pp. 38–45.

Scholl, R.B. (1988), 'The International Investment Position of the United States in 1987', *Survey of Current Business*, June, pp. 76–84.

Scholl, R.B. (1989), 'The International Investment Position of the United States in 1988', *Survey of Current Business*, June, pp. 41–9.

Scholl, R.B. (1990), 'International Investment Position: Component Detail for 1989', *Survey of Current Business*, June, pp. 54–65.

Scholl, R.B. (1991), 'The International Investment Position of the United States in 1990', *Survey of Current Business*, June, pp. 23–35.

Scholl, R.B., R.J. Mataloni and S.D. Bezirganian (1992), 'The International Investment Position of the United States in 1991', *Survey of Current Business*, June, pp. 46–59.

Schoone, P. and J.-M. Viaene (1988), 'Direct Foreign Investment and Exchange Rate Dynamics', paper Erasmus University, Rotterdam.

Schuurman, P. and J.P. Huner (1996), *Internationale Investeringen*, (International Investments), Discussienota BEB 9601, The Hague: Ministry of Economic Affairs.

Semlinger, K. (1991), 'New Developments in Subcontracting: Mixing Market and Hierarchy', in Amin, A. and M. Dietrich (eds), *Towards a New Europe*, Aldershot: Edward Elgar, pp. 96–115.

Sezer, H. and A. Kilmister (1993), 'Foreign Direct Investment (FDI)', in Piggott, J. and M. Cook (eds), *International Business Economics: A European Perspective*, London: Longman.

Sheehy, J. (1994), *Foreign Direct Investment in the CEECs*, European Economy, Reports and Studies No. 6, Chapter 4.

Siegel, M.H. (1983), *Foreign Exchange Risk and Direct Foreign Investment*, Research for Business Decisions No. 60, Ann Arbor, MI: UMI Research Press.

Sjöholm, F. (1996), 'International Transfer of Knowledge: The Role of International Trade and Geographic Proximity', *Weltwirtschaftliches Archiv*, Vol. 132, pp. 97–115.

Slemrod, J. (1990), 'Tax Effects of Foreign Direct Investment in the US: Evidence from a Cross-country Comparison', in Razin, A. and J. Slemrod (eds), *Taxation in the Global Economy*, Chicago: University of Chicago Press and NBER, pp. 79–122.

Slemrod, J. (1996), 'Tax Cacophony and the Benefits of Free Trade', in Bhagwati, J.N. and R.E. Hudec (eds), *Fair Trade and Harmonization, Prerequisites for Free Trade?*, Vol. 1, Economic Analysis, Cambridge, MA: MIT Press, pp. 283–310.

Sleuwaegen, L.I.E. (1984), 'Location and Investment Decisions by Multinational Enterprises, Theoretical and Empirical Essays on the Operations of Multinational Enterprises in Belgium and Europe', Dissertation, Katholieke Universiteit Leuven, Reeks van de Faculteit der Economische en Toegepaste Economische Wetenschappen, Nieuwe reeks nr. 55.

Sleuwaegen, L.I.E. (1985), 'Monopolistic Advantages and the International Operations of Firms: Disaggregated Evidence from U.S.-based Multinationals', *Journal of International Business Studies*, Fall, pp. 125–33.

Sleuwaegen, L.I.E. (1987), 'Multinationals, the European Community and Belgium, Recent Developments', *Journal of Common Market Studies*, Vol. XXVI, No. 2, pp. 255–72.

Sleuwaegen, L.I.E. (1994), 'The Structure and Internationalization of Public Procurement Industries in Europe', mimeo.

Sleuwaegen, L.I.E. (1996), 'Foreign Direct Investment, Cross-border Mergers and Competition Policy in the European Union', paper presented at the OECD workshop 'Beyond Regionalism: European and Asian Multinationals in a Globalising Economy', Paris.

Sleuwaegen, L.I.E. and H. Yamawaki (1988), 'The Formation of the European Common Market and Changes in Market Structure and Performance', *European Economic Review*, Vol. 32, pp. 1451–75.

Sleuwaegen, L.I.E. and H. Yamawaki (1990), *Foreign Direct Investment and Intra-Firm Trade: Evidence from Japan*, Discussion Paper Series No. 9002/G, Institute for Economic Research, Erasmus University, Rotterdam.

Sleuwaegen, L.I.E. and H. Yamawaki (1991), 'Foreign Direct Investment and Intra-Firm Trade: Evidence from Japan', in Koekkoek, A. and L.B.M. Mennes (eds), *International Trade and Global Development, Essays in Honour of Jagdish Bhagwati*, London: Routledge, pp. 143–61.

Smeets, M. (1991), 'Het Succes van de Aziatische Draken', (The Success of the Asian Dragons), *Economisch Statistische Berichten*, pp. 764–72.

Smeets, M. (1992), 'Mondialisering, Vrijhandel en Regionale Integratie', (Globalisation, Free Trade and Regional Integration), *Economisch Statistische Berichten*, pp. 488–91.

Social–Economic Council (SER) (1995), *Kennis en Economie*, (Knowledge and the Economy), Rapport Commissie Economische Deskundigen, No. 95/04, Den Haag: SER.

Social–Economic Council (SER) (1996), *Sociaal–Economisch Beleid 1996–2000*, (Social–Economic Policy 1996–2000), No. 96/05, Den Haag: SER.

Somers, F.J.L. (ed.) (1991), *European Economies, A Comparative Study*, London: Pitman.

Steinherr, A. (ed.) (1992), *The New European Market Place*, London: Longman.

Stevens, G.V.G. (1974), 'The Determinants of Investment', in Dunning, J.H. (ed.), *Economic Analysis and the Multinational Enterprise*, London: Allen & Unwin, pp. 47–88.

Stokman, A.C.J. (1995), 'Effect of Exchange Rate Risk on Intra-EC Trade', *De Economist*, Vol. 143, No. 1, pp. 41–54.

Stopford, J.M. and J.H. Dunning (1983), *Multinationals, Company Performance and Global Trends*, London: Macmillan.

Strange, R. (1993), *Japanese Manufacturing Investment in Europe: Its Impact on the UK Economy*, London: Routledge.

Takeuchi, A. (1991), 'Spatial Conflicts Arising from the Restructuring of Japanese Industry', in Rich, D.C. and G.J.R. Linge (eds), *The State and the Spatial Management of Industrial Change*, London: Routledge, pp. 58–73.

Taylor, M.Z. (1995), 'Dominance through Technology: Is Japan Creating a Yen Bloc in Southeast Asia?', *Foreign Affairs*, Vol. 74, No. 6, pp. 14–20.

Thomsen, S. (1992), 'Inward Investment in the European Community', in Commission of the European Communities, *Panorama of EC Industries 1991/1992*, Luxemburg, pp. 39–64.

Thomsen, S. and P. Nicolaides (1991), *The Evolution of Japanese Direct Investment in Europe, Death of a Transistor Salesman*, Hemel Hempstead: Harvester Wheatsheaf.

Tinbergen, J. (1954), *International Economic Integration*, Amsterdam: Elsevier.

Tinbergen, J. (1962), *Shaping the World Economy, Suggestions for an International Economic Policy*, New York: Twentieth Century Fund.

Trebilcock, M.J. and R. Howse (1995), *The Regulation of International Trade*, London: Routledge.

Trevino, L.J. and J.D. Daniels (1994), 'An Empirical Assessment of the Preconditions of Japanese Manufacturing Foreign Direct Investment in the United States', *Weltwirtschaftliches Archiv*, Vol. 130, pp. 576–99.

Tuller, L.W. (1991), *Going Global, New Opportunities for Growing Companies to Compete in World Markets*, Homewood, IL: Business One Irwin.

United Nations (1989), *Foreign Direct Investment and Transnational Corporations in Services*, UN Centre on Transnational Corporations, New York/Geneva.

United Nations (1992), *Determinants of Foreign Direct Investment, A Survey of the Evidence*, UN Centre on Transnational Corporations, New York/Geneva.

United Nations (1993a), *Transnational Corporations from Developing Countries, Impact on their Home Countries*, Transnational Corporations and Management Division, Dept. of Economic and Social Development, New York/Geneva.

United Nations (1993b), *World Investment Report, Transnational Corporations and Integrated International Production*, New York/Geneva.

United Nations (1993c), *World Investment Directory*, Volume III Developed Countries, New York/Geneva.

United Nations (1993d), *International Trade Statistics Yearbook*, Volume I, New York/Geneva.

United Nations (1994), *World Investment Report, Transnational Corporations, Employment and the Workplace*, New York/Geneva.

United Nations (1995a), *World Investment Report, Transnational Corporations and Competitiveness*, New York/Geneva.

United Nations (1995b), *Foreign Direct Investment in Africa*, Current Studies, Series A, No. 28, New York/Geneva.

United Nations (1996), *World Investment Report, Investment, Trade and International Policy Arrangements*, New York/Geneva.

Vanderkamp, J. (1977), *The Gravity Model and Migration Behaviour: An Econometric Interpretation*, Institute of Social and Economic Research, University of York, Reprinted from *Journal of Economic Studies*, Vol. 4, No. 2.

Venables, A.J. (1995), 'Economic Integration and the Location of Firms', *American Economic Review*, Vol. 85, No. 2, pp. 269–300.

Vernon, R. (1966), 'International Investment and International Trade in the Product Cycle', *Quarterly Journal of Economics*, pp. 190–207.

Vernon, R. (1979), 'The Product Cycle Hypothesis in a New International Environment', *Oxford Bulletin of Economics and Statistics*, Vol. 41, No. 4, pp. 255–67.

Vernon, R. (1992), *Are Foreign-owned Subsidiaries Good for the United States?*, Occasional Paper No. 37, Group of Thirty, Washington, DC.

Viaene, J.M. and V. Severins (1988), *The Macroeconomics of Direct Foreign Investment, A Probabilistic Assessment*, Working Paper No. 8804, Departement des Sciences Economiques, Université Catholique de Louvain, Louvain-la-Neuve.

Viaene, J.M. and C.G. de Vries (1992), 'International Trade and Exchange Rate Volatility', *European Economic Review*, Vol. 36, No. 6, pp. 1311–21.

Viner, J. (1950), *The Customs Union Issue*, New York: Carnegie Endowment for International Peace.

Visser, H. (1995), *A Guide to International Monetary Economics, Exchange Rate Systems and Exchange Rate Theories*, Aldershot: Edward Elgar.

Wallace, C.D. (ed.) (1990), *Foreign Direct Investment in the 1990s: A New Climate in the Third World*, Center for Strategic and International Studies, Dordrecht: Nijhoff.

Wang, J.-Y. and M. Blomström (1992), 'Foreign Investment and Technology Transfer: A Simple Model', *European Economic Review*, Vol. 36, pp. 137–55.

Wang, Z.Q. and N.J. Swain (1995), 'The Determinants of Foreign Direct Investment in Transforming Economies: Empirical Evidence from Hungary and China', *Weltwirtschaftliches Archiv*, Vol. 131, pp. 359–82.

Weber, A.A. (1991), 'EMU and Asymmetries and Adjustment Problems in the EMS: Some Empirical Evidence', in European Economy, *The Economics of EMU*,

Background Studies for European Economy No. 44 'One Market, One Money', special edition No. 1, Luxemburg, pp. 187–207.

Weiermair, K. (1991), 'The Japanization of European Industry' in Amin, A. and M. Dietrich (eds), *Towards a New Europe*, Aldershot: Edward Elgar, pp. 74–95.

Wheeler, D. and A. Mody (1992), 'International Investment Location Decisions: The Case of US Firms', *Journal of International Economics*, Vol. 33, pp. 57–76.

Wilkins, M. (1970), *The Emergence of Multinational Enterprise: American Business Abroad from the Colonial Era to 1914*, Cambridge, MA: Harvard University Press.

Wilkins, M. (1989), *The History of Foreign Investment in the United States to 1914*, Cambridge, MA: Harvard University Press.

Wilkins, M. (ed.) (1991), *The Growth of Multinationals*, Aldershot: Edward Elgar.

Williamson, O.E. (1985), *The Economic Institutions of Capitalism, Firms, Markets, Relational Contracting*, New York: Free Press.

World Bank (1994), *The World Tables*, Washington, DC.

World Trade Organisation (WTO) (1996), *Trade and Foreign Direct Investment*, Geneva: WTO.

Yannopoulos, G.N. (1990), 'Foreign Direct Investment and European Integration: The Evidence from the Formative Years of the European Community', *Journal of Common Market Studies*, Vol. 28, No. 3, pp. 235–59.

Yannopoulos, G.N. (1991), 'Foreign Direct Investment in the European Community: Evidence from the Formative Years', paper presented at the seminar on 'Foreign Direct Investment' at the Université de Louvain-la-Neuve.

Yannopoulos, G.N. (1992), 'Multinational Corporations and the Single European Market', in Cantwell, J. (ed.), *Multinational Investment in Modern Europe, Strategic Interaction in the Integrated Community*, Aldershot: Edward Elgar, pp. 329–48.

Yoshida, M. (1987), *Japanese Direct Manufacturing Investment in the United States*, New York: Praeger.

Young, K.H. (1988), 'The Effects of Taxes and Rates of Return on Foreign Direct Investment in the US', *National Tax Journal*, Vol. 41, pp. 109–21.

Young, S. and J. Hamill (eds) (1992), *Europe and the Multinationals, Issues and Responses for the 1990s*, Aldershot: Edward Elgar.

Yue, C.S. (1993), 'Foreign Direct Investment in ASEAN Economies', *Asian Development Review*, Vol. 11, No. 1, pp. 60–102.

Zafar Shah Khan (1991), *Patterns of Direct Foreign Investment in China*, World Bank Discussion Papers No. 130, China and Mongolia Department Series, World Bank, Washington, DC.

Zou, J., R.L.A. Morsink, and T. Liu (1996), 'Foreign Direct Investment and Economic Restructuring: A Case Study of Pudong', in Sander, H., K.S. Kim, S.F. Foster and M.S.S. El-Namaki (eds), *Economic and Corporate Restructuring: Experiences and Challenges of the Decade*, Leiderdorp: LANSA, pp. 113–29.

Zwet, A.M.C. van der (1996), 'Globalisering en de Nederlandse Economie', (Globalisation and the Dutch Economy), *Economisch Statistische Berichten*, pp. 138–42.

Index